MUSICAL PERFORMANCE AND RECEPTION

General editors

JOHN BUTT AND LAURENCE DREYFUS

This series continues the aim of Cambridge Musical Texts and Monographs to publish books centred on the history of musical instruments and the history of performance, but broadens the focus to include musical reception in relation to performance and as a reflection of period expectations and practices.

Published titles

Playing with History: The Historical Approach to Musical Performance
JOHN BUTT

*Palestrina and the German Romantic Imagination: Interpreting Historicism
in Nineteenth-Century Music*
JAMES GARRATT

Eight Centuries of Troubadours and Trouvères: The Changing Identity of Medieval Music
JOHN HAINES

The Keyboard in Baroque Europe
CHRISTOPHER HOGWOOD (ED.)

The Modern Invention of Medieval Music: Scholarship, Ideology, Performance
DANIEL LEECH-WILKINSON

Performing Brahms: Early Evidence of Performance Style
MICHAEL MUSGRAVE AND BERNARD SHERMAN (EDS)

Stradivari
STEWART POLLENS

Beethoven the Pianist
TILMAN SKOWRONECK

French Organ Music in the Reign of Louis XIV
DAVID PONSFORD

Histories of Heinrich Schütz
BETTINA VARWIG

Bach's Feet: The Organ Pedals in European Culture
DAVID YEARSLEY

Engaging Bach: The Keyboard Legacy from Marpurg to Mendelssohn
MATTHEW DIRST

The Musical Work of Nadia Boulanger: Performing Past and Future between the Wars
JEANICE BROOKS

The Guitar in Tudor England: A Social and Musical History
CHRISTOPHER PAGE

The Guitar in Stuart England: A Social and Musical History
CHRISTOPHER PAGE

Musical Authorship from Schütz to Bach
STEPHEN ROSE

Compositional Artifice in the Music of Henry Purcell
ALAN HOWARD

COMPOSITIONAL ARTIFICE IN THE MUSIC OF HENRY PURCELL

Alan Howard

SELWYN COLLEGE, UNIVERSITY OF CAMBRIDGE

CAMBRIDGE
UNIVERSITY PRESS

CAMBRIDGE
UNIVERSITY PRESS

University Printing House, Cambridge CB2 8BS, United Kingdom

One Liberty Plaza, 20th Floor, New York, NY 10006, USA

477 Williamstown Road, Port Melbourne, VIC 3207, Australia

314–321, 3rd Floor, Plot 3, Splendor Forum, Jasola District Centre, New Delhi – 110025, India

79 Anson Road, #06–04/06, Singapore 079906

Cambridge University Press is part of the University of Cambridge.

It furthers the University's mission by disseminating knowledge in the pursuit of education, learning, and research at the highest international levels of excellence.

www.cambridge.org
Information on this title: www.cambridge.org/9781107006669
DOI: 10.1017/9781139030458

First published 2020

Printed in the United Kingdom by TJ International Ltd, Padstow, Cornwall

A catalogue record for this publication is available from the British Library.

Library of Congress Cataloging-in-Publication Data
Names: Howard, Alan, 1979– author.
Title: Compositional artifice in the music of Henry Purcell / Alan Howard.
Description: Cambridge, United Kingdom ; New York, NY : Cambridge University Press, 2019.
| Series: Musical performance and reception | Includes bibliographical references and index.
Identifiers: LCCN 2019008505 | ISBN 9781107006669 (alk. paper)
Subjects: LCSH: Purcell, Henry, 1659–1695 – Criticism and interpretation. | Music – 17th century – Analysis, appreciation. | Composition (Music) – History – 17th century.
Classification: LCC ML410.P93 H68 2019 | DDC 780.92–dc23
LC record available at https://lccn.loc.gov/2019008505

ISBN 978-1-107-00666-9 Hardback

Contents

Figures

Tables

Music Examples

Acknowledgements

Much of this book, and all of the approach it embodies, originated in my PhD thesis (King's College, London, 2006). Consequently, my first and greatest debt is to my research supervisor, Laurence Dreyfus, without whose tactful guidance and insightful criticism my hazy ideas about Purcell's approaches to composition would not have developed to anything like their present form. It was also he, and John Butt, who encouraged me to consider publishing my work in their series for Cambridge University Press, and I am grateful to Victoria Cooper, then Commissioning Editor, for her initial receptivity to my proposal – and all the more to her successor, Kate Brett, for her support and patience in more recent years as I brought the long-overdue project to fruition. I also benefitted hugely during my doctoral studies (and indeed on several occasions since) from extended discussions with John Milsom, who generously shared then-unpublished material. The closeness of my analytical aims and methods to those of Dreyfus towards Bach, and Milsom in the field of sixteenth-century *fuga*, will be obvious to any readers already familiar with their work, and I hope that alongside these my work on Purcell will make a useful addition to the development of what Milsom calls 'forensic analysis' – an approach to the understanding of early musical texts that has attracted increasing interest in recent years.

My original plan, to complement what I had written as a doctoral student on Purcell's early instrumental music with a series of related studies of his later concerted vocal music, took shape during 2006–9, while I was employed in the University of Manchester as a Research Assistant on the research project 'Musical Creativity in Restoration England', funded from 2006 to 2010 by the UK's Arts and Humanities Research Council. I am much indebted to Rebecca Herissone, who led that project, both for her advice and encouragement during the process of devising my original proposal, and more generally for her support and guidance at that time and in the years since. My involvement with her project provided an unparalleled opportunity to deepen my knowledge of the music of Purcell and his contemporaries, and to develop archival and source-related skills that have transformed the way I think about this repertoire and about the relationship of my analytical approaches to wider musicological concerns.

Particular thanks are due to Bruce Wood, Martin Adams, and again to Rebecca Herissone, all three of whom have read multiple chapters of the book, sometimes in several different drafts, and whose responses have helped immeasurably as I have shaped and reshaped my arguments and analyses over the years since that first proposal, as well as alerting me to numerous problems and oversights in earlier versions. Among many other colleagues who have read and responded to portions of the whole, commented upon research papers developing my ideas, or simply spared their time for valued discussion, I am grateful in particular to John Cunningham, Peter Holman, Stephen Rose, Alon Schab, Bryan White and Andrew Woolley.

At various times progress on the book has been helped along by short periods of research leave, first from the University of East Anglia, Norwich, and later from my present position at Selwyn College, Cambridge. More recently I have received invaluable help from two colleagues: James Hume, in Manchester, who took on the gargantuan task of imposing some measure of uniformity on my music examples, and Natassa Varka here in Cambridge, who helped with the preparation of the final typescript and checking of the bibliography. Without their assistance over the summer of 2018, publication would doubtless have been delayed by several more months (if not years). Needless to say, I take full responsibility for any errors that remain.

Images reproduced in the book have been sourced from the British Library, the National Library of Scotland, the Bayerische Staatsbibliothek, Munich, the Foyle Special Collections Library, King's College, London, and the Music Library of Western University, London, Canada. I would like to thank these institutions, and in particular their many staff who assisted with these requests, as well as all those of other libraries who provided assistance in the course of my research. The costs of reproduction and of editorial support have been supported by research funds made available by Selwyn College and the Cambridge Faculty of Music, my gratitude to whom I also record here.

Finally, my deepest thanks go to my wife, Katie, who has been a constant source of loving support and encouragement since before this project began to take shape. I dedicate this book to her, and to our children Milly and Thomas, who have joined us in the intervening years and bring us great joy – not to mention a healthy sense of perspective.

Note on Music Examples

The unusually large number of music examples in this book is intended to make its argument comprehensible at first reading without the necessity of recourse to a large pile of separate scores. Many encode specific musical insights of a type and/or frequency that would be prohibitively cumbersome given recourse to verbal expression alone; any novel or specialized notational conventions in such cases should be graspable intuitively, though they are also explained in the associated text.

Since nearly all of the examples are intended to convey information about the music they contain, rather than the visual properties of its notation in original sources, modern and consistent conventions have for the most part been adopted in respect of score layout, barring, clefs, beaming, accidentals, text underlay and matters of spelling and punctuation. (Of course, matters pertaining to the visual representation of music in original sources may bear directly on one's understanding of 'the music they contain', though in the present study such cases are sufficiently rare that they can be dealt with on an individual basis – or indeed relate to matters at most tangential to the analytical approaches I take.) On the other hand, original note-values have been retained, as have original stave signatures (key signatures in modern terminology), slurs and ties; original clefs appear on prefatory staves before the parts concerned. Bass figuring, where reproduced, is notated as in the sources, but updated to follow modern accidental conventions and placed consistently below the stave. Editorial accidentals appear in small type above the stave, and any slurs or ties marked with a vertical slash are also editorial – as is any material that appears in square brackets.

Where instrumentation is obvious it has not been explicitly indicated, though trio sonata excerpts are visually distinguished by the joining of bar-lines across the two violin staves only, in contrast with passages for consort in which bar-lines extend across the whole ensemble. In examples featuring extensive annotation bar-lines are confined to the staves themselves, as they are in all vocal music. Where examples are drawn from trio sonatas the continuo bass and figures have generally been omitted unless directly relevant to the discussion in hand; where they do appear, they share a stave with the melodic bass (the latter taking upward stems in passages where the two parts diverge). It should be noted that the omission or conflation of these parts results from their often-oblique relevance to the contrapuntal matters under discussion here, and should not be taken to imply anything about performance practice. Similarly, excerpts from concerted vocal works have been presented on vocal staves only in order to focus on relevant parts as well as save space on the page. Minimal cues and verbal annotations are provided to assist the reader in imagining the complete texture, though these are rarely sufficient to permit the detailed reconstruction of the full score; notwithstanding this, readers should not infer that the abbreviated parts are in any way optional.

Abbreviations

AoD   Henry Purcell, 'A Brief Introduction to the Art of Descant', in John Playford, *An Introduction to the Skill of Music*, 12th edition (London: Henry Playford, 1694), 85–143.

Grove Online *Grove Music Online*, ed. Deane Root, Oxford University Press, www.oxfordmusiconline.com.

PS/PSr   The Purcell Society Edition, 32 vols (London: Novello, 1878–1962)/revised (London: Novello, 1964–2007; Stainer & Bell, 2007–).

PERIODICALS

EM   *Early Music* (Oxford University Press)
JAMS   *Journal of the American Musicological Society* (University of California Press)
JRMA   *Journal of the Royal Musical Association* (Taylor & Francis)
ML   *Music and Letters* (Oxford University Press)
MQ   *The Musical Quarterly* (Oxford University Press)
MT   *The Musical Times* (Musical Times Publications)

LIBRARY SIGLA (ACCORDING TO RISM USAGE)

Cfm   Cambridge, Fitzwilliam Museum
Drc   Durham Cathedral Library
Lbl   London, British Library
Lgc   London, Gresham College (held at Guildhall Library)
Ob   Oxford, Bodleian Library
US-NYp New York Public Library and Art Gallery
US-SM   San Marino, CA: Henry E. Huntington Library and Art Gallery

INSTRUMENTATION AND SCORING

Tpt	Trumpet
Ob	Oboe
Vn	Violin
Va	Viola
BC	Basso Continuo
KD	Kettledrum(s)
tr.	Treble (viol)
ten.	Tenor (viol)
S	Soprano
CT	Countertenor
T	Tenor
B	Bass

Pitch is indicated according to the Helmholz system, in which middle C is c', and the octaves proceed from the bass in the order $C-c-c'-c''-c'''$ (etc.); this formatting applies from the given C to the next B above.

Glossary of Analytical Terms

The specialized terminology employed in this book has been chosen and deployed with the intention that it rarely requires further explanation. Nevertheless, this glossary has been provided (a) as a source of quick reference, and (b) as a means of explaining terminology, and giving due credit to its inventors where necessary, without burdening the main text. (References are expanded below; where no citation appears, the definition is my own.)

Complex   A polyphonic passage usually in more than two parts, in which all parts of the texture are thematic. It may be constructed from interlocks of a single subject, juxtapose multiple subjects and countersubjects, or combine these two procedures. Two-voice polyphony may form a complex where it is constructed from entries of two different subjects (as distinct from the single-subject interlock).

Countersubject   A melodic fragment heard consistently against a subject, but which does not function as a subject in its own right (for example, due to its later introduction, or infrequency of occurrence by comparison with the subject(s) proper).

Cumulation   'The compositional strategy of postponing the boldest and most sophisticated ideas to the end of a movement' (Schab, 51). This applies primarily here to contrapuntal devices and inventions, but may equally refer to other factors such as harmony, chromaticism, texture or virtuosity in performance.

Flex·ed|ing   'Terms used to reflect the modification of a subject's interval content or durations as it is passed from voice to voice' (Milsom, 'Cipriano', 328). This concept allows, for example, for the use of a tonal answer, and equally for rhythmic modifications (but not the use of wholesale augmentation or diminution, which leave the relative durations of notes unchanged).

Fugeing	The process of constructing polyphony from successive statements of a subject in multiple parts, usually involving transposition; and by extension, a passage of such polyphony (AoD, see the discussion in Chapters 1 and 2 below).
Interlock	A passage of two-part polyphony constructed solely from overlapping subject-statements (see Milsom, 'Crequillon', 344).
Module	'A contrapuntal combination that repeats, both melodies and vertical intervals' (Schubert, 487). Since a module may be either imitative or non-imitative, this term has been found useful in the present study to describe passages of repeated polyphony in which one or more parts incorporate material not derived from the subject(s) or countersubject(s).
Point	*see* Subject
Rotat·e|ed|ing	The contrapuntal redistribution of two or more parts within a given texture, such that a part previously functioning as the bass is heard as an upper part, and vice versa (see Dreyfus, 14, 18). Such operations typically involve the manipulation of parts through invertible counterpoint at the octave, and (less commonly) at the tenth or twelfth.
Shadow·ed|ing	Terms for the situation in which 'one voice sings in parallel with a [subject-]statement … in another voice, typically at the interval of a third, sixth or tenth' (Milsom, 'Cipriano', 329). As Milsom further notes, the metaphor is chosen deliberately to indicate the hierarchical relationship between the structural entry and its 'shadow'.
Singleton	'A free-standing statement of the subject, not interlocked with another statement or a counter-subject' (Milsom, 'Cipriano', 329).
Stretto *fuga*	'Two-voice polyphony in which the melodic line of the leading voice is transferred to the following voice … [and] where the voices are temporally separated by what may be termed the "unit" of the counterpoint itself' (Milsom, '*Imitatio*', 146). Subjects suitable for such treatment at the unison, octave, fifth or fourth could be composed at will simply by following the requisite 'interval-stock' (see the discussion in Chapter 2).
Subject	A melodic idea that is repeated and passed between the parts of a polyphonic texture, usually in transposition.

	In the present study, and following Purcell's usage (AoD, 108–9, 112, etc.), the term 'point' signifies the same thing.
Viability	The property of an interlock that measures its ability to serve as a well-formed two-part fragment according to the conventions governing counterpoint and/or handling of dissonance. An interlock capable of serving as such by virtue of its own intervallic content is said to be 'intrinsically viable', whereas a 'conditionally viable' interlock will require specific contextual handling (for example, a given metrical placing, or harmonic clarification supplied by non-imitative parts).

References

Dreyfus, Laurence, *Bach and the Patterns of Invention* (Cambridge, MA: Harvard University Press, 1996).

Milsom, John, 'Crecquillon, Clemens, and four-voice *fuga*', in *Beyond Contemporary Fame: Reassessing the Art of Clemens non Papa and Thomas Crequillon*, ed. Eric Jas (Turnhout: Brepols, 2005), 293–345.

Milsom, John, '"*Imitatio*", "Intertextuality" and Early Music', in *Citation and Authority in Medieval and Renaissance Musical Culture: Learning from the Learned*, ed. Suzannah Clark and Elizabeth Eva Leach (Woodbridge: Boydell, 2006), 141–51.

Milsom, John, 'Cipriano's Flexed *Fuga*', in *Cipriano da Rore: New Perspectives on His Life and Music*, ed. Jessie Ann Owens and Katelijne Schiltz (Turnhout: Brepols, 2016), 293–329.

Purcell, Henry, 'A Brief Introduction to the Art of Descant', in John Playford, *An Introduction to the Skill of Music*, 12th edn (London: Henry Playford, 1694), 85–143.

Schab, Alon, *The Sonatas of Henry Purcell: Rhetoric and Reversal* (Rochester, NY: University of Rochester Press, 2018).

Schubert, Peter N., 'Hidden Forms in Palestrina's *First Book of Four-Voice Motets*', *JAMS*, 60/3 (2007), 483–556.

Two in one upon a Ground.

Chaconne for Flutes, in the Third Act.

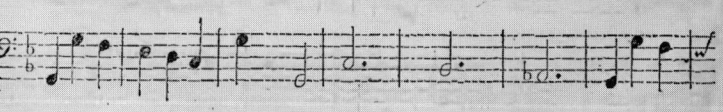

[61]

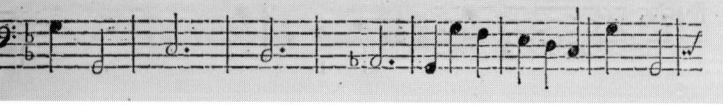

Fig. I.1 Henry Purcell, 'Chaconne for two flutes', from Act III of *The Prophetess, or The History of Dioclesian* (London: John Heptinstall for the Author, 1691), 60–61 (Opera Collection, Music Library, MZ0.523; Western University, London, Canada)

Introduction

What was Purcell aiming to do when he wrote his Chaconne for two flutes in Act III of *The Prophetess, or the History of Dioclesian* (1690; see facing page)? Such questions are not always easy to answer, but in this particular case there are strong grounds for optimism. Even without the informative heading, it is quickly obvious how the piece is constructed. Neither the repetitive ground bass nor the canon at the unison between the recorder parts could plausibly have arisen fortuitously, so at least in the context of compositional technique we can disregard many of the usual caveats about intention: in this work, Purcell was seeking to compose a canon 'Two in one upon a Ground', with the second recorder following the first, two bars later, at the unison. It is a short step from here to begin to reconstruct a process by which this might have been achieved, perhaps with the help of contemporary theoretical discussions; indeed, Purcell himself famously reveals something of his thinking on this particular topic at the very end of his contrapuntal primer 'The Art of Descant', the final part of John Playford's *Introduction to the Skill of Musick* in its twelfth edition of 1694:

Composing upon a *Ground* [is] a very easie thing to do, and requires but little Judgment: 'tis generally used in *Chacones*, where they regard only good Air in the *Treble*, and often the *Ground* is four Notes gradually descending, but to maintain *Fuges* upon it would be difficult, being confined like a *Canon* to a *Plain Song*.[1]

Purcell is admittedly referring here to the maintenance of 'fuges' or imitation over a ground, but earlier in 'The Art of Descant' he makes clear that he understands canon itself only as a stricter species of imitation, 'the eighth and noblest sort of Fugeing ... the Method of which is to answer exactly Note for Note to the end'.[2] Once this is recognized, there are clues in Purcell's description as to how this particular Chaconne might have been invented, though they do not always yield straightforward insight. The final clause, for example, lacks the necessary punctuation – a comma after 'confined' in the quotation above – to clarify that it is 'a *Canon* to a *Plain Song*' that is being compared to the maintenance of 'fuges' on a ground, on the basis that both are 'confined'.

[1] AoD, 144.   [2] Ibid., 114.

1

As it happens, Christopher Simpson had devoted some attention to the matter of composing canons to a plainsong in his *Compendium of Practical Musick* of 1667, though his examples of 'syncopated' or 'driving' canon involve much shorter intervals of time between the canonic entries. If, however, we instead consider the nature of the 'confinement' in Purcell's Chaconne, we can soon understand better the essentially simple solution he found for this 'difficult' task. Most obviously the piece is 'confined' to the ground. Yet tacked on to the end of the usual 'four notes descending' in the ground bass of this piece are an extra two bars – an extension whose duration exactly matches the interval of time between the canonic entries above. It follows that whatever melodic part the second recorder performs to these additional bars of the ground must have been compatible with the third and fourth bars of the ground, and from here that bars 3–4 and 1–2 of the ground, and indeed 1–2 and 5–6, must meet the same condition.

The success of the piece, then, hinges on the design of the ground itself: having decided first upon the nature of the conceit, Purcell devised a ground that proceeded in pairs of bars with identical – or at least greatly overlapping – harmonic implications, both such that a given melodic realization of one pair of bars was almost certainly repeatable in the next pair of bars, and that the range of such melodic realizations was sufficiently varied to support a piece lasting a full thirteen accompanied statements of the ground. While the canon is indeed 'confined', its true confinement is to this recurring two-bar metrical unit and not to the ground as a whole; as such, it is closely akin to much simpler compositional tasks such as the composition of catches (which Simpson also describes with helpful clarity).

This book is fundamentally about how Purcell's music works, and therefore has frequent recourse to the question 'what was Purcell aiming to do', with similar analytical goals to those briefly rehearsed at the start of this Introduction. Of course, not all pieces offer so helpful an analytical window onto their inner workings as this Chaconne, but we do have Purcell's extensive taxonomy of fugal techniques from elsewhere in 'The Art of Descant', and by applying these in his works we can often recover similar starting-points – at least where the various species of counterpoint, imitation and canon are concerned. I began to approach Purcell's music in this way in my doctoral thesis,[3] which sought to develop a historically sensitive analytical approach to the composer's early instrumental music; that is, the consort Fantazias preserved in his great autograph scorebook, *Lbl* Add. MS 30930, and the twenty-two trio sonatas published in the *Sonnata's of III Parts* (1683) and the posthumous

---

[3] 'Purcell and the Poetics of Artifice: Compositional Strategies in the Fantasias and Sonatas' (unpublished PhD thesis, King's College, London, 2006).

Sonata's in Four Parts (1697).[4] Much of the material in Chapters 1–4 (and some of that in Chapters 6 and 7 as well) is derived from this thesis, whose emphasis on this repertoire was inspired in part by Martin Adams's conviction, expressed at the start of his own book on Purcell's music – which remains the sole comprehensive overview of the composer's musical style and development – that

Despite the extraordinary surface changes in Purcell's style ... he was a deeply conservative composer, who had to struggle to reconcile the tide of the times – which he helped along its way, and which he identified primarily with Italian music – with the compositional priorities of his earlier music.[5]

It seemed to me in the first place that if this were the case, then a priority of any serious analytical engagement with Purcell's music ought to be the recovery of those 'compositional priorities', hence the emphasis in what follows, as in the brief discussion of the 'Chaconne for two flutes' above, on recovering how and why Purcell approached the task of composition in particular technical circumstances. From this starting-point, it would then be possible to understand better Purcell's continued promotion of these priorities in his later music; the fruits of which aim form the bulk of Chapters 5–7 of this book.

The idea of Purcell's conservatism, however – at least inasmuch as I understood this to mean some sort of ideological commitment to the preservation of past styles *per se* – seemed so fundamentally dissonant with the characteristics of Purcell's music as I experienced it that I began to look around for an alternative explanation for his interest in apparently arcane imitative and contrapuntal methods. What I hit upon was the notion of compositional 'artifice', the idea that music could be raised to a higher plane through the systematic application of imitative devices and other self-conscious conceits to produce a highly organized, tightly constructed and equally expressive, even meaningful (if sometimes self-referential) kind of composition. Here, then, is another answer to the question of what Purcell was aiming at in the 'Chaconne for two flutes', this time in a more general poetic sense: he was taking a simple chaconne, 'where they regard only good Air in the *Treble*' and transforming it into an altogether

---

[4] In spite of the difference of title, both sets contain sonatas for two trebles and a contrapuntally active bass (analogous to the Italian designation *a* 3) with thoroughbass; the confusion arises from the question of whether or not the thoroughbass is counted separately. According to the Preface to the 1683 publication this part was in any case only provided at the last minute, and evidently Purcell did not consider it sufficiently independent to feature in the naming of the set; by contrast, the editor of the 1697 publication opted to reflect the number of physical partbooks printed rather than the musical texture. On this and related issues see Peter Holman, *Henry Purcell* (Oxford University Press, 1994), 85–6; Martin Adams, *Henry Purcell: The Origins and Development of His Musical Style* (Cambridge University Press, 1995), 27; Alon Schab, *The Trio Sonatas of Henry Purcelll: Rhetoric and Reversal* (University of Rochester Press, 2018), 2.

[5] Adams, *Henry Purcell*, ix.

more exalted species of composition through the application of 'the noblest sort of Fugeing'. And what is more, the reader is aided in the identification of this aim through the careful labelling of the piece 'Two in one upon a Ground': the compositional artifice is both a creative conceit and an outward marker of poetic register, a sign that this is music to be taken seriously in spite of (or perhaps all the more importantly because of) its theatrical context.

Undoubtedly this poetic basis for the understanding of Purcell's style requires circumspection, but by drawing on his own theoretical writings and those of other musicians of the time, we can build up a picture of his ideas about compositional artifice, which compare revealingly with the contemporaneous conceptual basis for art in other domains. Artifice thus offers an attractive alternative to conservatism – or, as I would recognize more readily now, at least a more satisfactory explanation of its origins.

The careful consideration of how Purcell contrived his most 'artificial' music also offered an ideal inroad into the project of finding methods of engaging with the music without the need to resort to anachronistic analytical tools, or aesthetic assumptions derived from the study of much later music. Here I must acknowledge the hugely important role played by my research supervisor Laurence Dreyfus, and in particular his approach to the music of J. S. Bach in *Bach and the Patterns of Invention*, which was in many ways the model for my own engagement with Purcell's early instrumental music. Under his guidance I began to see that Purcell's instrumental music, and in particular his approach to contrapuntal invention and its elaboration, could be much better understood in the context of theoretical discussions with which he would have been familiar, and that considerable insight could be gained into how this music was constructed by asking how and why he might have approached the task of composition in the light of what contemporary treatises say (and indeed omit) about how to write music.

Although a significant portion of this book is devoted to the consideration of these principles in connection with Purcell's later, vocal music, the origins of these ideas in conjunction with the instrumental music are worth emphasizing because they bring into focus some of the reasons why this kind of approach to Purcell's music has not developed before. The reception of Purcell's instrumental music is in itself a complicated topic;[6] since it forms the background to Adams's identification of the key role of these early instrumental works, and this notion is in turn so central to my own understanding of how Purcell approached the task of composition

---

[6] Study of the reception of Purcell's music is yet to develop to the degree found in scholarship on other composers. For a comprehensive overview that lays the groundwork for future studies, see Rebecca Herissone, 'Performance History and Reception', in *The Ashgate Research Companion to Henry Purcell*, ed. Rebecca Herissone (Farnham: Ashgate, 2012), 303–51. See also John Higney, 'Henry Purcell: A Reception/Dissemination Study, 1695–1771' (unpublished PhD thesis, University of Western Ontario, 2008).

throughout his career, an outline of this reception at this point would serve as a useful background against which to turn to analytical matters themselves in Part I.

THE RECEPTION OF PURCELL'S INSTRUMENTAL MUSIC

Purcell occupies a somewhat unusual position in the history of English instrumental music. For a composer of his stature, his output of consort music (thirteen complete fantazias and two In nomines, together with four pavans) is considerably smaller than might be expected of a composer of the previous two generations, when the consort tradition was at its height.[7] Even if one adds to these works the twenty-two 'trio' sonatas and the assorted orchestral works of the earliest part of Purcell's career, his complete catalogue of instrumental chamber music seems meagre in comparison with that of Jenkins or Locke, William Lawes or Coprario. Given that these composers were all (with the exception of Locke) employed principally as composers of consort music, this is perhaps no surprise. Indeed, the fact that there was no longer a place, in the post-Restoration court, for a composer who dedicated his time almost exclusively to consort music, is a good indication of the decline of English consort music that lies behind Purcell's comparatively modest contribution to its repertoire.

Yet while this contribution was indeed modest in numerical terms, this is far from the case in terms of the accomplished nature of Purcell's highly individual approach to the genres of fantazia and In nomine. Christopher D. S. Field describes Purcell's fantazias as a 'surpassing tribute' to the genre, praising their 'unique brilliance and intensity', and it is these qualities that have contributed to their establishment as 'cornerstones of the modern viol consort repertory', in Peter Holman's words.[8] From a historical point of view, too, these works are of great importance. While the consort music brings to a close a tradition stretching back almost two centuries, the sonatas provide valuable evidence of the pressures of encroaching Italian fashions, bearing witness both to the reasons behind the eventual obsolescence of chamber music for viols and to the response of a talented composer in a particular culture to the music of another.

It is surprising, therefore, that Purcell's instrumental chamber music has not received more attention from scholars. While a number of articles have

[7] Several other works often described as 'consort music' are written for quite different ensembles, hence their absence here. Peter Holman associates the 'Three Parts upon a Ground' with the three violin and bass grouping of the 'Broken Consort', and the same may be said of the four-part Pavan in G minor; both contrast strongly with the more homogeneous scoring of the fantazias. The four-part Chacony in G minor, meanwhile, appears to be orchestral; see Holman, 'Compositional Choices in Henry Purcell's *Three Parts upon a Ground*', *EM*, 29/2 (2001), 250–61 (254–5).

[8] Christopher D. S. Field and Michael Tilmouth, 'Fantasia: 1. To 1700', §8 ('Great Britain'), in *Grove Music Online* (accessed 22 November 2018); Peter Holman and Robert Thompson, 'Purcell: (3) Henry Purcell (ii)', §3 ('Instrumental Music'), in *Grove Music Online* (accessed 22 November 2018).

explored the stylistic origins of Purcell's works, and they are given significant space in most comprehensive surveys of the composer's music, the
number of studies is small in comparison to the breadth of scholarship
surrounding his sacred music, music for the theatre and vocal music for the
court. One reason for this under-representation is that instrumental music
sits uncomfortably with a number of the orthodoxies that have built up
around Purcell since his lifetime, not least the conviction that his position
as the foremost composer of vocal music in English formed the greatest
part of his legacy.

This was a view that crystallized very early on in the reception of
Purcell's music, in the years immediately following his death, particularly
in the enduring trope of Purcell as *Orpheus Britannicus*. This sobriquet
seems to have first arisen with the publication of Henry Playford's anthology of Purcell's songs of the same name, perhaps suggested by Dryden's
reference in the elegy that headed the collection.[9] As Richard Luckett
notes, Purcell was by no means the first to be honoured with this particular
epithet: 'the significant factor … is not any inherent originality in the
forms and language with which Purcell's contemporaries mourned him …
but the way in which these commonplaces became definitive; the substance
of what men felt was for once appropriate to, and indeed appropriative of,
the available means of expression.'[10] In other words, the mythical figure of
Orpheus, so long a commonplace of Renaissance discussions of music,
became much more than a simple analogy in the discourse surrounding
Purcell's death. As well as providing a convenient classical metaphor for the
rhetorical force of musical expression, it furnished a whole system of
understanding Purcell's music and its importance to the national identity.
For the author of another anonymous ode to Purcell,

> The truthless Tales, which frantick Poets tell
> Of *Thebes*, and moving Stones, and Journeys down to Hell,
> Were only Prophecies of Musick's force, which we
> Have wonderfully seen fulfill'd in Thee.[11]

When viewed in the context of the ensuing reception, it is not only the
general allusion here to Orpheus' musical powers that proves to have been
influential. The specific application of this epithet to Purcell in the context
of late seventeenth-century musical politics in England represented an
overt claim for the supremacy of English music, and Purcell's fundamental

[9] John Dryden, 'An Ode on the Death of Mr Henry Purcell', in Henry Purcell, *Orpheus Britannicus* (London: Henry Playford, 1698), iv.
[10] Richard Luckett, '"Or rather our musical Shakspeare": Charles Burney's Purcell', in *Music in Eighteenth-Century England: Essays in Memory of Charles Cudworth*, ed. Christopher Hogwood and Richard Luckett (Cambridge University Press, 1983), 59–77 (62).
[11] Anonymous, 'Another Ode on the same occasion. By a Person of Quality', in Purcell, *Orpheus Britannicus*, iv; also in Franklin B. Zimmerman, *Henry Purcell, 1659–1695: His Life and Times* (London: Macmillan, 1967), 329.

contribution to that tradition, the repercussions of which can still be detected in the earliest modern musical scholarship of the twentieth century. Among the examples in *Orpheus Britannicus*, Henry Hall was perhaps the most explicit author to make such a claim, in addressing himself 'To the Memory of [his] Dear Friend Mr. Henry Purcell':

> How can I e're enough the Man admire,
> Who's rais'd the *British* o're the *Thracian* Lyre!
> That *Bard* could make the Savage-kind obey,
> But thou hast tam'd yet greater Brutes than they:
> Who e're like *Purcell* cou'd our Passions move!
> Who ever sang so feelingly of Love![12]

Hall's poem draws attention to two key features of Purcell reception in the years following his death, both of which proved crucial to the subsequent understanding of the composer. Firstly, the power of Purcell's music is associated principally with his vocal output: the notion of Purcell himself 'singing' through his music is common to much of the poetry printed in *Orpheus Britannicus*. Secondly, it is notable that Purcell is styled, both by Hall and others, the '*British* Orpheus', not 'New', 'Modern', or any number of appropriate adjectives that could equally have been chosen. The national element here reflects the contemporary struggle to find a prominent place for English music in a wider European context, and in the later eighteenth century would nourish an important attempt to define a native musical tradition in the face of the dominance of Italian opera. Still later, the nationalist element of Purcellian scholarship resurfaces in the context of the leading Austro-German musical aesthetic of the nineteenth and early twentieth centuries; the notion of Purcell as a national musical icon is therefore an important part of the reception of Purcell up to the present day.

In one sense, it is not at all surprising that the poems and elegies printed at the front of *Orpheus Britannicus* celebrate Purcell's achievements as a national vocal composer: the collection was, after all, an anthology of songs, not instrumental music. On the other hand, the very existence of such a volume, and the fact that it was this collection of works above all others that came to symbolize the most treasured part of Purcell's output, attests independently to the particular importance of his songs as the musical legacy to which Purcell's contemporaries clung. Henry Playford makes it clear in the course of his address 'The Bookseller to the Reader' that the book was much expanded from its original proportions in order to have it 'as compleat as possibly could be made, both in regard to the Memory of that great Master, and the Satisfaction of all that buy it'.[13] He goes on to explain the concentration on vocal music, noting that

---

[12] Henry Hall, 'To the Memory of my Dear Friend Mr. *Henry Purcell*', in Purcell, *Orpheus Britannicus*, vi; also quoted in Zimmerman, *Life and Times*, 348.
[13] Henry Playford, 'The Bookseller to the Reader', in Purcell, *Orpheus Britannicus*, iii.

The Author's extraordinary Talent in all sorts of Musick is sufficiently known, but he was especially admir'd for the *Vocal*, having a peculiar Genius to express the Energy of *English* Words, whereby he mov'd the Passions of his Auditors.[14]

It was this view that set the tone for much of the eighteenth century. By way of example, we might consider Charles Burney's account of Purcell. Although he was well acquainted with Purcell's instrumental music as well as his vocal – he gives a brief mention to the sonatas and notes that Purcell's symphonies and act tunes were used in the London theatres in his own memory – by far the greater part of his discussion is given over to the vocal music.[15] The form and contents of the two volumes of *Orpheus Britannicus* occupy no fewer than ten pages of the twenty-seven devoted to Purcell. Even more revealingly, when he adopts a more philosophical tone Burney inevitably returns to the vocal music:

Though his dramatic style and recitative were formed in a great measure on French models, there is a latent power and force in his expression of English words, whatever be the subject, that will make an unprejudiced native of this island feel, more than all the elegance, grace, and refinement of modern Music less happily applied, can do.[16]

Clearly Burney understands Purcell's greatest achievement to be in the musical setting of the English language. Yet even this characteristic could not rescue Purcell from increasing obscurity. 'So much is our great musician's celebrity already consigned to tradition, that it will soon be as difficult to find his songs, or at least to *hear* them, as those of his predecessors Orpheus and Amphion, with which Cerberus was lulled to sleep, or the city of Thebes constructed.'[17]

Burney's *History* is primarily, at least in its treatment of English music from 1650 onwards, a history of how the Italian style came to dominate and, in particular, the rise of Italian opera in English musical culture. He was heavily reliant on the writings of Roger North (who was himself notoriously biased towards the Italian style) in many details, not least in the section following that on Purcell describing the 'Progress of the Violin in England, to the end of the last century', in which he reprints whole pages from North's *Memoirs of Musick* verbatim.[18] Burney compares Purcell's sonatas to those of Corelli and finds the former 'barbarous' by comparison; given his greater interest in vocal music in the first place, it is little surprise that Purcell's instrumental music is given short shrift.[19] And given Burney's importance to the subsequent

---

[14] Ibid., iii [original emphasis].

[15] Charles Burney, *A General History of Music, from the Earliest Ages until the Present Period* (London: the author, 1789), ed. Frank Mercer, 2 vols (New York: Dover, 1957), II, 403 (sonatas); 389, footnote 'n' (theatre act tunes).

[16] Ibid., II, 404.   [17] Ibid., II, 380.

[18] Compare ibid., II, 407–9 with John Wilson, ed., *Roger North on Music* (London: Novello, 1959), 355–7.

[19] Burney, *History*, II, 403.

history of music scholarship in Great Britain, it is little surprise to see this pattern repeated well into the Purcell scholarship of the twentieth century.[20]

It could admittedly be argued that the neglect of Purcell's instrumental music is legitimate, given the comparative sizes of Purcell's contributions to each of these genres. Conversely, the importance of a particular body of works is not necessarily in proportion to its size: as I suggested above, Purcell's composition of fantazias and trio sonatas relatively early in his career, and the degree of their concentration on particular compositional problems – the solutions to which would occupy him for the rest of his life – makes them crucial to the understanding of his development as a composer. As such, they occupy a far more important position amongst his works than has often been recognized.

The problem with the literature surrounding Purcell's instrumental chamber music is compounded by an overwhelming preoccupation with a limited range of central issues, the most prominent among which are the surviving manuscript sources, the differing motivations behind the composition of Purcell's works in the two genres of fantazia and sonata, issues of performance practice, and the dates of composition of the sonatas. Behind almost all of these discussions is a more fundamental and all-embracing concern to determine on the one hand the nature and extent of the influence of the Italian sonata on Purcell and, on the other, the importance of his engagement with the native consort music of the earlier seventeenth century. Again, a number of orthodoxies prevail in this discourse, concerning Purcell's supposed conservative attitude and his ultimate failure to adopt the idiom of the Italian sonata.

One of the frustrations of studying Purcell's approach to the composition of these works is the paucity of contemporary documentation concerning his artistic goals and his attitudes towards different musical styles. The surviving sources tend to offer tantalizing snippets of information, often asking new questions rather than resolving existing ones. As a result, successive writers have been forced to rely on the same evidence, often speculating against similar backgrounds and even repeating the opinions of previous commentators. Roger North, a figure who is almost ubiquitously cited in studies of Purcell's sonatas, could almost have been foreseeing this problem when he wrote in his *Memoires of Musick* (1720) that:

In matters of Antiquity there are two extreams, 1. a totall neglect, and 2. perpetuall guessing; between which proper evidences are the temper; that is, if there be any, to make the best of them; if none, to desist.[21]

If the study of Purcell's instrumental chamber music has come to a similar impasse, North's plea for silence given the absence of 'proper

[20] For a more detailed account of this twentieth-century scholarship see Howard, 'Purcell and the Poetics of Artifice', 24–7.
[21] Wilson, *Roger North on Music*, 317.

evidences' seems unsatisfactory, since it leaves so much unclear about how Purcell viewed his compositions in this genre. Indeed, there are aspects of the existing literature that might suggest new ways of proceeding, principally through an examination of its methodology. Of particular importance in this respect is the dominant mode of analysis, which ever since the late eighteenth century has sought to account for aspects of Purcell's style by establishing patterns of influence.

The idea that Purcell's music gradually took on more and more Italianate characteristics was certainly evident in the works of Burney and John Hawkins, and in the earlier eighteenth-century works on which they drew; Roger North's oft-quoted line concerning 'the Orfeus Britannicus Mr H. Purcell, who unhappily began to shew his great skill before the reforme of musick *all'Italliana*, and while he was warm in the persuit of it, dyed' essentially articulates the same premise.[22] Ultimately, the issue can be traced directly to the preface of Purcell's 1683 Sonatas, in which the composer is said to have 'faithfully endeavour'd a just imitation of the most fam'd Italian Masters'.[23]

The first twentieth-century commentator to have taken up the question of just who these 'fam'd Italian masters' were seems to have been J. Frederick Bridge.[24] In a 1915 paper he championed the cause of Nicola Matteis, whose name he had presumably encountered in Burney's *History* before following the trail back to its source in the description of Matteis' importance in North's *Memoires of Musick*.[25] In the ensuing discussion, Hubert Parry reiterated Fuller-Maitland's speculation, from the preface to the Purcell Society's 1893 edition of the *Sonatas of Three Parts*, that the principal influence was G. B. Vitali, and called attention as well to 'G. B. Bononcini, whose Opus No. 1 came out in 1665 [*recte* G. M. Bononcini, Op. 1 Venice 1666]' and G. B. Bassani.[26] Some two years later, William Barclay Squire took up the debate in a letter to the *Musical Times* drawing attention to Purcell's quotation of a sonata by '*Lelio Calista*' in 'The Art of Descant'.[27] Lelio Colista (1629–80) was virtually unknown in 1917, and Barclay Squire assembled a selection of historical references to him and noted the similarity of some sonatas attributed to him in the Bodleian

[22] Wilson, *Roger North on Music*, 307. As J. A. Westrup notes (*Purcell*, 6th edn (New York: Oxford University Press, 1995), 241) this is indeed a 'rather muddled sentence', but the intended meaning (which, unfortunately, Westrup does little to clarify) is apparently that Purcell was 'warm in the persuit' of the Italian style, and would have mastered it had he not died so young.

[23] Henry Purcell, *Sonnata's of III Parts* (London: the author, 1683), preface [n. p.]; quoted in PSr 5, x. For more on this preface, including its authorship, see Chapter 2.

[24] J. Frederick Bridge, 'Purcell's Fantazias and Sonatas', *Proceedings of the Musical Association*, 42 (1915–16), 1–13.

[25] Ibid., 4–7; compare Burney, *History*, ii, 406–10 with Wilson, *Roger North on Music*, 355–8.

[26] Bridge, 'Purcell's Fantazias and Sonatas', 11. For biographical details of the composers listed in this paragraph see *Grove Music Online*.

[27] William Barclay Squire, 'Purcell and Italian Music', *MT*, 58 (1917), 157. The quotation from 'Calista' is in AoD, 124; the work in question turns out to be by Carlo Ambrogio Lonati (see Chapter 1, note 21).

Library to those of Purcell. Apart from the suggestion of Colista as a possible influence on Purcell, Barclay Squire's letter is most important for its introduction of Purcell's theoretical treatise to the debate surrounding Purcell's chamber music.

Little more was added to this debate until Michael Tilmouth came to consider the evidence afresh in 1959.[28] Tilmouth reviewed the previous suggestions, adding the name of Maurizio Cazzati to the list of Italian sonata composers and further suggesting that Purcell may have been influenced by Frescobaldi's keyboard works.[29] In presenting the Italian influence on Purcell as that of a body of well-known works by famous composers whose works reached England during the 1670s, Tilmouth managed to leave behind the ultimately futile attempts of earlier commentators to pin down the exact names of the Italian masters whom Purcell professed to have imitated. Nevertheless, and despite the obvious insights available from such an approach, its limitations and potential pitfalls are still too seldom subjected to critical examination. In the first place, it is susceptible to the kind of 'perpetuall guessing' that North so disliked, since its conclusions can rarely amount to more than informed speculation. Secondly, and more seriously, it focuses attention away from the activities of the composer, instead understanding the characteristics of Purcell's music according to its fidelity, or otherwise, to the stylistic expectations established by the putative influence.

This observation forms the background to my own approach to the analysis of these works, which attempts to restore priority to Purcell's agency as a composer by examining how the music might have been composed, by using the techniques of imitation and canon as an analytical framework to understand the decisions that he took as he worked. By concentrating not simply on the similarities between Purcell's works and the music of his predecessors and contemporaries (or indeed his successors), but on how Purcell made use of what he learnt from these sources, and what it was about them that seemed to interest him, it is possible to gain a much clearer picture of his priorities as a composer, and the reasons behind some of the important stylistic characteristics that we recognize in his work. This approach has the added attraction of focusing analytical observations on techniques that might have been familiar to the composer,

---

[28] Michael Tilmouth, 'The Technique and Forms of Purcell's Sonatas', *ML*, 40/4 (1959), 109–21 (112–13).

[29] Ibid. Direct evidence of Purcell's knowledge of music by Frescobaldi is lacking, and in any case this suggestion seems more obviously relevant to the consideration of Purcell's organ music. At least two organ voluntaries associated with John Blow are now known to be derived from works by Frescobaldi: see David J. Smith, 'Continuity, Change and the Emergence of Idiomatic Organ Repertoire in Seventeenth-Century England', in *Studies in English Organ Music*, ed. Ian Quinn (London: Routledge, 2018), 122–41; also Brian Hodge, 'A New Frescobaldi Attribution', *MT*, 122 (1981), 263–5, and Barry Cooper, 'Problems in the Transmission of Blow's Organ Music', *ML*, 75/4 (1994), 522–47 (523–5).

rather than relying on methods developed in conjunction with other, often later repertoires. At the same time, one can begin to see how these aspects of Purcell's music relate to the wider artistic and intellectual concerns of his close contemporaries.

At the heart of this understanding of Purcell's chamber music is a re-evaluation of his relationship with the music of past composers, and in particular the status of complex imitative textures in his style. These have often been taken as markers of conservatism on Purcell's part, perhaps in part because the virtual omission of the Fantazias from the reception of Purcell's music up to the early 1900s had resulted in a notion of his style much more skewed towards the later, Italianate music. Again, it was Bridge who drew attention to them:

> I do not think it is widely known that Purcell followed the prevalent custom and set to work to compose Fancies before he took the remarkable step of writing his *First Set of Sonnatas* for Two Violins and Bass. I do not think these Fancies have ever been published, but I have had most of them played at various times.[30]

Following this reference, the fantazias received their first publication in the edition of 1927 by Peter Warlock and André Mangeot.[31] Not until 1959, however, would Thurston Dart edit these and the remaining instrumental works for the Purcell Society, making Warlock's the only English edition of Purcell's fantazias for thirty years.[32] This fascinating performers' score, replete with liberal expression marks and brackets to draw the eye to Purcell's contrapuntal ingenuity, may be considered an English equivalent to Busoni's editions of Bach's fugues. Indeed, the comparison with Bach is one that Warlock makes explicit in the essay that accompanies the edition, observing that 'we must go forward to Bach before we can find any music which displays such a consummate mastery of all the devices of counterpoint allied to so wide a range of profoundly expressive harmony'.[33] Such an appeal anticipates the similar suggestions of Westrup, the common motivation being an improved reputation for Purcell by association with the later masters. Warlock's nationalist agenda becomes more explicitly nationalist in the following passage:

> Despite their startling originality, the Fantasias are essentially in the tradition of [the] Elizabethan polyphonists. They are the last heirs of the sixteenth century rather than the ancestors of the eighteenth. They stand at the end of a great period of English instrumental music, the crowning glory of a century and a half of rapid and continuous development. After them, there was complete silence in England,

[30] Bridge, 'Purcell's Fantazias and Sonatas', 1.
[31] Henry Purcell, *Fantasias for Strings*, ed. André Mangeot, transcrib. Peter Warlock (London: Boosey & Hawkes, 1927).
[32] PS 31 (1959). In fact, the works were presented to a much higher editorial standard than the Mangeot/Warlock edition as early as the 1930s in a German edition ed. Herbert Just (2 vols; Berlin: Nagels Musik-Archiv, 1930–35).
[33] Purcell, *Fantasias for Strings*, ed. Mangeot/Warlock, 'Historical Preface' [n. p.].

as far as chamber-music was concerned, until the beginning of the twentieth century.[34]

Such chauvinistic pride in Purcell's achievements in this genre is decidedly a twentieth-century phenomenon, however. The obscurity of Purcell's fantazias in the eighteenth and nineteenth centuries reached back even to Purcell's day, to the extent that we are not even sure whether the works were ever performed in his lifetime. Apart from Fantazia II in three parts, none of the fantazias survives in a set of parts suitable for performing.[35] One of the most pressing issues in connection with the fantazias, therefore, has always been the question of why they were written at all. The main alternative to a performance is that they were exercises in contrapuntal technique. This would certainly be in keeping with the rigorous exploration of imitative ideas contained in each fantazia, but even if the original inspiration was didactic, it is surely almost inconceivable that Purcell should expend so much effort only to keep the works hidden from his colleagues, especially given that these included such enthusiastic viol players as John Gostling (better known as the 'stupendious Base' for whom Purcell wrote many of the virtuoso solos in his anthems and court odes).[36] Furthermore, the inclusion of performance instructions such as 'Drag', 'Brisk' and 'Quick' suggests that Purcell at least imagined the possibility that the works would be performed. If they were, it must have been on the rarest of occasions and in the most intimate of surroundings, since no surviving account from any contemporary musician so much as mentions their existence.

Purcell's three fantazias in three parts and nine in four are all contained in the same manuscript as most of the 1697 Sonatas, *Lbl* Add. MS 30930, into which they were apparently copied during 1680. The same scorebook also contains an incomplete tenth fantazia in four parts, a four-part pavan, the five-part Fantazia upon One Note, and two In nomines in six and seven parts, respectively.[37] These, together with the four three-part pavans found only in *Lbl* Add. MS 33236, make up the complete set of Purcell's consort music.[38]

In general terms these works conform to earlier descriptions of these genres from Morley to Simpson, and their immediate ancestors were the very examples by Jenkins and Locke to which Roger North referred as the last works of their kind.[39] As a result, their impact on the literature

---

[34] Ibid., [n. p.].

[35] Robert Shay and Robert Thompson, *Purcell Manuscripts: The Principal Musical Sources* (Cambridge University Press, 2000), 106–13.

[36] Watkins Shaw and Robert Ford, 'Gostling, John', in *Grove Music Online* (accessed 22 November 2018). The famous epithet is Evelyn's; see Esmond S. de Beer, ed., *The Diary of John Evelyn* (Oxford University Press, 1955), IV, 404 (28 January, 1685).

[37] Shay and Thompson, *Purcell Manuscripts*, 90–97.

[38] The few dance movements and overture also contained in *Lbl* Add. MS 30930 need not concern us here, since they are not directly related to Purcell's sonatas or fantazias.

[39] Thomas Morley, *A Plaine and Easie Introduction to Practicall Musick* (London: P. Short, 1597); Christopher Simpson, *A Compendium of Practical Musick* (London, H. Brome, 1667). On

concerning Purcell's instrumental music has been to highlight supposedly
conservative elements of his style, engendering what must be seen as a clear
reaction against the prevailing view of Purcell's modernity, as documented
above, in the first half of the twentieth century.

Purcell's instrumental music has always been regarded as having elements that belong more to the English music of the previous century than
to the continental repertoire. Roger North's comment on the character of
Purcell's sonatas is quoted almost universally in connection with such
observations:

Witness Mr H. Purcell in his noble set of sonatas, which however clog'd with
somewhat of an English vein, for which they are unworthily despised, are very
artificiall and good musick.[40]

Quite how they were 'clog'd with somewhat of an English vein', however, we
are not told by North. There are perhaps two obvious grounds for his
observation. Firstly, it could refer to those local details of cadence, voice-
leading and melodic character that are often identified (if somewhat superficially) as peculiarly English. In his chapter on Purcell's 'Style and
Development', for example, Westrup gives examples of phenomena such
as expressive chromaticism, the 'overlapping' of two alternative cadential
progressions, false relations and irregularly resolved suspensions.[41] Unlike
some earlier writers, Westrup did not necessarily understand such features as
English in themselves. Rather, their significance was that the English, and
Purcell in particular, continued to use them long after they had become
obsolete on the continent: 'The chief interest of Purcell's use of false relations
is that it shows him, like some of his contemporaries, still attached to older
traditions.'[42] By the 1950s a better awareness of the music of the earlier
seventeenth century had begun to result in the questioning of even this
approach to Purcell's harmonic 'individualities'. While such phenomena had
seemed irregular, and even 'barbarous' by the standards of Corelli and
Handel, they began to seem more and more familiar when compared to
earlier works, either English or Italian. Tilmouth observed that 'some
commentators have isolated, as purely English or Purcellian characteristics,
traits which were the common property of all western music of the period',
inserting a *Largo* from Colista's sixth sonata to illustrate his point.[43] At the
very least, then, the conventional view of Purcell's harmonic eccentricity
seemed in need of refinement: it was clear that the 'English vein' of his
sonatas could not be explained simply by reference to this aspect of his style.

This leads to the second obvious interpretation of North's assessment of
the Sonatas, that he was referring in particular to their contrapuntal

contemporary descriptions of musical genres see Rebecca Herissone, *Music Theory in Seventeenth-Century England* (Oxford University Press, 2000), 209–14.
[40] Wilson, *Roger North on Music*, 310 (note 65).   [41] Westrup, *Purcell*, 246–53.   [42] Ibid., 251.
[43] Tilmouth, 'The Technique and Forms', 120.

density. The analytical implications of this possibility are worked out in more detail in Chapter 4; in the reception history outlined here, by contrast, this observation continued to be framed primarily in the context of patterns of influence among composers. In this context the 'rediscovery' of Purcell's fantazias and other consort music in the early twentieth century afforded a new opportunity to assess the relationship between Purcell's instrumental music and that of his predecessors. Ultimately it was this newly recognized stylistic background, together with the realization that several of the works associated with Purcell's most Italianate manner – not least the music to *The Tempest* which had been ascribed to him since the eighteenth century – were in fact not by Purcell at all, that permitted the reassessment of his style that was underway at the time that Adams was writing his book in the early 1990s.

An early indication of the new understanding of Purcell's chamber music appears in Franklin Zimmerman's 1967 biography of the composer. Having introduced the 1683 Sonatas, like Westrup and others before him, by quoting the newspaper advertisements concerning subscription and referring to Purcell's address 'to the reader', Zimmerman turns to the much discussed question of the 'great Italian masters' Purcell claimed to have imitated, suggesting that

These putative Italian models, should they be discovered one day, were probably not very important. Purcell's trio-sonatas are so like some of his fantasias in style and expression that it is fairly safe to assume that here as elsewhere he had been for the most part his own instructor in studying English masterpieces of the immediate past. Furthermore, it was a very common thing to claim Italian provenance for all sorts of compositions. Such claims should be interpreted rather as a kind of window-dressing than as confessions of deliberate eclecticism on the part of the composer.[44]

Zimmerman's biography was the second of a projected series of three volumes on Purcell – the *Analytical Catalogue, Life and Times*, and *Analytical Essays on his Musical Forms* – that has, regrettably, never been completed; thus we never really see how such views would have affected his reading of the music. The general thrust of this argument was nevertheless to gain ground in the following years, strengthened in particular by the increasing interest in Purcell's study and assimilation of 'ancient' styles. In his PhD thesis Robert Shay concluded that, even in the context of the general trend in early Restoration church music to look toward pre-Commonwealth examples, Purcell's engagement with older styles was in itself remarkable, and contributed greatly to his development, almost alone among his English colleagues, of a conservative, contrapuntal style:

The diligence with which Purcell pursued an interest in old polyphony in the years around 1680, copying a number of late sixteenth- and early seventeenth-century

---

[44] Zimmerman, *Life and Times*, 103.

anthems and emulating the style of these in newly-composed works (not to mention similar interests in the viol fantasia, then also an antiquated polyphonic genre), remains remarkable, if for no other reason than because Purcell alone among the important composers of Restoration England seems to have been so deeply affected by a sense of historical consciousness.[45]

The two most recent published studies of Purcell's consort music both draw heavily on such a view of Purcell's attitude towards the music of previous generations, though each puts a slightly different emphasis on it. Peter Holman, who examines the repertoire most comprehensively in his article for *The Purcell Companion*, concentrates on establishing the English precedent for Purcell's fantazias, and in a shorter discussion of the sonatas emphasizes their reliance on counterpoint and other 'conservative' traits.[46] Martin Adams, meanwhile, uses the fantazias as a paradigmatic representation of Purcell's early training in the old polyphonic style, which he views as central to any understanding of the later music.[47] Against this background, the sonatas are seen as a kind of early attempt at the reconciliation of English and continental practice that Purcell would ultimately achieve (at least according to this model) in the mature works of the 1690s.

Holman gives far more emphasis to the archaic nature of Purcell's fantazias than any study we have encountered hitherto. He seemingly rejects any idea that they might have been written with performance in mind, preferring to suggest (much as Shay implied) that they were undertaken for didactic purposes.[48] A short survey of his comments on each of the important consort works is revealing in its tendency to emphasize Purcell's links with tradition: the four-part pavan is in a style from 'around 1600', and the three-part pavans are indebted to Locke.[49] The seven-part In nomine is 'in many respects ... closer in style to sixteenth- rather than seventeenth-century In nomines', the three-part fantazias 'owe much to Orlando Gibbons's published set (c1620)', and the 'main models [for the four-part fantazias] are Locke's fantasias, particularly those in the Consort of Four Parts'.[50] In more general terms it is clear that Holman sees Purcell's fascination with counterpoint as a direct result of his interest in earlier styles:

When all is said and done there are several aspects of Purcell's fantasias that cannot be accounted for in the music of his immediate predecessors ... One has to go back to the reign of James I, to John Bull and Elway Bevin (whose canons were praised by Purcell in *An Introduction to the Skill of Music* ['The Art of Descant']), before encountering a body of English music so taken up with formal contrapuntal devices.[51]

[45] Robert S. Shay, 'Henry Purcell and "Ancient" Music in Restoration England' (unpublished PhD thesis, University of North Carolina, Chapel Hill, 1991), 107.
[46] Peter Holman, 'Consort Music', in *The Purcell Companion*, ed. Michael Burden (London: Faber & Faber, 1995), 254–98.
[47] Adams, *Henry Purcell*, 8–14, 26–36, 91–117.   [48] Holman, 'Consort Music', 271–2.
[49] Ibid., 267.   [50] Ibid., 272–3.   [51] Ibid., 278.

This interest in Purcell's cultivation of dense polyphonic textures also influences Holman's discussion of the sonatas. In fact, he even suggests that it may have been one of the main reasons why Purcell should have been interested in the Italian trio sonata at all.[52] Throughout his account of the sonatas, Holman emphasizes their contrapuntal pedigree; indeed, his discussion consists almost entirely of a survey of the various types of fugal movement, to the extent that he does not mention at all some of those types of movement – such as the opening *Grave* or slow triple-time *Largo* – which are arguably more 'modern' and Italianate than the various canzonas and other fugues. Furthermore, the apparently persuasive underlying implication, that the pursuit of contrapuntal mastery creates a continuity between the two genres in which Purcell worked, is fundamentally problematic. This is because Purcell's approach to the writing of counterpoint, as we shall see in Chapters 2 and 3, encompasses a substantially different set of aims and techniques in the canzona movements of the sonatas when compared with the fantazias. Other movements in the sonatas come closer to the techniques of the fantazias, but Holman does not mention these either.

The central premise underpinning Adams's influential thesis of Purcell as conservative is that Purcell's whole style rested on his study of the contrapuntal music of previous generations of English composers, and that these techniques continued to exert an influence on even his most Italianate-sounding music of the 1690s. This view of the importance of Purcell's consort music is clearly in line with that of Peter Warlock some seventy years before:

He produced the final flowering of a tradition which had proved remarkably persistent and immutable – even esoteric: not only did it last through the Civil War and the Restoration into Purcell's lifetime but, in his hands and those of his immediate forbears, it also continued to use the Renaissance-based genres from which it arose, long after most of these and their equivalents had fallen out of use in France and Italy.[53]

Adams also seems to agree with Holman that Purcell's interest in consort music stretched beyond the works of his immediate forbears, as for example when he observes that Purcell's In nomines 'lie at the most conservative end of In nomine practice, in that they show little absorption of modern instrumental styles'.[54] An important part of Adams's understanding of Purcell's conservatism, however, is that it represents a conscious choice on the part of the composer:

Purcell was a natural conservative, not in the sense of being old-fashioned, but in that he seems to have been dissatisfied by modern developments which abandoned that polyphonic and motivic rigour characteristic of those earlier styles which interested him. Much of his unusually wide stylistic development was involved

---

[52] Ibid., 281.   [53] Adams, *Henry Purcell*, 7.   [54] Ibid., 10.

with a struggle to adapt the priorities of [the] fantasias to more modern styles – and quite a struggle it sometimes seems to have been, for the necessary conflation of textural types and structural methods did not come easily.[55]

As the latter part of this passage shows, Adams regards the experience of this self-conscious emulation of the contrapuntal fantazia as crucial to the understanding of Purcell's later music, a point that becomes clear in his discussion of the sonatas – a genre in which, Adams seems to suggest, this 'struggle' was not quite resolved. Rather the two styles sit uncomfortably in the sonatas, 'embody[ing] the paradoxical tension between his modernistic and conservative aspirations'.[56] In the context of his overall view of Purcell as a conservative, Adams regards the best movements of the sonatas to be those that most closely resemble the technique of the fantazias, while those with 'overtly Italianate' qualities tend to be criticized: 'short-breathed periodicity is nigglingly persistent, and the triple-invertible counterpoint mere mechanistic juggling.'[57] This is a long way, then, from the championing of Italianate qualities in Purcell's music as signs of its importance in a European context.

During the two hundred years in which Purcell's 'conservatism' has been first suppressed, then rediscovered and, eventually, lauded, the very idea of Purcell's relationship with older styles has undergone a fundamental transformation, or at least an important shift of context. Holman in particular observes that the image of Purcell the conservative is particularly attractive in the modern climate, suggesting that 'we tend to like music clogged with the English vein'.[58] It may be that this modern taste is partly related to the constant search for new and unexplored repertoire demanded by the recording industry. Purcell's sonatas and fantazias are written in an idiom that seems fresh and individual to the modern ear, but is close enough to the familiar staples of the Corelli–Vivaldi repertoire to appeal to the general listener who is not familiar with earlier styles.

The changing attitudes and approaches towards Purcell's instrumental music offer a salutary reminder of the problems of founding aesthetic judgements on historically contingent categories. 'In matters of taste', wrote Roger North in his *Memoires of Musick*, 'there is no criterium of better and worse, and men determine upon fancy and prejudice, and not upon intrinsick worth'.[59] In this context 'fancy', and in particular, 'prejudice', are not to be understood with the negative connotations we ascribe to them today, but simply as alternatives to a judgement based on 'intrinsick worth'; in other words, North's statement amounts to a recognition that musical taste is highly conditional upon fashion and subjective judgement, and that it is only in the context of these that musical works acquire aesthetic significance and 'value'. With the benefit of hindsight, our

---

[55] Ibid., 14.   [56] Ibid., 34.   [57] Ibid., 34–5.   [58] Holman, *Henry Purcell*, 93.
[59] Wilson, *Roger North on Music*, 317.

understanding of Purcell's instrumental music can only be enhanced by an awareness of the continual flux of musical tastes and fashions during and since his lifetime, and their role in shaping the responses of commentators at varying removes from one another and ourselves. Such an attitude towards the vagaries of aesthetic judgement is also, indeed, one that can be observed in Restoration discourse itself, informing subjects as diverse as John Dryden's attitude to Shakespeare and Chaucer, Sir Christopher Wren's understanding of the origins of classical architecture, and Thomas Tudway's account of the history of English sacred music.[60]

* * *

In addition to explaining the background to Adams's convictions about Purcell's conservatism, this picture of the reception of Purcell's instrumental music identifies many of the issues I address in the chapters that follow. Most importantly, and for all that Purcell was interested in the music of his English (and continental) predecessors, I try to get away from the assumption that he was conservative by instinct. Rather I would suggest that his profound interest in, and sustained engagement with, the music of earlier seventeenth-century composers in the years around 1680 stemmed from his fascination with the degree of technical skill which they so often demonstrated: the level of musical artifice that they achieved, which was so lacking in the most fashionable styles of the 1670s. Not only does this fit well with his exploration of the genres of consort music, but it is also equally applicable to the sonatas. Rather than observing in them a flawed attempt to imitate the latest Italian style, which ultimately fails because of Purcell's perceived conservatism, it becomes possible to view both Purcell's enthusiastic embracing of the Italian genre and his continued interest in fugal techniques as different aspects of the same underlying principle of compositional artifice as an artistic goal.

The recovery of Purcell's compositional approaches in the context of this goal – the exploration of what he was trying to do in a given piece, as a way of demonstrating how it works – has the potential to transform how we approach Purcell's music, as I attempt to show in the eight chapters that follow; and not only for the instrumental music itself, which forms the basis for the establishment of my analytical method and its preliminary application in Part I, but also in terms of the relationship between this earlier repertoire and some of Purcell's best-known works of the 1690s, which is the subject of Part II. Perhaps most importantly, this analytical approach emphasizes the *agency* of the composer. In many cases it is

---

[60] Dryden, preface to *Troilus and Cressida* (1679), repr. in John Dryden, *Selected Criticism*, ed. James Kinsley and George Parfitt (Oxford University Press, 1970), 159–62; Lydia M. Soo, *Wren's 'Tracts' on Architecture and Other Writings* (Cambridge University Press, 1998), 131–2, 53–5; Tudway, prefaces to *Services and Anthems*, in Ian Spink, *Restoration Cathedral Music, 1660–1714* (Oxford University Press, 1995), 435–49 (esp. 448–9).

possible to reconstruct the compositional devices and processes that Purcell used as he worked. By examining these, we can often see how he used those materials he garnered from English and Italian repertoires, and from here suggest why it was that these interested him (or, indeed, how he might have found them lacking). In this way, one can arrive at much stronger conclusions about Purcell's attitudes towards composing and towards music as an art, with which we can perhaps begin to fill in those lacunae in the 'proper evidences' that have previously given rise to so much of the kind of 'perpetuall guessing' that so frustrated Roger North.[61]

---

[61] Wilson, *Roger North on Music*, 317.

PART I

Purcell's 'Art of Descant'

CHAPTER I

In Counterpoint: Sources and Analysis

Given that the presence of arcane fugal devices in Purcell's instrumental music is widely recognized as a stylistic marker of conservatism, it is surprising how little detailed and historically sensitive analytical work there has been in order to support this critical response. If the study of this music is to retain any place in modern musicological discourse it will require strong historiographical and analytical models capable of interrogating such commonplace ideas, and thereby illuminating the music to which they refer. Purcell's 'conservatism', if such it is, is a matter of much more than simple stylistic affinity with music that was, by the 1680s, decidedly old-fashioned: one must consider what it was about such music that attracted Purcell, and how it acquired meaning for him and others in the cultural context of late seventeenth-century London. Similarly, the mere identification and description of some of the unfashionably elaborate contrapuntal textures in his music is an impoverished analytical endeavour: far more interesting are the skills and strategies Purcell required to produce them, and their interaction with, and contribution to, what contemporaries might have understood as the poetic aspect of the developing traditions of instrumental music.

The three chapters that follow this preamble in Part I aim to develop a starting-point for the analysis of Purcell's contrapuntal artifice, both in terms of its theoretical backgrounds and its manifestation in the two instrumental genres to which he devoted so much time and energy in the late 1670s and early 1680s: the consort fantazias and the twenty-two Italianate trio sonatas. My analytical approach focuses on the goal of understanding Purcell's music through the recovery of contemporary approaches to creativity, using seventeenth-century theory to understand the compositional strategies Purcell might have deployed, and to expose both the problems he would have faced in following these and the solutions he found in specific circumstances.

There are obvious advantages to this approach to Purcell's music. It focuses attention securely on the agency of the composer, rather than reducing him to an inert medium for the transmission of stylistic and historiographical trends, and it derives analytical insight from the techniques and terminologies of Purcell's own theoretical training, helping to guard against the more damaging forms of anachronism. It is for similar reasons that several other studies from varying methodological standpoints have sought to analyse seventeenth- and eighteenth-century repertoires through the recovery of creative processes and techniques: the 'workbench methods of the composer',[1] or the 'historical modus operandi that informs the practice of Bach's daily craft'.[2] The common approach of all such work is its attempt to discern the creative activities of the composer through sensitive analysis rather than through close examination of autograph sources – what I characterized in an earlier essay as a 'palaeographical' approach to Purcell's creativity.[3]

The difficulties of such a 'palaeographical' approach in relation to the repertoire in question demonstrate further, indeed, the need for the analytical methodology developed in the ensuing chapters. 'Palaeographical' studies of creativity have traditionally focused on the extent to which a composer's working methods can be revealed through the close analysis of variant details in the earliest manuscript sources, typically in the form of additions, deletions and corrections notated by the composer or substantial variation between texts of comparable authority. The pioneering work of Gustav Nottebohm in the 1860s and 1870s on Beethoven's compositional sketches paved the way for well over a century of further investigation, and in the past half-century a number of important studies have attempted to examine the practices of earlier composers, including J. S. Bach, Mozart, and Handel, from a similar viewpoint.[4]

---

[1] Christopher Wintle, 'Corelli's Tonal Models: The Trio Sonata Op. III, n. 1', in *Nuovissimi Studi Corelliani III*, ed. Sergio Durante and Pierluigi Petrobelli (Florence: Olschki, 1982), 29–69 (31).

[2] Laurence Dreyfus, *Bach and the Patterns of Invention* (Cambridge, MA: Harvard University Press, 1996), 30, and see Chapter 5, 'Matters of Kind' (135–68). Similar approaches are increasingly being brought to bear on sixteenth-century music – notably by John Milsom, most recently in 'Cipriano's Flexed *Fuga*', in *Cipriano da Rore: New Perspectives on His Life and Music*, ed. Jessie Ann Owens and Katelijne Schiltz (Turnhout: Brepols, 2016), 293–329; this article develops methodology introduced most fully in Milsom, 'Crecquillon, Clemens, and Four-Voice *fuga*', in *Beyond Contemporary Fame: Reassessing the Art of Clemens non Papa and Thomas Crequillon*, ed. Eric Jas (Turnhout: Brepols, 2005), 293–345. Both articles include helpful glossaries of terms. Peter Schubert's work shares many of Milsom's aims, but develops a parallel (and at times mutually complementary) terminology. This is detailed most fully in Schubert, 'Hidden Forms in Palestrina's *First Book of Four-Voice Motets*', *JAMS*, 60/3 (2007), 483–556; for a fascinating recent demonstration of the power of historical theoretical sources to illuminate modern analytical methods see Schubert, 'Thomas Campion's "Chordal Counterpoint" and Tallis's Famous Forty-Part Motet', *Music Theory Online*, 24/1 (2018), http://mtosmt.org/issues/mto.18.24.1/mto.18.24.1.schubert.html (accessed 22 November 2018). Further studies by both Milsom and Schubert will be found in the Bibliography, as will relevant work by Denis Collins, Julie Cumming, Julian Grimshaw, Jonathan Oddie and Joshua Rifkin.

[3] Alan Howard, 'Understanding Creativity', in *The Ashgate Research Companion to Henry Purcell*, ed. Rebecca Herissone (Farnham: Ashgate, 2012), 65–113.

[4] On Nottebohm and the subsequent history of Beethovenian 'sketch studies' see Douglas Johnson, 'Beethoven Scholars and Beethoven's Sketches', *Nineteenth-Century Music*, 2/1 (1978), 3–17 *passim*; Robert Lewis Marshall, *The Compositional Process of J. S. Bach* (Princeton University Press, 1972); Alan Tyson, *Mozart: Studies of the Autograph Scores* (Cambridge, MA: Harvard University Press, 1987); and David Ross Hurley, *Handel's Muse: Patterns of Creation in his Oratorios and Musical Dramas, 1743–1751* (Oxford University Press, 2000).

The identification and description of manuscript sources containing Purcell's music, together with related issues such as the qualities of his handwriting, have always occupied a central place within the scholarship surrounding the composer, and more recently these same sources have been the focus of a more explicit attempt to understand how Purcell composed, and the attitudes that shaped his compositional priorities.[5] Our understanding of these issues has been transformed by the much more ambitious approach taken by Rebecca Herissone in her *Musical Creativity in Restoration England*,[6] which for the first time allows us to view Purcell's creative process as recorded in the sources of his music in the context of both the philosophical and pragmatic aspects of creativity among his contemporaries in seventeenth-century England.

A number of insights into Purcell's working methods can be derived from this literature: he was a composer who often left substantially different versions of the same piece, suggesting a desire to improve upon earlier versions or, in some cases, provide alternative versions appropriate for use in different circumstances; he frequently excised or replaced short unsatisfactory passages of works that were otherwise complete, and he seems never to have considered a completed movement beyond improvement, correcting obvious grammatical and notational errors, and making small changes to voice-leading (especially at cadences), and chromatic alterations to clarify the sense of key, almost whenever he was engaged in copying an earlier work. Such characterizations are based on particular physical observations concerning the surviving sources (scratched-out or crossed-out notes or passages; torn-out pages, pasted or pinned 'correction slips' inserted over a replaced passage; changes in ink type) and, often tellingly, on the comparison of variant sources. These methods frequently reveal surprisingly detailed aspects of Purcell's working habits, such as Rebecca Herissone's remark that Purcell typically composed the outer parts of orchestral and choral movements first, before going back to complete the inner parts: the number of sources to survive with the inner voices missing, or completed in a different ink (often with alterations to the original outer voices added in the new ink) makes this a compelling interpretation.[7]

---

[5] The principal source studies are listed in part (b) of the bibliography provided by Robert Thompson in the 'Purcell' article for *Grove Music Online*; most have been superseded with the publication of Shay and Thompson, *Purcell Manuscripts*. The most recent publication to deal specifically with Purcell's working methods is Rebecca Herissone, '"Fowle Originalls" and "Fayre Writeing": Reconsidering Purcell's Compositional Process', *The Journal of Musicology*, 23/4 (2006), 569–619. Among older studies, Adams's *Henry Purcell* contains many relevant passages (see for example the discussion of the Overture in G, pp. 118–19); see also Rebecca Herissone, 'Purcell's Revisions of his own Works', in *Purcell Studies*, ed. Curtis Price (Cambridge University Press, 1995), 51–86 (containing material from an unpublished dissertation, 'The Compositional Techniques of Henry Purcell as Revealed Through Autograph Revisions Made to his Works' (unpublished MMus thesis, King's College, London, 1993)), and Herissone, 'The Theory and Practice of Composition in the English Restoration Period' (unpublished PhD thesis, University of Cambridge, 1996); also Robert S. Shay, 'Purcell's Revisions to the Funeral Sentences Revisited', *EM*, 26/3 (1998), 457–67.

[6] (Cambridge University Press, 2013).   [7] Herissone, 'Purcell's Revisions', 56–7.

The earliest sources of Purcell's consort music exhibit numerous examples of all the kinds of changes described here, and thus might be thought to offer considerable potential for the exploration of his compositional methods.[8] For the present purposes, however, there is unfortunately very little to be gleaned from this approach. This is partly because of the nature of the sources, which generally preserve texts from comparatively late in the compositional process (and are therefore poor records of Purcell's actual composition of fugal passages), and partly to do with the nature of the fugal textures, which frequently invalidate the common models of Purcell's compositional process, thereby precluding what have proved to be some of the most fruitful lines of inquiry in other genres.

The fantazias and In nomines have a comparatively simple source background. The only autograph source is Purcell's scorebook, *Lbl* Add. MS 30930, and the only other contemporary source to preserve the full set of consort music (*NYp* Drexel MS 5061) contains no substantive variant readings, and probably derives directly from the autograph.[9] This means that any information about the composition of the works is most likely to be contained within *Lbl* Add. MS 30930 itself. Armed with this knowledge, the large number of corrections apparent in the source would seem to be revealing, were it not for the fact that in almost all cases these must belong to the final stages of the compositional process, long after the working out of the fugal sections took place. This is in marked contrast to the situation with Matthew Locke's similar scorebook of instrumental music (*Lbl* Add. MS 17801), for example, in which the copies of the *Flat Consort* in particular (fols 27–37) appear to have been the original working manuscripts, and contain many passages that have been revised at different, and sometimes multiple, stages of their composition. Purcell's own scorebook is more like some of the other sections of Locke's, in which the music is copied from other sources and small revisions made over time, some perhaps planned in advance, and others made on reviewing the work or somewhat later. We know that most of Fantazia II predates the copying of *Lbl* Add. MS 30930, for instance, since it also exists in an earlier, shorter version in *Lbl* Add. MS 31435.[10]

---

[8] For the most up-to-date discussion of this most intensively studied group of sources, see Shay and Thompson, *Purcell Manuscripts*, 84–100, 106–25. More detail concerning the actual texts and their comparative readings is available in the relevant volumes of the Purcell Society's complete edition of Purcell's works: Henry Purcell, *Twelve Sonatas of Three Parts*, rev. edn, ed. Michael Tilmouth, PSr 5 (London: Novello, 1976), ix–xvii, 144–6; Purcell, *Ten Sonatas of Four Parts*, rev. edn, ed. Michael Tilmouth, PSr 7 (London: Novello, 1981), ix–xxiii, 145–52; Purcell, *Fantazias and Miscellaneous Instrumental Music*, rev. edn, ed. Michael Tilmouth, PSr 31 (London: Novello, 1990), ix–xvi, 117–27.

[9] See Shay and Thompson, *Purcell Manuscripts*, 106–9.

[10] See Alan Howard, 'Compositional Strategies in Purcell's Second Three-Part Fantazia', *Music Theory Online*, 21 (2015), www.mtosmt.org/issues/mto.15.21.3/mto.15.21.3.howard.html (consulted 16 July 2018), §10–13.

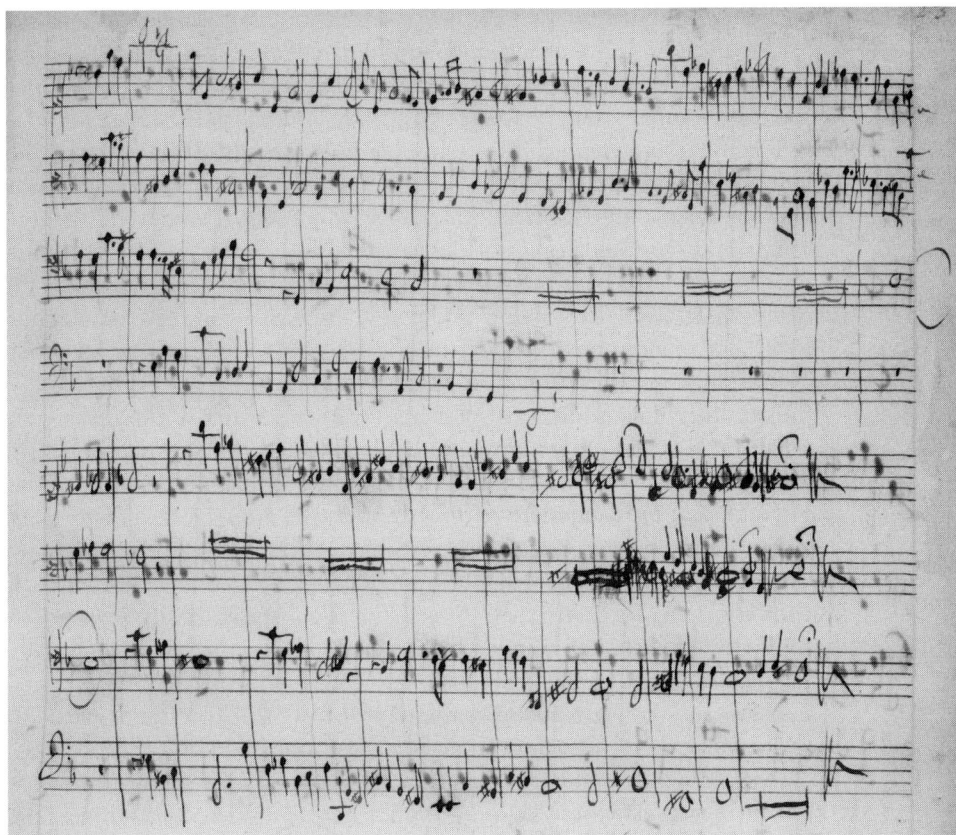

Fig. 1.1   *Lbl* Add. MS 30930, fol. 58v (detail): Fantazia XII, conclusion
(© British Library Board)

Furthermore, certain corrections in the manuscript themselves seem to be the results of copying from an earlier source, which we must speculate is now lost. This is most obvious at the end of Fantazia XII on fol. 58v (Fig. 1.1), where Purcell apparently began to notate the final four bars of the two uppermost parts a bar early, only to realize his mistake when he began the tenor and bass – forcing him to scratch out and correct the treble and alto. Other corrections found in the manuscript are less likely to be directly linked to the copying process, but are nevertheless the kinds of changes that one would make on returning to a completed work and examining it afresh, such as the removal of consecutive fifths in bar 49 of Fantazia VII (tenor).

With the sonatas, the source situation is somewhat more unwieldy, since these works were widely copied in the late seventeenth and early eighteenth centuries. The various manuscripts and editions were well scrutinized by

Michael Tilmouth for the editions in Purcell's *Works*, however, and this information is summarized and consolidated once more in Shay and Thompson's *Purcell Manuscripts*. As with the fantazias, the resultant picture is of a small group of sources of strictly limited value in the examination of fugal processes. This is particularly true of the 1683 Sonatas, the autographs for which are all lost, and all early manuscript sources of which appear to derive directly from the published edition.[11] Manuscript annotations in the printed copies of the first edition indicate a similar attitude towards the 'final' text to that displayed in Purcell's corrections to small details in *Lbl* Add. MS 30930, and the fact that many of these corrections were later incorporated into the second impression lends them authority even though none are in Purcell's own hand.[12]

Even the 1697 Sonatas, of which several works survive in copies with major revisions and, in two cases, completely rewritten movements, fail to supply any more information about the earlier stages of fugal composition. Here the printed versions of the sonatas are thought to derive from a manuscript, now lost, that contained different readings from the copies of Sonatas I–III and VII–X (1697) preserved in *Lbl* Add. MS 30930.[13] In contrast to the works in which Purcell makes only insignificant revisions in the latter stages of copying, these few works that survive in substantially revised or variant forms (Sonata VII (1697), central three movements; Sonata VIII (1697), fourth movement) are obviously the result of extensive re-composition rather than simple emendation of an existing text.

The problem with interpreting these different versions is the difficulty of discerning which, if any, Purcell would have considered definitive. The traditional assumption that the printed versions of the 1697 Sonatas represented their final state was challenged by Christopher Hogwood, and it now seems likely that the versions preserved in *Lbl* Add. MS 30930, including the violinistic figuration introduced into the canzona from Sonata VII (1697) and the attractive inversion of the subject in the fourth movement of Sonata VIII (1697), represent a later text, not an original, superseded reading.[14] This argument rests heavily on stylistic grounds, however, and in any case, far from supplying additional information about compositional process, the sources simply preserve two alternative *finished* versions of these works. There are no signs of compositional activity at all, for example, on fol. 33 of *Lbl* Add. MS 30930 (Fig. 1.2), which contains the section of the fourth movement of Sonata VIII (1697) with the new inversion of the subject. In the absence of demonstrable

---

[11] Shay and Thompson, *Purcell Manuscripts*, 124–5.   [12] See PSr 5, xv.

[13] All other sources of these works have been shown to derive either directly or indirectly from one of these sources; see the *stemma* in Purcell, PSr 7, xii, and the discussion in Shay and Thompson, *Purcell Manuscripts*, 113–24.

[14] See Herissone, 'Purcell's Revisions', 60–63; Henry Purcell, *Ten Sonatas in Four Parts*, ed. Christopher Hogwood (London: Ernst Eulenberg, 1978), i, vi.

Fig. 1.2   *Lbl* Add. MS 30930, fol. 33: part of the fourth movement of
Sonata VIII (1697) (© British Library Board)

notated revisions to the text, the ambiguous relationships between the different sources of the 1697 Sonatas means that the different surviving versions of Sonatas VII and VIII cannot be placed within a strong chronological sequence; indeed, the very importance of stylistic observations in the dating of the sources threatens to make any hypothesis concerning the evolution of Purcell's techniques self-fulfilling. This is all the more problematic since there is no reason to suppose that Purcell necessarily intended one version to replace another. As Robert Thompson points out, the corrections that Purcell made on pinned inserts in *Lbl* Add. MS 30930 were easily reversible, and it is easy to imagine him making the revisions to Sonatas VII and VIII in response to the demands of a specific context.[15]

Unfortunately the one statement that it is possible to make concerning Purcell's working methods in *Lbl* Add. MS 30930 results in something of a truism. Herissone's observation concerning Purcell's habit of composing the outer parts first and then returning to fill in the inner voices, adjusting the existing text where necessary, has a revealing exception in the copy of Sonata VII (1697) on fol. 34v, where changes in the colour of the ink show that Purcell was instead entering the music from the top part downwards.[16] The implication is that in genres where the inner parts were of equal importance with the treble and bass (and the trio sonata *a* 3 is one of the most emphatic examples of this) Purcell did not follow his usual pattern of working. In other genres the outer parts were sufficient if the intention was to notate his ideas quickly or to serve as an *aide mémoire* until more complete texts were required for performance, at which point the inner voices could be fleshed out by composing directly into the score. The stricter fugal and contrapuntal textures of the sonatas, however, demanded full notation whatever purpose the copy was intended to serve, and the same is surely true to an even greater extent of the fantazias contained in the same manuscript.[17] Given this, there was no reason to notate the outer voices first and Purcell simply copied the music from the top downwards. When composing, meanwhile, we might expect that Purcell must have been working in all voices concurrently in order to produce such an equal polyphonic texture. Exactly how he went about this, however, the manuscripts alone cannot reveal.

The decision to develop an analytical approach to Purcell's contrapuntal creativity, then, stems in part from the limitations of 'palaeographical' studies of Purcell's creative process in the early instrumental works in particular. This does not mean that source-based study of this repertoire has nothing to offer from an analytical perspective: in some works, such as

[15] Robert Thompson, 'Purcell's Great Autographs', in *Purcell Studies*, ed. Curtis Price (Cambridge University Press, 1995), 6–34 (15–16).

[16] See Herissone, 'Purcell's Revisions', 57 (note 22).

[17] Fresh examination of the manuscript has revealed no further changes in ink colour within the fantazias or related pieces that could be used either to support or to undermine this assumption.

Purcell's second Fantazia of three parts, careful study of the sources can offer valuable corroboration of ideas developed first analytically.[18] Nevertheless, in the chapters that follow it is the analytical approach that is privileged, with the aim of establishing a set of principles that can be used more widely in conjunction with well-established 'palaeographical' approaches thereafter.

* * *

The three chapters that follow in this section deal broadly with Purcell's contrapuntal methods in the Fantazias (Chapter 2) and Sonatas (Chapters 3 and 4) respectively. Or, to be more precise, they follow a technical distinction reflected in a notable linguistic peculiarity of Purcell's treatment of fugue in his counterpoint manual 'The Art of Descant' (a publication that will be introduced properly in Chapter 2): his adoption of the verb 'to fuge' throughout. This apparent idiosyncrasy emphasizes the active process of *fugeing* on the part of the composer, unlike the more conventional, and largely indiscriminate use of 'fuge' as a label for an imitative point or section of music fashioned around that point.[19] Indeed, so useful is this construction as a way of characterizing Purcell's attitude towards the composition of imitative counterpoint that the present study adopts his term *fugeing* widely in conjunction with his creative approach to the fantazias and to many passages of the sonatas that follow the same principles, much as John Milsom has encouraged the use of the term *fuga* for the techniques of sixteenth-century imitative polyphony.

The modern use of such contemporary terminology in this case has a number of advantages. Most importantly, perhaps, it focuses attention away from the kind of vague observations about fugue as a stylistic marker in Purcell's music to which I referred above, concentrating instead on what Purcell's fugal technique can tell us about how he composed. It also helps to avoid a number of knotty problems with the modern usage of fugal terminology when applied retrospectively to earlier repertoires. If we follow general seventeenth-century English usage, all imitative counterpoint is simply referred to as 'fuge'; however, since the nineteenth century this word has acquired formal connotations which are in some manifestations so inflexible as to render them ill-suited to the analysis even of the eighteenth-century repertoire from which they were derived.[20] The closer modern term for the technique Purcell describes as *fugeing* is 'imitation', but as will become obvious in Chapter 2, this causes potential confusion with the Renaissance distinction between *fuga* and *imitatione*, a distinction

---

[18] See Howard, 'Compositional Strategies', §13–15.

[19] See, for example, Simpson's *Compendium of Practical Musick*, in which he uses the word 'fuge' for the point (e.g. 104, 110), a fugal section (105, 110) and the relationship between parts ('in fuge', 109), but never as a verb.

[20] For a discussion of this point, see Dreyfus, *Patterns of Invention*, 135–44.

that remains relevant in Purcell's own theory even though he does not use this terminology.

By contrast with the emphasis on *fugeing* in Chapter 2, Chapters 3 and 4 focus on Purcell's compositional techniques in a group of works that might be identified as belonging to a genre of 'fugue' in his sonatas; this includes all of those fugal movements labelled as 'canzonas', but also a wider range of pieces that share a number of outward characteristics with these movements. This difference between this usage and the reference to *fugeing* can be illustrated in the discrepancy between some of Purcell's own illustrations in 'The Art of Descant' on the one hand and, on the other, the style that he advocates as a model for aspiring composers – especially in his discussion of 'double descant' (what we would now call invertible counterpoint) in three parts on pages 122–4. Purcell's example is based on the same short, harmonically open point that he had used throughout the discussion of 'fuge', contrived so that it is triple-invertible and presented in three different permutations in order to demonstrate the suitability of each part to function as a bass (Fig. 1.3a). Aware of the difference between this kind of invertible counterpoint and that found in the Italian repertoire, however, Purcell inserted a second illustration in the form of the well-known quotation from 'the famous Lelio Calista [*sic*], an Italian' (Fig. 1.3b).[21] This new example employs two further discrete subjects alongside its main point, which is harmonically self-contained.

It is no surprise, given his reference elsewhere to the supremacy of the Italian sonata, to find Purcell quoting from an Italian composer, but the absence of any discussion of the differences between these two approaches cannot hide the resulting fissure in his contrapuntal theory. On the one hand, he apparently recommends the modern style, quoting from an Italian sonata and couching music examples in trio texture. On the other, he appeals to strict composition, quotes from an outdated Italian composer and devises examples that resemble fantazias more than sonatas. In attempting to provide a comprehensive overview of triple-invertible counterpoint in its practical application, Purcell has in fact confused the issue in much the same way as would later writers on his music. Manfred Bukofzer, for example, seriously misrepresents the relationship between Purcell's works in the two genres by commenting:

The trio sonatas are divided into four or five contrasting movements and fall into the pattern of the church sonata of the Vitali type. On the other hand, the close bonds with the English fancy, which come to light in highly imitative movements, belatedly called canzonas, should not be overlooked.[22]

[21] Though Purcell, like Wessely-Kropik, confused Colista with Carlo Ambrogio Lonati, the true author of this canzona; see Peter Allsop, 'Problems of Ascription in the Roman *Simfonia* of the Late Seventeenth Century: Colista and Lonati', *The Music Review*, 50/1 (1989), 34–44.
[22] Manfred F. Bukofzer, *Music in the Baroque Era* (New York: Norton, 1947), 214.

(a) 'Double descant' in three parts (p. 123)   (b) Quotation from 'Lelio Calista' (p. 124)

Fig. 1.3   Purcell, 'The Art of Descant' (1694): examples of 'double descant'
(reproduced by permission of the National Library of Scotland)

Michael Tilmouth's article of a decade later represented a marked improvement on this confusion, by observing that the fugal procedure of Purcell's
fantazias was most evident not among the canzonas, but in slow or
moderately-paced imitative sonata movements like the opening movements of Sonatas VI and VII (1683).[23] Far more than just a difference in
technical approach, the distinction demonstrates two different ways of
thinking about the whole ontological status of 'fuge' that can be observed
in Purcell's treatise, one that comes down to the difference between understanding it as a technique, and as a genre.

According to the latter understanding, the general characteristics of
fugeing as a technique still apply, but in combination with specific qualities
of the fugal materials and the existence of a recognizable *a priori* formal

---

[23] Tilmouth, 'The Technique and Forms', 109–21 (111).

principle.[24] Thus for example Fig. 1.3b begins from fixed notions of the harmonic and rhythmic relationship between the parts, against which the melodic material has been contrived and into which any number of alternative sets of material might have been substituted without altering the basic plan of the passage. As Chapter 3 will show, this distinction gives rise to a very different set of creative strategies in canzonas and other similar movements in the sonatas, when compared with the deployment of *fugeing* in the Fantazias and Sonatas alike. Then in Chapter 4, the analytical insights of the preceding chapters are brought to bear on the questions of reception examined above in the Introduction, in order to offer a deeper interpretation of the earliest surviving commentary on Purcell's sonatas. Part II of this study broadens the application of both fugal principles in order to trace the fruits of Purcell's experience in the early instrumental works in his later compositional career. First, however, we must turn to the establishment of the basic analytical approaches to both conceptual models.

---

[24] Though note that this does not require the categories of form and genre to collapse together; on the relationship of form, genre and technique in a fugal context see Dreyfus, *Patterns of Invention*, 135–41.

CHAPTER 2

Artifice, Fugeing *and Fantazia*

One way we can get at the kinds of creative strategies Purcell employed in his most contrapuntally intricate music is to examine it alongside contemporary theoretical writings, including his own. This chapter, then, is principally concerned with the establishment of a methodological basis for the analysis that follows later. This basis is unfolded in three parallel strands: the examination of theoretical texts by Purcell and his immediate contemporaries, the situation of these within the wider context of Restoration cultural discourse, and the analysis of Purcell's music in the light of the insights gained from both. It culminates in a more detailed study of the first part of one of Purcell's most accomplished fantazias, with the aim of recovering the composer's working methods through a careful analysis of his use of counterpoint, or *fugeing*, as he called it in 'The Art of Descant'.

ARTIFICE AND CREATIVITY

Before going on to examine the basis of Purcell's compositional technique in detail, it would be helpful to place it in context by asking what it was that attracted Purcell to the intricate contrapuntal textures he cultivated in the fantazias and sonatas. This is important because, like the more conventional source-based studies discussed above, the legitimacy of any claim to understand compositional process rests upon a demonstrable insight into what the composer was seeking to achieve through the techniques and strategies employed. Traditional 'sketch studies' and other 'palaeographical' accounts (see Chapter 1) have been able to rely to a certain extent on the chronological ordering of successive stages of revision in this regard: since the composer demonstrably replaced one version with another, it is assumed that the final version represents the most authentic realization of the composer's intentions, and thus the differences between versions can be understood as successive stages in the gradual accomplishment of that goal. Robert Shay's perceptive description of Purcell's concern to improve upon the imitative texture of certain sections of his Funeral Sentences (particularly 'Thou knowest, Lord') is successful for exactly this reason. Working with three sources of known relationship to one another, he is able to offer a strong interpretation of the development of the composer's compositional priorities: Purcell increasingly sought to elide the entries of imitative points more closely, and to ensure that they provided a harmonically explicit exordium by entering on the first and fifth degrees.[1]

This methodology in itself is not without potential pitfalls: it tends to assume, for example, that revisions are always intended to supersede earlier versions, that composers were always successful in achieving the goals of their reworkings, and that those differences between versions that seem most significant from a modern perspective were also the most important in their original contexts. Furthermore, such problems become far more acute when the analytical burden shifts – as I am proposing here – from manuscript sources to less tangible creative acts: those that were perhaps carried out using more ephemeral materials, or even never written down at all. Such an approach rests on the hypothesis that it is not only the physical aspects of the original notation, but also the music encoded therein, which exhibit tell-tale signs of the processes and techniques used in its creation.

Above all, it is Purcell's use of formal contrapuntal devices that offers the opportunity to examine his creative methods, though the decision to concentrate on this one facet of Purcell's creativity rests on more than its simple ubiquity in the repertoire in question. Fugal counterpoint is the aspect of musical technique that Purcell discusses in the most detail in his own theoretical discussions, providing the best opportunity to understand the demands of a particular aspect of his compositional technique. Furthermore, the importance of these compositional strategies to Purcell's creative methods ties in well with contemporary notions of creative artifice, which forms a recognisable category in the criticism of and commentary upon all art, including music, during the composer's lifetime. The idea that Purcell's fugal and imitative writing represents a musical manifestation of this concern for the artificial qualities of artistic creations, furthermore, offers a more subtle way of understanding the very nature of Purcell's 'conservatism'. The notion that he was interested in reviving or sustaining an outdated style of composition *per se*, which is both historiographically and stylistically suspect, can be replaced with the observation that the particular aspects of older compositions which he emulated – namely their preoccupation with the very techniques of formal counterpoint elevated to such levels in Purcell's fantazias and sonatas – actually represented for him a means of achieving the level of artifice in music which contemporaries sought in other forms of creative expression.

Purcell's own comments on the 'poetics' of his instrumental music are not only small in number, but also difficult to apply in a wider context. As a result, their meaning is often ambiguous. Indeed, one of the most famous

---

[1] Shay, 'Purcell's Revisions', 462–5; also Robert Ford, 'Purcell as His Own Editor: The Funeral Sentences', *Journal of Musicological Research*, 7/1 (1986), 47–67.

examples, the preface to the 1683 Sonatas, is further complicated by ambiguity over its authorship, referring throughout to the composer in the third person.[2] Whether its comments represent Purcell's own artistic ideals or reflect more upon the commercial ambitions of the composer and his publisher, however, passages such as the following serve as a useful introduction to contemporary discourse on musical poetics:

> Its Author, he has faithfully endeavour'd a just imitation of the most fam'd Italian Masters; principally, to bring the seriousness and gravity of that sort of Musick into vogue, and reputation among our Country-men, whose humor, 'tis time now, should begin to loath the levity, and balladry of our neighbours.[3]

On a simple level, it is easy to comprehend the binary opposition that is set up in this short excerpt: the opposition between 'levity' and 'gravity' suggests a simple analogy with the physical properties of materials derived from pre-Newtonian physics and alchemy. The light/heavy distinction, however, is by itself relatively undefined: we are left with little indication of how these properties might manifest themselves in the music.

A more useful context for the terms 'levity' and 'gravity' can be found in the use of these very terms to describe aspects of human behaviour, in accordance with the increasing interest in the human condition, and the causes of differing human characters, during the seventeenth century. Thomas Hobbes' *Humane Nature*, for example, was first published in 1650 and still very much current around the time that Purcell's comments were published, a second edition appearing in 1684. Having considered the nature of sensation, and its ability to move the passions, Hobbes turns in Chapter 10 to consideration of why it should be, since he holds that the capacity of the mind is similar for all healthy individuals, that the same experiences can alter the passions more or less intensely for different people and at different times. This leads him to a consideration of the differing 'constitutions' of individuals, among which he describes the characteristic of levity:

> There is another Defect of the Mind, which Men call *Levity*, which betrayeth also *Mobility* in the Spirits, but in Excess. An Example whereof is in them that in the

---

[2] Westrup (*Purcell*, 230, note 1) suggested that the preface may have been written by John Playford. In his biography Bruce Wood implies, without stating outright, that it was by Purcell himself (Bruce Wood, *Purcell: An Extraordinary Life* (London: Associated Board of the Royal Schools of Music, 2009), 72–3); John Cunningham and Peter Holman are less equivocal, introducing the passage quoted here with the words 'Purcell wrote (in the third person)' (John Cunningham and Peter Holman, eds, *Restoration Trio Sonatas*, Purcell Society Edition Companion Series, IV (London: Stainer & Bell, 2012), xi). Most recently, Alon Schab declines to pronounce on the issue, but ascribes considerable importance to the preface's contents; at the very least this text – as Westrup acknowledged – must have been authorized by the composer, as part of what Schab calls his 'act of self-promotion' (Schab, *The Sonatas of Henry Purcell*, 21). Cheryll Duncan has published a fine account of how the paratextual aspects of the 1683 publication contributed to this aim, though she does not discuss the preface at all; see Cheryll Duncan, 'Henry Purcell and the Construction of Identity: Iconography, Heraldry and the *Sonnata's of III Parts* (1683)', *EM*, 44/2 (2016), 271–88.

[3] Henry Purcell, *Sonnata's of III Parts* (London: the author, 1683), preface [n. p.].

midst of any serious Discourse, have their Minds diverted to every little Jest or witty Observation; which maketh them depart from their Discourse by a Parenthesis, and from that Parenthesis by another, till at length they either lose themselves, or make their Narration like a Dream, or some studied Nonsense.[4]

Reading the 1683 preface in this context, we can form an idea of why its author criticized 'levity' in music. On the part of the composer, levity would mean an inability to sustain the musical elaboration of a particular idea, resulting in an ill-disciplined and illogical succession of events, which failed to articulate a larger purpose at the level of the movement or work. By contrast, the preface's preferred attribute (and the opposite of levity) was gravity, in which, according to Hobbes, 'the End being the great and Master-Delight, directeth and keepeth in the Way thereto all other Thoughts'.[5] In other words, the overall subject of a discourse (or a musical work) imparted structure and coherence to its constituent parts.

There nevertheless remains a fundamental problem with using such descriptions of levity and gravity in human personalities to try to understand the use of these terms in the preface to Purcell's sonatas. The kinds of characteristics Hobbes attributes to levity of character could have any one of a number of musical analogues: disparate melodic elements, poor harmonic planning, inadequate part-writing, or even an inability to relate melodic and harmonic elements according to the rules of counterpoint and 'good air'. Where a more nuanced understanding of these terms can prove useful, however, is in the interpretation of the parallel binary opposition that the author of the preface sets up between Italian and French national styles. In the light of this opposition, pieces such as the first movements of Sonata X (1683) and Sonata IV (1697) have always made Purcell's comments seem rather disingenuous: why did he apparently criticize the French style so harshly, yet remain willing to employ characteristically French dotted rhythms in these instances? The confusion stems from the problematic ideological mapping of the two binary oppositions: stylistically, it would be ludicrous to suggest that all Italian music was grave and serious while all French music was balletic and frivolous, but this is exactly the stereotype to which the author of the preface appeals in attempting to take commercial advantage of the contemporary fashion for Italian music.[6] The arch-Italophile Roger North provides a good example of the power of such stylistic pigeon-holing in his famous descriptions of Charles II's musical tastes, which he advanced to explain the predominance of the French style immediately after the Restoration: Charles was 'a lover of slight songs', and 'never in his life could endure any [music] that he could

[4] Thomas Hobbes, *Humane Nature* (London: F. Bowman, 1650), 124–5.   [5] Ibid., 125–6.
[6] See Margaret Mabbett, 'Italian Musicians in Restoration England (1660–90)', *ML*, 67/3 (1986), 237–47 (esp. 241–2); Graham Dixon, 'Purcell's Italianate Circle', in *The Purcell Companion*, ed. Michael Burden (London: Faber & Faber, 1995), 38–51 *passim*.

not act by keeping the time; which made the common *andante* or else the step-tripla the onely musicall styles at Court in his time'.[7]

In the two movements cited above, however, Purcell deftly subverts the popular conception of the French style to create a version of it that is every bit as 'grave' as the more 'Italian' sections of his sonatas. One of the means by which he achieves this 'gravity' in these movements is through contrapuntal sophistication, which is the subject of the one passage of writing in which we get a better idea of the qualities Purcell valued in the music he admired. In 'The Art of Descant', Purcell commends the sonata as an example of the use of the various fugal techniques:

Most of these different sorts of *Fugeing* are used in *Sonata's*, the chiefest Instrumental Musick now in request, where you will find *Double* and *Treble Fuges* also reverted and augmented in their *Canzona's*, with a great deal of Art mixed with good Air, which is the Perfection of a master.[8]

Here is a much clearer indication of what Purcell considered admirable in the music of others and, we might infer, the qualities that he had endeavoured to incorporate into his own sonatas. 'Art' in this sense – a word that already carries connotations of skill or ingenuity – should also be understood to encompass the related notion of 'Artifice', and the context suggests clearly that what Purcell understood by it was fugal technique, and formal imitative devices. At the same time, he tells us, this must be balanced with the principles of 'good Air'. 'The perfection of a master', it seems, is to combine contrapuntal ingenuity with a clear and accessible sense of melody, rather than pursuing dry imitative processes to the detriment of the immediate aural impression of the music.

In appealing to the notion of artifice as a criterion for excellence in instrumental music, Purcell was echoing generations of his predecessors who had valued it as a measure of their skill and professional accomplishment. He may well have been consciously updating Christopher Simpson's similar description in the *Compendium of Practical Musick*; for both writers the aim is to illustrate the use of fugal techniques in an appropriate contemporary genre:

Of this kind [instrumental music], the chief and most excellent, for Art and Contrivance, are Fancies, of 6, 5, 4, and 3 Parts, intended commonly for viols. In this sort of Musick the Composer (being not limited to words) doth imploy all his Art and Invention solely about the bringing in and carrying on of these Fuges, according to the Order and Method formerly Shewed.[9]

What neither of these excerpts mentions, however, is whether this 'Art' has any impact upon the expressive qualities of the music: its poetic

---

[7] Wilson, *Roger North on Music*, 299–300.   [8] AoD, 125.
[9] Simpson, *Compendium*, 115. Purcell updates Simpson's treatise even more explicitly on pp. 115–16 of AoD: finding Simpson's example of three-part counterpoint 'too strict and destructive to good Air', he shows how the same passage might be handled with the two treble parts moving in parallel thirds.

consequences. By contrast, Thomas Morley (whose own description of the fantazia seems likely to have been the ultimate source of Simpson's discussion of the genre) explicitly precludes the possibility of the quality of artifice having any bearing on its ability to move the listener when he notes the common practice of performing motets without their words:

> This kind [the motet] of al others which are made on a ditty, requireth most art, and moveth and causeth most strange effects in the hearer, being aptlie framed for the dittie and well expressed by the singer, for it will draw the auditor (and speciallie the skilfull auditor) into a devout and reverent kind of consideration of him for whose praise it was made. But I see not what passions or motions it can stirre up, being sung as most men doe commonlie sing it: that is, leaving out the dittie and singing onely the bare note, as it were a musicke made onelie for instruments, which will in deed shew the nature of the musicke, but never carrie the spirit and (as it were) that livelie soule which the dittie giveth.[10]

In one sense Morley's formulation of the relative qualities of musical genres remained current in the late seventeenth century: he arranges them into a hierarchy beginning with the most 'grave' (which, incidentally, he contrasts with 'light'), consistently associating the gravest genres with those pieces that exhibit the highest 'art'. In his dismissal of the poetic qualities of artifice in the absence of words, however, Morley might well have been considered somewhat outdated by the Restoration period.

Neither Purcell nor Simpson touches upon this topic; indeed, when compared to their contemporaries in other artistic domains, Restoration musicians appear to have been remarkably reticent about committing their thoughts on the nature of art and musical poetics to posterity. At a time when Dryden and Rymer were contributing to the newly emerging discipline of literary criticism in England, the majority of musical treatises were concerned largely with practical rather than philosophical issues. All this makes it all the more surprising that the relationship between music and the other arts is so often neglected in discussions of the artistic standing of Restoration music. The obvious exception is the theatre, which shares genres such as the 'dramatick opera' with music – though even here discussion is generally confined to the history of institutions, collaboration between artists, and the technical apparatus of the conjunction between the two arts.[11] Rarely does one find extended discussion of any shared, or indeed contrasting, artistic aims.[12]

[10] Morley, *Introduction*, 179.
[11] See, for example, Curtis Price, *Henry Purcell and the London Stage* (Cambridge University Press, 1984).
[12] With perhaps two exceptions. Wilfrid Mellers makes a brief comparison between Purcell and Sir Christopher Wren, 'whose greatness is classical and baroque in a way as odd as Purcell's'; Mellers, 'The Heroism of Henry Purcell: Music and Politics in Restoration England', in *Music and the Politics of Culture*, ed. Christopher Norris (London: Lawrence & Wishart, 1989), 20–40 (38–9). The other comes not from musicology but from literary history: Harold Love, 'Constructing Classicism: Dryden and Purcell', in *John Dryden: Tercentenary Essays*, ed. Paul Hammond and David Hopkins (Oxford University Press, 2000), 92–112.

One of the potential problems with such discussion is that it is unclear to what extent musicians can be considered culturally literate by comparison with the university-educated intellectual elite from among whom the wider picture of Restoration poetics emerged. Most professional composers, Purcell included, came from comparatively lowly social backgrounds, and received the greater part of their education first as choirboys, and then (for the most talented at least) as apprentices to more senior musicians. Such a didactic model naturally facilitated the acquisition of practical musical skills, but was unlikely to equip the novice composer with the skills, and still less the time and incentive, that were required to engage in the broader intellectual discourse surrounding the role of the arts in contemporary culture and their relation to the human condition.

Nevertheless, it would be wrong to suppose that this 'vocational' model of pedagogy exempts Restoration music from the kinds of poetic considerations that were beginning to gather currency in other contemporary artistic domains. Most obviously, music often played a significant role in cultural events that required collaboration between musicians, poets, painters and other artists. Not only would this entail personal contact among the practitioners of the different arts, but it also made obvious the relationship between the arts in terms of their shared aims. The famous prefatory epistle to Purcell's published score of *The Prophetess, or the History of Dioclesian* (1691), for example, expresses the commonplace notion of sisterhood among the arts:

Musick and poetry have ever been acknowledged Sisters, which walking hand in hand, support (& *grace*) each other: And as poetry is the harmony of words, so musick is that of notes: and as poetry is a rise above prose and oratory, so is Musick the exaltation of poetry. Both of them may excel apart, but sure they are most excellent when they are joind, because then, nothing is wanting to either of their perfections: for then thus they appear, like wit & beauty in the same person.[13]

This preface has a complicated history: although signed by Purcell, the manuscript is in Dryden's hand and contains a large amount of material that never made it to the press – including, immediately after the passage quoted here, an extension of the sisterhood of the arts to painting as well ('being like [music and poetry], an imitation of Nature').[14] We can be sure, though, that Purcell was familiar with its contents; as with the preface to the 1683 Sonatas, he must at least have approved of those sentiments that were included in the edition. In this connection, the probability that Purcell spent a short period at the end of the 1670s as a student of the Westminster School, while of ambiguous educational significance, is strongly suggestive as a potential route by which he might have become

---

[13] Quoted in Michael Burden, ed., *Purcell Remembered* (London: Faber & Faber, 1995), 89.
[14] See Franklin B. Zimmerman, *Henry Purcell, 1659–1695: An Analytical Catalogue of his Music* (London: Macmillan, 1963), 306.

acquainted with many of the most influential writers on Restoration poetics, including Dryden himself. Although the two were nowhere near being contemporaries, there is evidence that Purcell retained a lifelong association with the school's charismatic master, Richard Busby, and alumni of the institution seem to have formed a tight grouping around their former teacher.[15]

Although the *Dioclesian* preface furnishes some useful ideas for the understanding of the poetics of Restoration vocal music, it is clearly of little use in the analysis of instrumental music: despite its sharing in the 'sisterhood' of the arts, music is understood as a kind of ornament to the text, an intensification of its rhetorical power similar to that of poetry when compared to prose forms. This will be of greater use when we turn to Purcell's pursuit of artifice in vocal music in the later chapters, but for now it is the end of the passage quoted that is more helpful. In particular, here we have a hint towards how the idea of the 'sisterhood' of the arts might illuminate contemporary ideas about the nature of expression in music without an accompanying text: music, poetry and painting, we are told, all share the ultimate goal of the imitation of nature.

This mimetic principle is central to Restoration poetics in all artistic domains, and was something that Dryden expressed far more explicitly elsewhere. His most celebrated work of criticism, the *Essay of Dramatick Poesie* (1668), for example, begins from the premise that 'a Play ought to be, *A just and lively Image of Humane Nature, representing its Passions and Humours, and the Changes of Fortune to which it is subject; for the Delight and Instruction of Mankind*'.[16] Later, in the essay that prefaced his translation of Charles Alphonse Du Fresnoy's *De Arte Graphica*, Dryden pressed the point at greater length:

The principal and most important parts of Painting, is to know what *is most beautifull in Nature, and most proper for that Art:* To imitate Nature well in whatsoever Subject, is the perfection of *both Arts*; and that *Picture* and that *Poem* which comes nearest to the resemblance of Nature is the best.[17]

Such ideas were not confined to Dryden, or even to the domains of literature and the visual arts. Sir Christopher Wren, another alumnus of Westminster, used a similar appeal to the imitation of nature as a legitimization of the classical forms of architecture: 'A Walk of trees is more beautiful than the most artificial Portico', he writes, but 'these not being easily preserved in Market-places, they made the more durable shades of Porticoes; in which we see they imitated Nature'.[18] In a later discussion he

---

[15] A similar point is made in Jonathan Keates, *Purcell: A Biography* (London: Pimlico, 1996), 26–8; see also Zimmerman, *Life and Times*, 55–6.

[16] John Dryden, *Of Dramatick Poesie, An Essay* (London: Henry Herringman, 1668), 8.

[17] John Dryden, 'A Parallel of Poetry and Painting', in Charles Alphonse Du Fresnoy, *De Arte Graphica*, trans. John Dryden (London: W. Rogers, 1695), xxxi–ii.

[18] Quoted in Soo, *Wren's 'Tracts'*, 156.

adds 'and still in the Ornaments of the Stone Work was imitated, (as well as the Materials would bear) both in the Capitals, Frizes and Mouldings, a Foliage, or sort of Work composed of Leaves, which remains to this Age'.[19] While the emphasis of these comments is different from that of Dryden, there is a strong underlying intellectual affinity: it is the fact that Wren appeals to the imitation of nature in order to justify the artistic (what might be called the aesthetic, rather than the scientific) aspects of his understanding of architecture that is crucial, rather than the exact terms of this appeal. It is at this level, I would suggest, that Purcell too would have found some points of contact with his own views about music.

The actual mechanism by which music in particular was able to imitate nature was always somewhat ambiguous, and at times subject to opposing views that could impact profoundly upon the reception of particular styles of music. In the present context, however, the principal concern is with how the idea of artifice impacted upon the fundamentally mimetic aims of artistic production, and what thus made the concept of artifice so attractive for Purcell.

Dryden understood that theatre was inherently artificial, and therefore that it could never be a true reflection of nature. His discussion of rhymed verse in the *Essay of Dramatick Poesie* provides a case in point. Crites, the most conservative participant in Dryden's dialogue and the sceptic in this argument, objects to the introduction of rhyme to the theatre on the grounds that it is unrealistic:

I am of opinion, that Rhyme is unnatural in a Play, because Dialogue there is presented as the effect of sudden thought. For a Play is the imitation of Nature; and since no man, without premeditation speaks in Rhyme, neither ought he to do it on the Stage; this hinders not but the Fancy may be there elevated to an higher pitch of thought then it is in ordinary discourse: for there is a probability that men of excellent and quick parts may speak noble things *ex tempore*: but those thoughts are never fetter'd, with the numbers or sound of Verse without study, and therefore it cannot be but unnatural to present the most free way of speaking, in that which is the most constrain'd.[20]

In reply, Neander contends that if one objects to rhymed verse on the basis that it is not natural then one must equally object to any 'composed' forms of speech. Having thus shown that any stage dialogue is inherently artificial, Dryden is free to build a case for the higher artifice of rhymed verse on its own merits, because of its superior sound:

You say the Stage is the representation of Nature, and no man in ordinary conversation speaks in rhime. But you foresaw when you said this, that it might be answer'd; neither does any man speak in blank verse, or in measure without rhime. Therefore you concluded, that which is nearest Nature is still to be preferr'd. But you took no notice that rhime might be made as natural as blank

---

[19] Ibid., 158.   [20] Dryden, *Of Dramatick Poesie*, 57–8.

verse, by the well placing of the words, &c. all the difference between them when they are both correct, is the sound in one, which the other wants.[21]

Rather than abandoning the ideal of the imitation of nature, this is in line with Dryden's discussions elsewhere of the proper relationship between nature and artifice. He proposed that artifice be used to present a heightened, or perfected representation of nature; it was therefore the responsibility of the artist to use all his skill – his artifice – in order to distil from nature in its imperfect, realized form those elements that he considered perfect, and present them together as an ideal, untainted image:

For *both* these *Arts* [poetry and painting] as I said before, are not onely true imitations of Nature, but of the best Nature, of that which is wrought up to a nobler pitch. They present us with Images more perfect than the Life in any individual: and we have the pleasure to see all the scatter'd Beauties of Nature united by a *happy Chymistry,* without its deformities or faults.[22]

Such a view of the artificial poetics of Dryden's writing offers a highly attractive model for Purcell scholarship. Here, it seems, is a potential direct analogy with the kind of elevation of artificial compositional devices in Purcell's fantazias and sonatas, and the concept of gravity and the ideal of 'artifice mixed with good air' which he espoused in his writings. For the first time it offers a way of assessing his use of complex fugal devices outside the potentially problematic binary oppositions (modern/conservative, Italian/French) that have traditionally been invoked in such discussions. Moreover, it situates Purcell's music squarely within the artistic context of the Restoration, a cultural climate that was itself fascinated by the difference between appearance and reality, the tension between the mimetic aims and artificial means of all of the 'sister arts' examined above. The musical manifestation of such ideas, as we find above all in Purcell's consort music and in his sonatas, was an even more intense concentration on artificial devices and processes than can be found in any of the other arts.

PURCELL'S THEORETICAL TREATISE

Fortunately, Purcell's own writings prove considerably more fruitful as a source of analytical vocabulary than in terms of his poetic goals. My aim in this section is to examine their potential as descriptive tools, before going on to consider what we might be able to recover of Purcell's compositional strategies. We can gain considerable insight into the former by considering the first movement of his first published sonata, Sonata I (1683), in the light of the composer's coverage of the techniques of imitative counterpoint in 'The Art of Descant'.

This short treatise formed the third and last part of John Playford's *Introduction to the Skill of Musick* in its twelfth edition, published by Henry

[21] Ibid., 62.   [22] Dryden, 'Parallel of Poetry and Painting', xxxiii.

Playford in 1694. As in previous editions of the *Introduction*, the other sections covered the rudiments of music (part 1) and instructions for the playing of the bass viol and violin (part 2). Part 3 was the least consistent: absent from the first edition of 1654, it comprised Thomas Campion's *Art of Setting, or Composing of Musick in Parts* (1655) with annotations by Christopher Simpson from the second edition (1655) onwards, until that was replaced in the tenth edition (1683) by John Playford's own 'Brief Introduction to the Art of Descant'.[23]

Purcell seems to have been enlisted as editor for the entire twelfth edition, but it was only 'The Art of Descant' that demanded extensive revision.[24] Beginning with the basics of consonant and dissonant intervals, it covers simple counterpoint, the correct handling of dissonances 'either ... by way of Pass, or Binding', common cadence patterns, and the principles of good voice-leading, before giving a detailed, note-by-note example of how to harmonize a given melody. There then follows a short passage treating the handling of keys and the proper cadences in a major and a minor key, before Purcell begins a detailed discussion 'Of fuge, or Pointing'.[25] From this point onwards the treatise is completely new. Purcell's account of the various kinds of 'fuge' is comprehensive, and in general follows the pattern established by previous English writers on the subject including Morley, Coprario and Simpson.[26]

The value Purcell placed on the most artificial devices in his compositional armoury is demonstrated by the hierarchical arrangement of his account of fugal and canonic techniques. Beginning in two voices with simple 'fuge' and an explanation of the tonal answer, he continued with 'Imitation, or Reports' (a 'diminutive sort of Fugeing' in which the bass should 'answer the *Treble* in some few notes as you find occasion'), before moving on to encompass 'Double Fuge', with two subjects, 'Fugeing *per arsin et thesin*' (by inversion), '*per augmentation* [*sic*]', '*recte et retro*' (retrograde), 'double descant' (invertible counterpoint) and finally canon, 'the noblest sort of Fugeing'. Each of these is illustrated with a passage constructed from the same subject or 'point', and the whole is then repeated for *fugeing* in three parts and then four.[27]

One notable feature of Purcell's treatment of fugal techniques in 'The Art of Descant' is his consistent use of the verbal form 'to fuge'. As noted in Chapter 1, this seemingly idiosyncratic usage, while obviously cognate with the conventional noun used for imitative music, strongly evokes Purcell's emphasis on the composer's active creation of music through *fugeing*, rather than functioning merely as a taxonomic category for the

---

[23] For a detailed account of the successive editions of Playford's *Introduction*, see Herissone, *Music Theory*, 8–10, and Appendix C (251–70).
[24] Ibid., 265–7.   [25] AoD, 85–106 *passim*.   [26] Herissone, *Music Theory*, 194–205.
[27] AoD, 107–43 *passim*.

finished product. This usage may be somewhat personal to Purcell[28] – but then so, arguably, is the degree of interest shown by Purcell in imitative counterpoint *per se*, certainly among his Restoration teachers and contemporaries. Its use in a modern context provides a helpful way of referring to contrapuntal discipline as Purcell understood it, without invoking each time the terminological 'baggage' that comes along with terms like 'fugue' or 'imitation' as defined since his lifetime.

Purcell's terminology for the various kinds of *fugeing* can be readily applied to an analysis of the first movement of Sonata I (1683), though in practice the divisions between the various techniques he describes are less clear-cut, and the ways in which they are used display an ingenuity that is barely hinted at in the treatise. At the start of the movement, Purcell employs two different fugal interlocks so contrived as to serve different harmonic ends: the first employs a flexed answer after one bar to produce a cadence on G in bar 4, and the second, beginning on the same pitch class, uses an exact real answer after a minim, thereby creating a fleeting modulation to D minor in bars 5 and 6 (Ex. 2.1a and b).[29] By thus using the availability of either an exact or flexed answer to this subject, Purcell could create a harmonic 'proposition' moving from the key-note to the fifth, in much the same way as he used what Alon Schab has recently called the 'Italian Gambit' in more homophonic movements like the third movement of the same sonata (Ex. 2.1c) – but without the need for literal transposition of material.[30] In other words, the harmonic content of the first movement is generated by the specific contrapuntal combinations Purcell chose; this is the first of many instances we shall encounter in which contrapuntal and harmonic events are mutually inclusive.

Although this movement begins in the manner of simple *fugeing*, with no apparent use of the rotation of fugal interlocks, both forms of answer here actually create two-voice interlocks with viable 'double descant'; that is, they are invertible at the octave. Indeed, with this observation we move closer to the identification of the creative origins of this piece. In bars 7–16, Purcell constructs the most densely woven passage of counterpoint in the piece from successive statements of these two interlocks, themselves

---

[28] The more familiar use of the word 'Fuging' is of course in connection with eighteenth-century psalm singing, particularly in North America (see Nicholas Temperley, 'The Origins of the Fuging Tune', *Royal Musical Association Research Chronicle*, 17 (1981), 1–32). As far as I am aware there is no connection between this practice and Purcell's use of the word.

[29] The term 'flexed' describing the modification of a subject's intervallic structure (and its converse, the 'exact' statement) is from John Milsom's analyses of *fuga*; it is frequently deployed in situations we would recognize as demanding a tonal answer, though this case is not quite so simple – were the order of leading and following entries in Ex. 2.1a and b to be reversed, the relationship would indeed be one of subject and tonal answer.

[30] Schab, *The Sonatas of Henry Purcell*, 31–3. As Schab notes, this sort of harmonic 'proposition' is extremely common in the slow movements of Purcell's Sonatas, as it is in the Italian repertoire that he is most likely to have known; for earlier discussions of its importance see Helene Wessely-Kropik, 'Henry Purcell als Instrumentalkomponist', *Studien zur Musikwissenschaft. Beihefte der 'Denkmäler der Tonkunst in Österreich'*, 22 (1955), 85–141 (111); Tilmouth, 'The Technique and Forms', 115; Adams, *Henry Purcell*, 29–30.

Ex. 2.1   Sonata I (1683), excerpts

(a)   First movement: opening interlock

(b)   First movement: further interlock used in bb. 4–6

(c)   Third movement

combined to create one short passage of invertible counterpoint in three voices (X) which is stated three times in quick succession (Ex. 2.2; the repeated three-voice complex is shaded).

The full invertibility of complex X is never demonstrated, since only two of its component subject entries appear in the bass: this may be because statement ⅱ itself overlaps so closely with ⅰ, dictating the appearance of

Ex. 2.2   Sonata I (1683), first movement, bb. 7–16: complex X (shaded)

the first entry in the bass. For the same reason, this passage is another good example of the harmonic impact of Purcell's contrapuntal decisions: the overlapping of statements i̅ and i̅i̅ creates the modulation towards C minor, and in the following bars the necessity of avoiding a further flatwards modulation prompted Purcell to alter the end of statement i̅i̅ in order to make a different interlock viable. Statement i̅i̅i̅ of complex X could then be transposed and delayed by a minim, bringing the harmony back towards the key-note.

Virtually all of the *fugeing* in this movement can be extrapolated from these three overlapping statements of complex X. This can be seen by comparing Ex. 2.2 with Ex. 2.3, which shows all of the two-part interlocks at conventional intervals (unison, fourth/fifth and octave) to be found in the movement. These are listed in descending order of artifice, with the closest imitations first; each is given in rhythmically simplified form, together with sigla describing the imitation they embody.[31] Of the five two-voice interlocks found in the movement, three are derived from X, since the combination of interlocks A̅ and C̅ already noted also produces the incidental interlock D̅ between bass and violin 2 in statement i̅ of Ex. 2.2. Together, these three two-voice interlocks account for sixteen of a total of twenty-one statements of the subject in the movement, as shown in

---

[31] These sigla will be used henceforth in order to describe the imitative combination of a subject with itself. 'S' stands for 'subject', while the superscript characters indicate the intervals of pitch and time between the two entries. The interval of transposition is measured between the second notes of the respective entries, to avoid potential confusion caused by flexing of the opening interval. Laurence Dreyfus adopts a similar system of describing fugal complexes in *Patterns of Invention*, 147–52.

Ex. 2.3   Sonata I (1683), first movement: imitative materials

the outline score in Ex. 2.4. In other words, the invention of the two alternative interlocks in Ex. 2.1, and the discovery that they could be combined to create one invertible three-voice complex, formed the entire creative effort with which Purcell composed just under three quarters of the *fugeing* in this movement.

Although all of the two-voice interlocks in Ex. 2.3 involve *fugeing* at the perfect intervals, this is not exclusively the case in the first movement of Sonata I. One case of (flexed) imitation at the second has already been identified as a consequence of the overlapping of statements ⟨ii⟩ and ⟨iii⟩ of the three-voice complex (Ex. 2.2; see also Ex. 2.4, bb. 12–13); another, more significant, instance (more significant since it involves greater overlap between the entries) is that identified by the asterisks in bars 5 and 17 of Ex. 2.4. Both of these bars use imitative counterpoint at the second after one minim, and in bar 5 this also incidentally produces imitation at the sixth after a semibreve. Clearly there is a need here to establish the limits of Purcell's fugal terminology: does *fugeing* account for such cases of imitative counterpoint at intervals other than the fourth, fifth or octave?

In Renaissance music these different imitative relationships were characterized by differentiating between *fuga*, or imitative counterpoint at the perfect intervals, and *imitatione*, used to denote imitative counterpoint on a less restricted basis. This distinction is commonly traced to Zarlino's description of these terms in *Le istitutioni harmoniche*, despite the fact that, as Paul Walker has shown, Zarlino actually based his categories on the exactness of imitation, which ranged from what would today be called strict canon from beginning to end (Zarlino's *fuga legata*) to a freely contrapuntal texture incorporating brief and inexact melodic references

Ex. 2.4   Sonata I (1683), first movement: outline score, showing distribution of two-voice interlocks

between the parts (*imitatione sciolta*).[32] The linking of these terms with the presence or otherwise of imitation at the perfect intervals was a later generalization on the part of Italian theorists based on Zarlino's observation that, according to his criteria of exactness, *fuga* would only work at the octave, or at the fourth or fifth (when correctly chosen according to the mode), whereas imitation at any other interval would require changes to the interval species of the subject, thereby producing *imitatione*.[33]

Such a distinction is of limited use in connection with Purcell's music, since he seems to have abandoned the binary terminology in favour of a single category of *fugeing* that privileged the perfect intervals but nevertheless acknowledged (if only implicitly) the possibility of imitation at other relative pitch levels. In one sense this resembles the common

[32] See Paul Mark Walker, *Theories of Fugue from the Age of Josquin to the Age of Bach* (University of Rochester Press, 2000), 9–12 and 63, and the summary on 348.
[33] Ibid., 12–14, 55–6, 348.

rejection of Zarlino's dual description by German authors since Calvisius (who had used the word 'fugue' indiscriminately for all imitative counterpoint), but it is important to note that Purcell did not simply ignore the issue.[34] In 'The Art of Descant' he advocated, in common with most other English theorists, a theoretical restriction to the perfect intervals by stating that 'A *fuge* is, when one part leads one, two, three, four, or more Notes, and the other repeats the same in the *Unison*, or such like in the *Octave*, a *fourth* or *fifth* above or below the Leading Part'.[35] For Zarlino the definition of *fuga* in opposition to *imitatione* had been an issue of nomenclature, derived from a certain degree of theoretical purism which in turn was one of the reasons why Calvisius rejected it as 'somewhat subtle'.[36] For Purcell, however, the theoretical restriction of *fugeing* to the perfect intervals was more of a practical response to the demands of modern instrumental music: the entry of the subject at these intervals kept it within the bounds of the key or 'air' of the music. In this respect he was in line with the similar advice offered by Charles Butler, Simpson and Playford earlier in the century.[37]

This more practical emphasis resulted in a degree of pragmatism that is evident not in the written portions of 'The Art of Descant', but in Purcell's illustrations, two of which incorporate fugal entries at imperfect intervals despite his description of 'fuge' referring only to imitation at the octave, fourth or fifth. In the example of *Fugeing per Augmentation* [*sic*] in two voices there is a sequence of entries beginning in bar 4 on the pitches C *aug* (bass) – G (tr.) – B (tr.) – E (bass) – C (tr.) – G (bass), while in the example of *fugeing per arsin et thesin* in three voices the final four entries (all *thesin*) are on G (tr.1) – C (bass) – D (tr. 2) – G (bass).[38] In both cases the entries at irregular intervals can themselves be understood to belong to interlocks at the fourth or fifth, but the coincidence of these interlocks with entries in other parts results in *fugeing* at the intervals of a second and a third as well as the fourth and fifth, for which Purcell provides no alternative term.[39]

The transposition of the subject was of course a basic aspect of fugal composition, and was explicitly recommended by Simpson in his *Compendium*.[40] In Purcell's examples, though, the density of subject entries meant that this transposition inevitably created counterpoint that seems to be at odds with his definition of *fugeing*. For this reason, it may be more sensible to treat Purcell's written description as equivalent to Simpson's advice about the appropriate keys for cadences in the course of a piece, which suggested a more restricted approach for the beginner while pointing out that experienced musicians were able to modulate to

---

[34] On German theorists see ibid., 79, 349, 424.   [35] AoD, 106.
[36] Walker, *Theories of Fugue*, 79.   [37] Herissone, *Music Theory*, 195.   [38] AoD, 111, 120.
[39] Purcell does in fact use the word 'imitation', but it is used in the specific context of adding a part to a pre-existent treble; see p. 45 above and the discussion on pp. 54–5 below.
[40] Simpson, *Compendium*, 111.

almost any key successfully.[41] The restricting factor seems not to have been any theoretical insistence on the appropriate intervals for *fugeing*, but the success or otherwise of the resulting music. Indeed, this had been recognized a century earlier by Morley:

> You must cause your fuge answere your leading parte either in the fifth, in the fourth, or in the eight, & so likewise every part to answer other, although this rule bee not general, yet is it the best manner of maintaining pointes, for those waies of bringing in of fuges in the third, sixth, and every such like cordes though they shew great sight yet are they unpleasant and seldome used.[42]

For Purcell, by contrast, it seems that the converse reasoning could legitimize fugal entries at any interval, provided that the air of the music was not impaired. Zarlino's division of imitative counterpoint into *fuga* and *imitatione* is thus replaced with a continuum, beginning with *fugeing* at the perfect intervals, which is most common, and adding further intervals in order to increase the range of possibilities for the use of the material.

This same continuum is very much in evidence in the fantazias and sonatas, as can be seen by returning to the first movement of Sonata I (1683): as noted above, most of the interlocks used by Purcell involve imitation at the perfect intervals, but other intervals (as in the examples from 'The Art of Descant') come about incidentally through the juxtaposition of perfect interlocks in close proximity. The boxed passage in Ex. 2.4, however, highlights something quite different: a subject entry in the second violin that more deliberately forms the interval of imitation of a second with that in the first violin, and a sixth with that in the bass. Here there is no recourse to an explanation of coincidence; we are forced instead to consider Purcell's motivation for exploring fugal interlocks beyond those at the perfect intervals.

In order to understand Purcell's reasons for introducing this entry, we need to look carefully at how he combines the two-voice interlocks in Ex. 2.3 into three-voice complexes suitable for use in the final composition. As we have seen, interlocks $\boxed{A}$ and $\boxed{C}$ combine easily to form complex X (Ex. 2.2). However, the apparent simplicity of this additive approach to the derivation of larger fugal complexes is deceptive: the mere fact that a two-part interlock is viable does not, of course, make it any more (or less) likely to be compatible with any other two-voice combination. Indeed, as we will see in future analyses, the converse reasoning is more often likely to be the case: if a series of two-voice interlocks easily combines into one larger complex, it is most likely that the larger complex was composed first and the individual interlocks extracted therefrom.

Evidence from other three-part complexes in the first movement of Sonata I (1683) confirms these observations. In bars 14–17 of Ex. 2.4, a

---

[41] Simpson, *Compendium*, 36.

[42] Morley, *Introduction*, 155. Despite the apparent clarity of this passage Morley is typically inconsistent on this point, earlier citing the sixth as a possible interval for fugal entries on p. 76.

statement of interlock B in the bass and second violin is joined to a further subject entry in the first violin, which would have formed interlock A with the bass. As the crossed noteheads show, this entry was incompatible with the second violin beyond its third note; Purcell was therefore forced to abandon it (shown in Ex. 2.2), moving instead from the $f\natural'$ to $f\sharp'$ (shown in Ex. 2.2 above), and thereby to a cadence on the key-note.

The attraction of this aborted complex, however, was that it was potentially more artificial than the existing complex X. While X contained fugal entries after a minim and then a further semibreve relative to the first note, bars 14–17 attempted a three-part complex with entries on successive minims, thereby increasing the artifice: in John Coprario's words, somewhat earlier in the century, 'to sooner [*sic*] you bring in your parts with the fuge, to more better will it shewe'.[43] Such a complex is not possible using only *fugeing* at the perfect intervals, however. In order to make a three-part complex that does work in this manner Purcell had to introduce other intervals, as shown in Ex. 2.5. Even then he had to make some small alterations to the end of the subject in order to make the counterpoint work: at stage (b) in the example the last note of the new complex is removed in order to avoid the sounding of a suspension against its resolution. Thus the expansion of the range of intervals used in *fugeing* beyond the perfect intervals in the first movement of Sonata I (1683) is a direct result of Purcell's desire to increase the artifice of the movement. Having used this combination once, the composer then considered it part of his pool of fugal materials along with the other interlocks from Ex. 2.3: the same two-part interlock at the upper second appears between the bass and second violin later in the movement (b. 17, again marked with an asterisk in Ex. 2.4).

'ALL HIS ART AND INVENTION'

Already in this analysis of the first movement of Sonata I (1683) we have seen that the very attempt to apply Purcell's theoretical terminology to his music leads to insights into the way in which he might have composed. The remainder of this chapter attempts to apply some of these insights to a more detailed analysis of the first section of Fantazia VIII, as well as looking more closely to see whether contemporary theory can further uncover Purcell's working methods rather than simply furnishing descriptive vocabulary.

Anyone eager to learn how to write imitative counterpoint from 'The Art of Descant' might have been forgiven a certain dissatisfaction with his or her chosen text. As Rebecca Herissone observes, the treatise is 'replete with breathtaking examples of imitative complexity, but contain[s]

---

[43] John Coprario, *Rules How to Compose* [Huntington Library, California, MS EL6863, *c*. 1610–14], ed. Manfred F. Bukofzer, facs. edn (Los Angeles, CA: Gottlieb, 1952), fol. 36v.

Ex. 2.5   Sonata I (1683), first movement: derivation of bb. 4–6

virtually no rules to explain how a student might go about producing his own imitation';[44] indeed, the examples resemble those of Elway Bevin's *Briefe and Short Introduction* of 1631 in that they are far more successful as demonstrations of the author's skill than as usable pedagogical exemplars.[45]

Nevertheless, there are clues within 'The Art of Descant' to some of Purcell's approaches to *fugeing.* Of particular interest is what he calls 'Imitation, or Reports'.[46] This kind of *fugeing,* next in difficulty after 'simple fuge', is noticeably set apart from all the other techniques in that it is the only one not illustrated using the same subject that Purcell uses for the other kinds

[44] Herissone, *Music Theory,* 195.

[45] Ibid, 203–4. Purcell in fact recommends Bevin's book to his own readers in AoD, 114, 125.

[46] Purcell's use of the word 'imitation' here creates further problems for the use of the same word in the modern sense when analysing his music, since (as the discussion below explains) he uses the term in a very specific sense. His choice of the word 'imitation' may well be related to the Zarlino-derived theoretical tradition described above, in that such 'Imitation, or Reports' are both less exact and less sustained than other kinds of *fugeing.*

Fig. 2.1 Purcell, 'The Art of Descant' (1694): example of 'Imitation, or Reports' (p. 108)
(reproduced by permission of the National Library of Scotland)

of imitative counterpoint. Instead, he provides a passage in two parts based on completely different materials, designed to show the imitation of a treble line 'in some few Notes as you find occasion when you set a *Bass* to it' (Fig. 2.1).[47] In other words, such 'Reports' involved fitting a bass to a given, pre-existing treble part. Purcell was even more explicit on this point in his discussion of *fugeing* in three parts: '*Imitation* or *Reports* ... needs no Example, because you are confined to a *Treble*, and so must make *Imitation* or *Reports* in the two Parts as the *Treble* will admit of.'[48]

By implication, therefore, the other kinds of *fugeing* were different in that they were not 'confined' to a pre-existing treble – or, for that matter, any other part.[49] This being the case, the alternative was to carry on *fugeing* in all parts concurrently. Although Purcell gives no specific example of how

---

[47] AoD, 108.   [48] Ibid., 118.
[49] The sole mention in AoD of composition to a *cantus firmus* is that already discussed in the Introduction (p. 1), to the maintenance of *fugeing* on a ground bass being 'confin'd like a *Canon* to a *Plain Song*' (144).

Ex. 2.6   Simpson, *Compendium* (1667): 'Example of the first Platform of a Fuge'[50]

this might be achieved, Simpson describes such a method in his *Compendium*, giving clear, practical advice on how to begin the 'first platform' of a fuge: the composer should first set out the entries of the point of imitation, leaving the remaining bars blank (Ex. 2.6). After this stage, the student is instructed to

> fill up the empty places with such Concords and Bindings as you think fittest for carrying on your Composition; until you repeat the Fuge, in one of those Parts that begun it; which may be done either in the same, or in any other Key that will best maintain the Aire of the Musick.[51]

Thus the composer fits together the entries of the point first, and it is these that determine the way the piece develops.

It is easy to imagine a similar compositional strategy for the beginning of Fantazia VIII, one of the most beautiful and the most artificial of all Purcell's fantazias (Ex. 2.7). In this case, though, the elimination of all material not belonging to the subject leaves a good deal more music than Simpson provides, since Purcell's entries overlap with each other to create several interlocks involving imitation at different pitches and times, not to mention different combinations of the subject *arsin* and *thesin* (that is, the subject and its inversion). While this may not seem very different from the way in which Simpson uses the end of his subject as a fragment of countersubject (bb. 2 and 4–5 of Ex. 2.6), Simpson's approach to this aspect of his 'fuge' seems too haphazard to have resulted in anything approaching the complexity of Purcell's opening platform: 'Perhaps the latter end of the Fuge-Notes which you have Prickt down, may agree [with the notes of the next entry]', he writes, or, 'If not, you may add such other Notes as may aptly meet the following part at its coming in'.[52] By contrast, the variety of imitations found in Purcell's first platform seems to be there by design rather than by chance. Each of the three two-part interlocks employed here is selected for its particular characteristics: the first (b. 1, ten./tr. 1) establishing the treatment of the subject by inversion, the second (bb. 1–2, tr. 1/2) grounding the harmony by implying a progression from the key-note to its fifth and back, and the third (b. 3, bass/ tr. 1)

[50] Simpson, *Compendium*, 136.   [51] Ibid., *Compendium*, 136.   [52] Ibid., 135.

Ex. 2.7   Fantazia VIII, first section: opening platform

beginning again from the key-note with greater intensity, owing to its closer imitation.

Simpson's method seems even less likely to have produced some of the more artificial passages in this first section of Fantazia VIII, beyond the 'opening platform'. Many imitative points will yield multiple two-voice interlocks, and even the odd three-voice complex might be attributed to chance – as we saw in the first movement of the G minor sonata – but a passage like that in bars 16–18 of the Fantazia, in which the subject appears in all four voices simultaneously, seems far less likely to have resulted from the fortuitous combination of entries: Purcell surely worked out such passages in advance of the composition of the rest of the section. In so doing, he was able to ensure that his fugal materials could support the highest levels of artifice, since at this stage in the process he was free to make any necessary changes to the subject. Thus the exact form of the subject is itself the *product* of Purcell's *fugeing*, and not simply its basic material as is conventionally assumed (and indeed as it was in Simpson's instructions for the first platform of a 'fuge').

Paradoxically, though, the moment of supreme compositional artifice in bars 16–18 is also a passage of extraordinary simplicity. This is because the intervals from which Purcell created his subject will always produce material capable of overlapping with itself at intervals of an octave or lower fifth and after periods of one metric unit, according to the technique that John Milsom calls 'stretto *fuga*'.[53] This 'interval-stock' (restricted here to a rising fourth, or falling third or fifth) can be seen in the reduction in Ex. 2.8, which adopts Milsom's notation for stretto *fuga*. (The inverse – at the octave or the lower fifth, moving down 4 or up 3 or 5 – also works; a 'hold' or repeated note is permissible in either collection.) Because Purcell began

[53] Milsom's most comprehensive exposition on this subject is to be found in his article 'Style and Idea in Josquin's *Cueur langoreulx*', *Journal of the Alarime Foundation*, 8/1 (2016), 77–91 (81–9). I am grateful to John Milsom for his insightful comments on my work on this piece, and for generously sharing what was then unpublished material. No contemporary theorist fully describes stretto *fuga*; Milsom suggests that it is the kind of practical advice that was passed on directly from teacher to pupil, and thus never appeared in published musical pedagogy.

Ex 2.8   Fantazia VIII, bb. 16–18: stretto *fuga*

this passage by imitating at the lower octave, the original two-voice stretto *fuga* would not be intrinsically viable (producing a fourth on minim 4 of the following part), but the bass entry a further fifth lower provided consonant support for the entire four-part structure.

Purcell's use of the technique of stretto *fuga* here meant that he need not actually have worked out the four-part complex in advance for it to have had an influence on the earliest stages of his compositional process. Instead, the complex was incipient in the melodic structure of the material itself: the composer could devise his subject from these intervals precisely in order that such an artificial passage would be possible, then go on to experiment with other imitative combinations. We know that some of the principles of stretto *fuga* must have been known to English musicians in the generations before Purcell – indeed, Morley even used them to formulate a 'Rule for first-species canon' in his *Plaine and Easie Introduction.*[54] And Purcell was far from the first to use this technique in his consort music; it is present at least from Byrd (the four-part Fantazia in G minor) to Locke (Fantazia no. 2 from the *Consort of Four Parts,* second section), while similar principles underpin vast swathes of Orlando Gibbons's music.[55]

Aside from Purcell's use of stretto *fuga* in this section of Fantazia VIII, there are further clues as to the creative origins of his fugal materials in the relationship between this fantazia and the previous work in *Lbl* Add. MS 30930. As will become apparent in Chapter 5, Purcell's fantazias are

---

[54] See Julian Grimshaw, 'Morley's Rule for First-Species Canon', *EM*, 34/4 (2006), 661–6.
[55] See Jonathan Oddie, 'Counterpoint, "Fuge", and "Air" in the Instrumental Music of Orlando Gibbons' (unpublished DPhil thesis, University of Oxford, 2016), esp. Chapter 1.

Ex. 2.9   Quotation in Fantazia VIII

(a)   Fantazia VIII, bb. 10–13

(b)   Fantazia VII, bb. 22–25

replete with relationships between sections of different works, many of which relate closely to the creative use of *fugeing* in the body of works as a whole. The first section of Fantazia VIII is no exception, most obviously in the music surrounding the climactic C minor cadence in bars 11–12, which is an almost literal quotation from the first section of Fantazia VII (Ex. 2.9). Events like this in Purcell's fantazias cannot be explained as the subconscious result of his intense concentration on the genre in June and August 1680; rather, they are the outward signs of a conscious creative process that stretches across the boundaries between individual fantazias to encompass the whole of what I call Purcell's 'fantazia project'. The quotation in Ex. 2.9 is no accident: the same basic contrapuntal complex, replete with pungent false relation, appears no fewer than five times in the earlier work (see bb. 4, 7, 8, 15 and 23), and is inserted into Fantazia VIII at precisely the moment when the music reaches the comparatively distant key of C minor – the overall key of Fantazia VII.

There are a number of reasons why Purcell might have chosen to insert this short passage from the previous fantazia into the first section of Fantazia VIII. He may simply have been particularly pleased with the effect of the dissonance; in addition, he might conceivably have sought to exploit such an expressive passage better by allowing it to be heard in relief, rather than in the context of so many other similar false relations. At the same time, it is worth noting that this quotation is not the only link between the two sections of *fugeing*. The subject at the start of Fantazia VIII is clearly derived from the second subject of the first section of Fantazia VII: it is as if the direct quotation is intended as a pointer to the origins of the materials in Fantazia VIII.

By examining the subject he took from the opening of Fantazia VII in the context of the technical premise of the first section of Fantazia VIII, we can get even closer to understanding how Purcell's subject took its final form. Many sections of Purcell's fantazias, and opening sections in particular, concentrate specifically on one of the different types of *fugeing* he would later describe in 'The Art of Descant': in Fantazia VII it is 'double fuge', while in Fantazia VIII the principal technique is *fugeing* '*per arsin et thesin*'. (Following Purcell's terminology, for the remainder of this analysis, I designate the two forms of the Fantazia VIII point *arsin* [rising] and *thesin* [falling] according to their overall contour – in this case, always the same as the direction of the first interval (see Ex. 2.10). In order to adapt the sigla used to describe fugal interlocks in my analysis of Sonata I (first movement), I use the letters A and T on either side of a colon to represent *arsin* and *thesin*, respectively; thus the opening interlock of the piece (Ex. 2.10c) can be described as T:A$^{+4, \circ}$, or *thesin* followed by *arsin*, a fourth higher after a semibreve.[56])

As Purcell must have found when he decided to experiment with *fugeing* '*per arsin et thesin*' using the second subject from the start of

Ex. 2.10   Fantazia VIII, first section: subject

(a)   *Arsin*

(b)   *Thesin*

(c)   Opening two-voice interlock

---

[56] The interval of transposition is always measured between the second notes of the respective entries, in order to avoid confusion caused by melodic inversion or flexing of the opening interval.

Ex. 2.11   Second subject of Fantazia VII, opening: problems with putative attempts at *fugeing* '*per arsin et thesin*'

(a)   Original subject a semibreve apart

(b)   Correction producing subject of Fantazia VIII

Fantazia VII, this subject is actually rather poorly suited to such treatment. The creation of two-voice interlocks from two entries *arsin* or *thesin*, respectively, he would already have known, was unproblematic, since the subject was constructed from the requisite interval-stock for stretto *fuga*. However, the most obvious interlocks involving both an *arsin* and *thesin* entry in either order – that is, after a semibreve in each case – prove problematic. As Ex. 2.11a shows, A:T$^{+4, \circ}$ produces an augmented fifth approached by parallel stepwise motion (marked with a star), while T:A$^{+4, \circ}$ suffers from consecutive perfect fifths. Both of these problems could be solved, however, by delaying the start of the subject by a minim, and shortening the third note of the subject to a crotchet (Ex. 2.11b); all that was left to produce the subject of Fantazia VIII was to fill in the empty minim at the start with the opening melodic fourth (shown smaller, in grey). So persuasive was the second of these interlocks, indeed, that it was the very combination that Purcell chose to open the fantazia.

Together with the stretto *fuga* passage (Ex. 2.8), Purcell's attempts to create successful interlocks involving melodic inversion are critical to the understanding of the full range of fugal materials he employs in Fantazia VIII. As in the first movement of Sonata I (1683), this is best appreciated by examining the potential of Purcell's subject matter in the abstract, before seeing how it is manipulated in the final piece. In common with the first movement of Sonata I (1683), Purcell created the opening section of Fantazia VIII from a series of two-voice subject interlocks. In this case, however, the melodic inversion of the subject means that the number of combinations involved is significantly greater: an interlock may be formed from two statements of the subject *arsin* or two statements *thesin,* or equally from one statement of each with either version coming first. Even given Purcell's almost exclusive use of imitation at the unison or octave, fourth or fifth, then, this material yields a maximum of thirty-six potential two-voice interlocks.

Naturally, not all of these interlocks are viable, and indeed the range of interlocks that do work is further reduced by Purcell's extremely strict attitude towards the harmonic contextualization of his fugal interlocks in this section of Fantazia VIII: throughout the first 13 bars, whenever the leading voice of a interlock has a subject *arsin,* its second note is interpreted as a local key-note; if it is *thesin,* the same note is the fifth of the key.[57]

Table 2.1 lists all of the conceivable two-part interlocks using the Fantazia VIII subject at the conventional intervals, arranged in order of artifice (that is, with those involving the closest imitation at the top) and differentiated according to their viability under the conditions described. The bar numbers of those interlocks that Purcell used in Fantazia VIII are also given, and may be verified in Ex. 2.12, which is an outline score of the first section of the piece.

As one might expect, Purcell made no use of the interlocks that were simply unredeemable in contrapuntal terms (those shaded dark grey in Table 2.1). At the other end of the scale are those interlocks we might describe as 'intrinsically viable', in that they make good two-part counterpoint by themselves, producing no solecisms in terms of counterpoint, voice-leading or handling of dissonance, and requiring no additional voices in order to make them usable.[58] These interlocks (without shading in Table 2.1) account for 22 out of 28 subject entries in this section of Fantazia VIII, or almost four-fifths. Furthermore, all of the most artificial such interlocks are present in the fantazia: it is only when we reach those that involve imitation at a separation of more than a semibreve that we find intrinsically viable complexes that Purcell discarded. The remainder of the possible interlocks (shaded light grey in Table 2.1) are what we might call 'conditionally viable', in that they contain incomplete harmonies,

---

[57] The exception is the subject *arsin* in bar 11 (tr. 1), where the second note is not the key-note but the fifth; this may perhaps be explained by the fact that this passage is the one quoted from the opening section of Fantazia VII (see above), where this note is often deliberately interpreted as a fifth in order to produce the false relation that is so characteristic of that section. It is probably not a coincidence that subsequent entries after this point in Fantazia VIII are couched in somewhat more varied harmonic contexts.

[58] Octave-inverted interlocks are considered to be equivalent, however, so that an interlock is called 'intrinsically viable' even if to exchange the octave transposition of the entries would require an additional bass part to accompany a fourth between the subject-carrying voices. Note too that the opening interval of the subject is permitted to flex between a fourth and a fifth in order to establish the viability of a given interlock.

Table 2.1 Two-part fugal interlocks in the first section of Fantazia VIII

Interlock	Sigla	(unis./±8)	4 (+4/−5)	5 (+5/−4)
A	A:A$^\downarrow$	19	(5)	
B	A:T$^\downarrow$			
C	T:T$^\downarrow$	3, 16	8, 14, 16	
D	T:A$^\downarrow$			
E	A:A°		1, 7	
F	A:T°			11, 19
G	T:T°	12	16	
H	T:A°		1, 9	
J	A:A°°		(11)	
K	A:T°°			19
L	T:T°°		8, 16 *twice*	
M	T:A°°		3 *inv. at* 12	

dissonances, or voice-leading problems that make them problematic on their own, but which can be made to work in particular harmonic and metrical contexts through the addition of other materials. Two such conditionally viable interlocks (A̅ and E̅4̅) are used in exact forms in the fantazia, and both seem to have been chosen for their particularly suggestive dissonances. The remaining two both required flexing (hence their presence in brackets in Table 2.1): Purcell extended the second note of the following part in interlock A̅4̅ (b. 6) in such a way that beyond this point its contrapuntal contents are identical to interlock E̅4̅; J̅4̅, meanwhile, has its last note transposed down a tone – a form that can be traced directly to the quotation from Fantazia VII discussed above.

While both Simpson and Purcell seemed to have worked in multiple parts concurrently, then, Purcell's systematic inclusion of the most artificial intrinsically viable interlocks in the first section of Fantazia VIII seems strongly suggestive of some kind of *a priori* process of research into the contrapuntal potential of his materials. The exact form which this 'research' took, however, is uncertain. One possibility is that Purcell actually notated a large number of possible interlocks in order to test their viability, thereby amassing a pool of imitative combinations from which he could select the most useful.

Unfortunately, no autograph material of this type survives, though there is some suggestion that Purcell sometimes used brief sketches to work out details of imitative counterpoint: a correction slip inserted into the autograph 'fowle originall' score of the anthem 'Let mine eyes run down with tears', *Ob* MS Mus.c.26, has music notated on the reverse that turns out to be a short two-voice sketch for part of the opening verse of the same anthem, featuring an interlock formed

Ex. 2.12 Fantazia VIII, first section: outline score

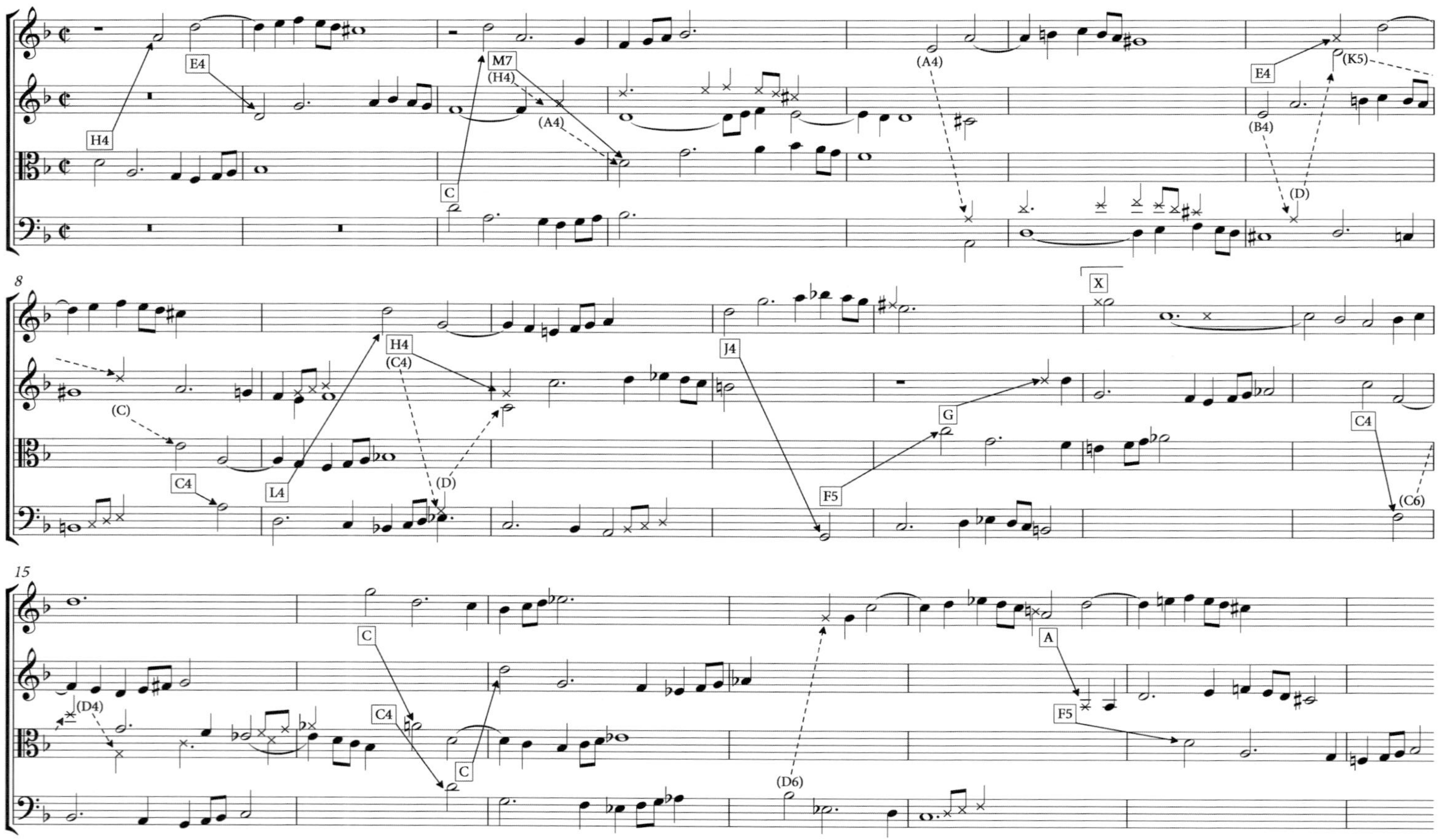

from *fugeing* at the upper sixth.[59] That this paper was cut up and used for another purpose suggests that such sketches were not considered worth keeping after they had performed their initial function, so any similar rough drafts that Purcell might have made while composing the fantazias may too have been subsequently destroyed. It is even possible that they were made on some sort of impermanent surface in a similar manner to Renaissance composers' use of the erasable *cartella* to work out the details of imitation and counterpoint.[60] Jessie Ann Owens has recently described a manuscript copied by the amateur composer James Sherard which had first been treated with a varnish in order to permit subsequent layers of notation to be erased and written over.[61] Owens further notes an entry in Samuel Pepys's diary as early as 1663 which seems to relate to his efforts to procure varnish for a similar purpose; whether use of this kind of erasable surface extended beyond amateurs and novice composers to professionals like Purcell is thus far unclear.[62]

The search for such materials beyond Purcell's own surviving manuscripts may, however, yield more fruitful results. Remarkable evidence for the notated trialling of multiple imitative possibilities survives in the manuscript collection of 'Rules in Musicke' (*Lbl* Add. MS 4910) copied perhaps around 1670 by Matthew Locke's friend Silas Taylor, *alias* Domville.[63] On fol. 56v of the manuscript Taylor copied an example intended – as Christopher D. S. Field and Benjamin Wardhaugh have shown[64] – to illustrate the sixth of the idiosyncratic music teacher John Birchensha's rules for composition, the 'Fuge rule'. The diagram (Ex. 2.13) shows an imitative subject on the fourth stave, and above and below are a series of possible imitations; the whole is not designed to be played

[59] Herissone, 'Purcell's Revisions', 63–5. Since it was first identified, this fragment has been discussed several times in the literature; see for example Robert Thompson, 'Sources and Transmission', in *The Ashgate Research Companion to Henry Purcell*, ed. Rebecca Herissone (Farnham: Ashgate, 2012), 13–63 (33–5); Howard, 'Understanding Creativity', 74 (and note 37); Herissone, '"Fowle Originalls"', 585. Herissone's most recent published remarks on this matter (*Musical Creativity*, 204) summarize and incorporate all of these interventions.

[60] See Jessie Ann Owens, 'The Milan Partbooks: Evidence of Cipriano de Rore's Compositional Process', *JAMS*, 37/2 (1984), 270–98 (276–83).

[61] Jessie Ann Owens, '"El foglio rigato" Revisited: Prepared Paper in Musical Composition', in *Uno gentile et subtile ingenio: Studies in Renaissance Music in Honour of Bonnie J. Blackburn*, ed. M. Jennifer Bloxam, Gioia Filocamo and Leofranc Holford-Strevens (Turnhout: Brepols, 2009), 53–61 (57–60). I thank Stephen Rose for drawing this to my attention; in a forthcoming article on Sherard he suggests that the manuscript in question may date from the 1690s.

[62] Owens, '"El foglio rigato" Revisited', 60; see also Herissone, *Musical Creativity*, 204–6.

[63] On the relationship between Locke and Taylor see Alan Howard, 'A Midcentury Musical Friendship: Silas Taylor and Matthew Locke', in *Beyond Boundaries: Rethinking Music Circulation in Early Modern England*, ed. Linda Phyllis Austern, Candace Bailey and Amanda Eubanks Winkler (Bloomington, IN: Indiana University Press, 2017), 127–49.

[64] See Christopher D. S. Field and Benjamin Wardhaugh, eds, *John Birchensha: Writings on Music*, Music Theory in Britain, 1500–1700: Critical Editions (Farnham: Ashgate, 2010), 242 note 14; for discussion of the manuscript in general see 217–24.

Ex. 2.13   'Fuge rule', as copied by Silas Taylor in *Lbl* Add. MS 4910, fol. 56v

together, but rather the selection of the fourth stave and any other line would produce a viable two-voice interlock. Furthermore, the layout on a single page makes it relatively straightforward to identify any larger interlocks produced by the fortuitous compatibility of otherwise alternative imitations. The purpose of the X beneath bar 4 of stave 7 is unexplained.[65]

Although the potential intervals for imitation are not systematically explored in Taylor's copy of Birchensha's chart, it does show a clear attempt to find entries at every minim interval up to and including three whole bars. There is also some indication of awareness of invertible counterpoint: the entries at the distance of one minim are related by inversion at the tenth; those after two minims by inversion at the octave, and those after four minims by inversion at the twelfth. Quite apart from the early date of this 'rule', Birchensha's position on the fringes of the musical establishment makes it unlikely that Purcell could have acquired such a strategy directly or indirectly from his teaching; more likely, Birchensha had himself gleaned, from his contact with court musicians in the 1660s, a habit of mind that was

---

[65] Field and Wardhaugh suggest that it may have been intended to apply to stave 8, where it would coincide with the premature ending of its barely viable imitation at the lower second.

passed on from master to pupil and reached Purcell that way later on. Moreover, it is ironic that the subject Birchensha chose to illustrate the rule is itself contrived from the interval-stock necessary for stretto *fuga*, a quality that arguably makes such notated trials less necessary (since each of the entries in the first two bars could be assumed to work based on the intervallic properties of the subject).

Another possible explanation for the lack of surviving written materials of this kind in Purcell's hand is that he was able to process such large amounts of material, in a manner analogous to Birchensha's 'rule', without resorting to notation. We can never know his capacity for musical memory, but at a time when writing materials were valued more highly and the boundaries between composition and improvisation were considerably more blurred than we readily appreciate today, it seems likely to have been highly developed. Furthermore, a closer look at the range of interlocks used by Purcell in the first section of Fantazia VIII reveals that nearly all of the intrinsically viable combinations can be related back to the creative origins of the materials themselves: like some of the entries in Birchensha's 'rule', interlocks $\boxed{C}$, $\boxed{C4}$, $\boxed{G4}$ and $\boxed{L4}$ all exploit the principles of stretto *fuga* (and in fact are derived from the climactic passage in bars 16–17); $\boxed{F5}$ and $\boxed{H4}$ are the two interlocks involving both the subject and its inversion at the semibreve discussed earlier, and $\boxed{G}$ is simply an inversion of $\boxed{G4}$ at the twelfth; the remaining two intrinsically viable interlocks that Purcell used both arise incidentally from the conjunction of other interlocks. Furthermore, both pairs of interlocks $\boxed{F5}$ and $\boxed{H4}$, and $\boxed{K5}$ and $\boxed{M4}$, are, respectively, exact melodic inversions of one another. What this section of Fantazia VIII demonstrates, then, is that technical devices such as stretto *fuga* and invertible counterpoint could serve as valuable creative shorthands, both facilitating the creation of materials suitable for such systematic displays of imitative resources, and reducing the demands upon the memory for their realization.

The most important interlocks having been thus derived from the original inventive materials, the only passages that required true 'research' were firstly those conditionally viable combinations that Purcell chose for use in particular contexts, and secondly those in which viable two-voice interlocks were combined in order to create larger complexes of subject entries involving three or four voices. The evidence for this process of research is not only in those interlocks (such as $\boxed{A}$ and $\boxed{E4}$) which Purcell incorporated unchanged into the first section of the fantazia, but also in those passages in which the material is derived from failed or problematic attempts at imitative entries.[66] A good example of the latter is the altered

---

[66] For a similar observation with respect to Bach's C major fugue, *WTC* I see Dreyfus, *Patterns of Invention*, 153.

form of interlock A4 in bars 5–7 (tr. 1/bass): Purcell lengthens the second note of the bass entry by a minim, thus displacing the augmented second interval to a weaker beat and ensuring that the end of the bass entry, and thus the arrival on the locally stable A major chord, falls on a strong beat at the beginning of bar 7. The result is a slightly distorted interlock which, as noted above, resembles A4 at the beginning and E4 at the end, but the derivation of this material from an attempted two-part subject interlock is beyond question.

It is possible that many more fragments of counterpoint in the first section of Fantazia VIII are derived from similar modified or aborted subject complexes. Nevertheless, a degree of caution is necessary when applying this generally convincing principle to specific instances in the music: the degree of speculation involved in any such observation inevitably increases as the resemblance of the passage in question to the imitative materials becomes more distant. Bars 3–5 of Fantazia VIII furnish a good example of a passage that has plausible origins in Purcell's imitative processes, but which nevertheless could not be sufficiently proven to carry any significant authority. These bars are clearly related to the opening two bars of the piece: Purcell transfers the opening tenor and treble 2 entries, at original pitch, to the bass and tenor parts, and composes out the harmonic motion from the key-note to its fifth over three bars instead of two. He further intensifies the music by introducing close *fugeing* on the subject *thesin* in bar 3, making use of interlock C between treble 1 and bass.

What is less certain, however, is the status of the second treble part in bars 4–5. Given the demonstrable connections with the opening two bars, it seems logical to suggest that Purcell originally planned to retain the subject *arsin* from bar 1, now as part of complex E4 with the first treble; thus bar 3 would have been the start of a series of four entries in which two entries *thesin* (bass/tr. 1) overlapped with two *arsin* (tr. 2/ten.). As in bars 5–6, the problematic interlock here is A4 (which would be between the inner voices in bars 3–4), and in this context more drastic alteration was required (Ex. 2.14): if left unaltered, this treble 2 entry would have produced an accented upper auxiliary on a strong beat (a dissonance Purcell reserves for the important arrival at on the fifth of the key in bar 20 immediately prior to the final cadence of the section), and a $c\sharp'$ on the last beat of bar 4 (thereby implying a premature arrival on the fifth and an earlier cadence). Purcell's final treble 2 line in bars 3–4 unquestionably follows the contour of the subject *arsin*, but whether it is truly a stretched-out and freely rhythmicized version of the point is perhaps open to debate.

The resemblance between Purcell's final treble 2 line in bars 3–5 and the subject *arsin* in augmented form (Ex. 2.14b) makes this an attractive interpretation of this passage, nevertheless, since Purcell clearly intended

Ex 2.14   Fantazia VIII, bb. 3–5 (ten. and tr. 2)

(a) Interlock A4

(b) Treble 2 augmented

(c) As in bars 3–5

to introduce an augmented entry in this section. Perhaps it was even his experience of working on these bars that suggested the idea, which resulted ultimately in the augmented entry *thesin* in bar 13 (tr. 1; marked 'X' in Ex. 2.12). Such a feature, particularly given the artifice of its combination with interlock G in original note-values, may seem likely to have originated close to the beginning of the creative process. In fact, however, Purcell must have worked these bars out rather later, since the augmented entry required flexing via a rhythmic alteration in order to accommodate the pre-existing interlock G and thereby avoid an unresolved suspension on the second beat of bar 13. In other words, Purcell incorporated the augmented entry at a stage when the melodic material was already fixed; otherwise, he could have altered the melodic content of the subject so that the augmented entry could be made to fit exactly, thereby increasing its artifice.

'MOST REGULAR TO YOUR DESIGN'

Having examined in detail how Purcell invented his materials and probed their imitative potential, it remains to comment on his approach to their successful disposition and contextualization within the first section of Fantazia VIII.[67] As in the first movement of Sonata I (1683), contrapuntal events play an integral role in the harmonic organization of the section, demonstrating again the mutual inclusivity of *fugeing* and harmony in Purcell's compositional technique. This is visible even in Example 2.12, in the extent to which the fugal working of the subject does all of the harmonic 'work': none of the material that is missing from the outline score results in any harmonic ambiguity either at a local level or in the context of the planning of the section.

---

[67]   The heading of this section is taken from AoD, 119.

Purcell often uses fugal entries for specific harmonic purposes. In bar 5, for example, he introduces an entry on e' in the first treble to intensify the treble 2 suspension and overlap with the ensuing cadence, a decision that additionally results in the first decisive harmonic move away from the key-note by introducing a $g\sharp'$ in bar 6_3. Some of the more distant modulations can also be attributed to particular fugal processes, in particular the notable tendency of the section to modulate flatwards towards E♭ major and C minor. Such flatwards motion is a common characteristic of stretto *fuga*, owing to the predominance of rising fourths and falling fifths in the necessary interval-stock. Furthermore, Purcell was obliged to modify the stepwise ascent through a fourth at the end of his subject *thesin* to preserve interval rather than mode when answering it at the fourth, in order to avoid an ungrammatical melodic succession of three whole tones (see Ex. 2.15). Interlock C4, which is affected by this consideration, is the controlling interlock at both of the most prominent moments of flatwards modulation in this section (bb. 8–9, and 16–18, where it forms part of the larger four-voice stretto *fuga*). Such a prominent harmonic trait has a notable impact on the remainder of the fantazia: the penultimate section strays as far as A♭ major, and the persistence of E♭s in the closing bars makes the final cadence sound almost more like an imperfect cadence in G minor than a full close on D.

Such intervallic properties may exert a powerful influence over the harmonic direction of the music, but Purcell retains tight control of the long-range organization of harmony. This is particularly apparent at the very end of the section, where having cadenced in E♭ at bar 18_3, he manages to perform a decisive return to the key-note (D) in the space of just three and a half bars. He achieves this by sidestepping from the E♭ major cadence to an entry *arsin* outlining C minor (tr. 1, b. 18_3), then immediately repeating the same form of the subject in D minor, creating a rising sequence. In order to accommodate this, the density of subject entries is noticeably reduced; instead, Purcell concentrates on providing a strong harmonic accompaniment, over a descending scale in long notes in the bass. Only in the latter stages of this transition does he reintroduce close imitation – making use of two interlocks, A and F5, that could be used to outline unambiguous key-note harmonies.

Apart from representing a simple but highly effective means of bringing the section to a close, the use of sequence in bars 18–20 reflects an important aspect of the overall harmonic planning of this section of Fantazia VIII. In returning to D minor by way of a sequential step up, Purcell mirrors the modulation to C minor in bars 7 to 12, which incorporated a step down: the subject entry in bar 7 (tr. 1) is repeated a tone lower in bar 10 (tr. 2), with the equivalent fragment of bass line accompanying it both times (see Ex. 2.12). The result is a large-scale structural symmetry (see Table 2.2) with the superb harmonic and registral

Ex. 2.15   Fantazia VIII, interlock C4: necessary modifications

(a)   Ungrammatical succession of three whole tones produced by preservation of mode

(b)   Correction preserving interval

climax of bars 11–12 placed almost exactly at the midpoint of the 22 bar section.

This climactic cadence is none other than the quotation from the first section of Fantazia VII and, as has already been noted, it appears at the moment that the music reaches the key of the earlier work; thus the importance of this relationship to the composition of Fantazia VIII is played out at a structural level as well as contributing to the invention of its fugal materials.

This process of give and take between harmony and *fugeing* does not, however, tell the whole story about the structure of the first section of Fantazia VIII. In a direct parallel with the presentation of his illustrations of *fugeing* in 'The Art of Descant' in order of increasing artifice, Purcell also paid careful attention to the ordering of his fugal inventions to produce a gradual cumulation of artifice. At the beginning of the piece, the counterpoint is generally made up of simple two-voice interlocks (see Ex. 2.12); as the passage continues, however, the level of artifice progressively accumulates. Purcell gradually builds up to the four-part stretto *fuga* by introducing its component two-voice interlock C in bar 3, and interlock C4 in bars 8 and 14 (a fragment of interlock C in the former case hinting at the larger complex to come). The augmented subject entry then appears in bar 13, before the full stretto *fuga* in bar 16. Harmonically, this passage marks the furthest modulation from the key-note, with a strong cadence on E♭ in

Table 2.2 Fantazia VIII, first section: structural symmetry

7–9	11–12	18–20
Repetition of subject and bass fragment in sequence, down a tone.	Prominent cadence in C minor	Subject *arsin* in C minor, followed by interlock A in D minor; hence sequential repetition of subject up a tone.

bar 18; at the same time, it integrates the two structural processes I have described by linking together the harmonic and registral climax (b. 11) with the passage of greatest artifice (bb. 16–18), couching them, respectively, in relative minor and major keys.

A similar process of structuring material according to a principle of gradual cumulation of artifice can be heard in some of Matthew Locke's fantazias.[68] In the second section of the Fantazia that begins the third *Consort of Four Parts*, Locke begins with simple imitation at the distance of one and a half bars, then introduces successively closer imitation, free inversion and augmentation, and finally a four-part complex towards the end of the section (see Ex. 2.16). Like Purcell, he uses stretto *fuga* to facilitate close imitation of the subject. Locke, however, is much freer in his treatment of material: unlike Purcell, he seems to have worked out the different ways of treating his subject successively, in combination with material not belonging to the point. Thus although the basic principle of organization is the same, Purcell's insistence on the integrity of the fugal subject, and the corresponding increase in the level of artifice, led him to develop a fundamentally different way of working. The successive appearance of Locke's increasingly artificial devices is accompanied by a gradual decrease in fidelity to the original intervallic and rhythmic identity of the point. Purcell, by contrast, seems to have begun by working on the most artificial passages, enabling him to retain the original form of his subject throughout.

* * *

The techniques explored in this chapter find applications throughout Purcell's consort music and sonatas, though not every piece will yield quite such striking examples. There are also many passages and obvious stylistic features that are not specifically accounted for by such analytical approaches, although it is clear from the foregoing analyses that the use of imitative procedure as a way in to the study of creative process can lead to considerably wider insights. Far from offering an analytical machine capable of revealing the secret behind each composition, such methods represent practical points of departure for the close analysis of the music, which has remained all too often a minor concern of the literature. Each analysis reveals something of the way the music was composed, which in turn can tell us about what it was that Purcell valued in music: not conservative stylistic tendencies or superficial contrapuntal tricks, but

---

[68] 'Cumulation' is a useful term recently proposed by Alon Schab for 'the compositional strategy of postponing the boldest and most sophisticated ideas to the end of a movement' (Schab, *Sonatas of Henry Purcell*, 51–6). In its general sense this principle is supported – as Schab notes – by Christopher Simpson's advice for the ordering of divisions over a ground: 'if you have any thing more excellent than other, reserve it for the Conclusion' (Simpson, *The Division-Viol*, 2nd edn (London: Henry Brome, 1665), 57). I will refer to the specific use of this principle to structure what Schab calls the 'contrapuntal unfolding' of a piece as 'cumulation of artifice'.

Ex. 2.16   Matthew Locke, *Consort of Four Parts*, Fantazia no. 3: second, fugal section

(a)   Simple *fugeing*

(b)   Two-part stretto *fuga*

(c)   Free inversions and augmentations of the subject

(d)   Final four-voice complex using compound stretto *fuga* artifice at a deep level that is fundamental to the very conception of each piece, thorough examination of musical resources, and creative use of the qualities of the material to produce particular harmonic effects and structural patterns. It is on this basis that we can begin to assemble a larger picture of Purcell's techniques in both the fantazias and sonatas, and indeed throughout Purcell's oeuvre as a whole.

CHAPTER 3

'The chiefest instrumental musick now in request': Canzonas and Other Sonata Fugues

Most of Purcell's sonatas contain at least one fugal movement in duple time, usually the second movement of the sonata and frequently entitled 'canzona'. In many respects this kind of movement enshrines in miniature the full range of issues behind the varied and contradictory reception of Purcell's instrumental music examined in the Introduction. It certainly brings into sharp focus the dichotomy between, on the one hand, those who wish to hear in Purcell's sonatas the echoes of a dying tradition of English consort music and, on the other, those for whom they sound a triumphant herald for the coming of the age of Bach and Handel.[1] For all that Purcell's canzonas superficially resemble the fugues familiar from eighteenth-century repertoire, however, the techniques he deploys in his canzonas and related movements can be clearly related back to his concern for compositional artifice.

Once this is established it becomes possible to escape the suspiciously conflicting modern responses to these works and examine Purcell's compositional strategies in the context of their earliest reception, asking – as I do in Chapter 4 – what his contrapuntal methods have to tell us about his understanding of the Italian style and how, in turn, this may have contributed to the comparatively short-lived popularity of his sonatas. This chapter, in the meantime, begins by examining the difference between Purcell's sonata fugues and the approach to *fugeing* found in passages such as the start of Fantazia VIII. Concentrating on the 'opening platforms' or expositions of his canzonas, I examine in contrapuntal terms how Purcell constructed these sections, before going on to explore the role of thoroughbass – one of the most important factors in his engagement with the Italian sonata – in the creation of the very materials he used.

As I argued in Chapter 1, the apparent confusion in the Purcellian literature over just how Purcell's sonata fugues related to his interest in the more arcane forms of counterpoint in the fantazias is traceable right back to the composer's own treatment of 'fuge' in 'The Art of Descant'. The difference between the two approaches to 'double descant' shown in Fig. 1.3 – the one a demonstration of *fugeing* as a technique, and the

[1] Bukofzer, *Music in the Baroque Era*, 214; Tilmouth, 'The Technique and Forms', 117–19.

other inserted to represent the Italian genre of the canzona – is undermined in Purcell's commentary by his association of all of the kinds of fugal procedure he describes with the Italian sonata. While such features are certainly important aspects of his own sonatas, they are in fact rare in those of the Italian composers whom Purcell so warmly commends elsewhere in 'The Art of Descant'; indeed, Peter Allsop considers such devices as augmentation, diminution, retrograde motion and inversion to be 'hardly ever associated with the Italian "trio" sonata in the seventeenth century'.[2]

The issue of 'double descant' is particularly germane to the analysis of Purcell's sonata fugues, since it is exactly the technique of the 'Calista' example (Fig. 1.3b) that he applies to almost all of his own canzonas: an extended passage of triple-invertible counterpoint is built from a subject and two countersubjects, each introduced in turn and then redistributed among the parts at each repetition of the basic unit of three-part counterpoint. No theoretical work discusses the technique of composing such a movement. Its requirements, however, are quite distinct from those of *fugeing*: whereas in the fantazias (and indeed in the many sonata movements based on the same techniques) Purcell cultivates a densely woven contrapuntal structure in which harmonic and motivic elements are mutually interdependent, with local cadences occurring at irregular intervals and in often distant key areas, in his canzonas the relationship between material, harmony and phrasing is fundamentally different: subjects take on a fixed relationship to the harmony, and cadences coincide with the ends of the subjects, recurring at regular intervals of time throughout the (often long) first platforms. This is true for all of the movements Purcell called 'canzona', but is most obvious in those – such as the second movement of Sonata III (1683) – that adopt a strict triple-invertible texture. The result is a strong sense of hypermetre and a periodic repetition that would be completely out of place in any of the fantazias.

Helene Wessely-Kropik accounts for this technique by pointing out that Purcell's invertible counterpoint can often be understood (allowing for octave transposition) as a strict three-part canon.[3] The corresponding implication of a high degree of compositional artifice neatly explains Purcell's interest in the techniques of the Colista–Lonati repertoire, where this technique is commonplace, and is also representative of contemporary understandings of 'double descant': as Rebecca Herissone observes, English theorists consistently associated invertible counterpoint with canon during the seventeenth century.[4] This kind of canon, though, is far less artificial in terms of its degree of compositional difficulty than the brief canonic passages or even the imitative treatment to be found in

---

[2] Peter Allsop, *The Italian 'Trio' Sonata from its Origins until Corelli* (Oxford University Press, 1992), 115.
[3] Wessely-Kropik, 'Henry Purcell als Instrumentalkomponist', 112.
[4] Herissone, *Music Theory*, 197–8.

the fantazias. Indeed, its construction over a periodically repeating harmonic background aligns it closely with another genre in which Purcell was well versed: that of the vocal catch.

CATCH AND CANZONA

Catches and rounds were highly popular among the patrons of London's taverns and clubs throughout the seventeenth century and beyond.[5] The similarity between the catch and the instrumental canzona in Purcell's hands has been noted before: in remarking on the familiarity of the catch to contemporary audiences, Michael Tilmouth effectively observed that the decrease in compositional effort compared with the *fugeing* in the fantazias is accompanied by a reduction in generic level, making such movements more accessible to the listener.[6] In this respect it is perhaps not out of place to recall Roger North's famous description of his older brother Francis's hosting of a performance of some of Purcell's Sonatas, with the composer at the harpsichord and Roger and another playing the violins.[7] While at one level this is clearly an act of patronage – Roger records that 'wee performed them more than once, of which Mr Purcell was not a little proud, nor was it a common thing for one of his dignity to be so enterteined' – on the other hand, this gathering shares in the sense of performance for the enjoyment of the participants, in a male homosocial environment in which music facilitated the crossing of social hierarchies, that Linda Austern associates with catch culture as a whole.[8]

The analogy may be pushed even further in terms of the detail of compositional technique, making clear Purcell's distinction between *fugeing* and his adoption of triple-invertible counterpoint in the sonata fugues. Characteristically, Christopher Simpson was the only seventeenth-century author to describe the composition of catches in detail:

The contrivance [of a catch] is not intricate: for, if you compose any short Strain, of three or four Parts, setting them all within the ordinary compass of a Voice; and then place one Part at the end of another, in what order you please, so as they may aptly make one continued Tune; you have finished a Catch.[9]

In lieu of Simpson's rather perfunctory example, Example 3.1 shows Purcell's homage to the viol, 'Of all the instruments that are', one of

[5] John Harley, *Music in Purcell's London* (London: Dobson, 1968), 141–3; on Purcell's catches see Holman, *Henry Purcell*, 29–31.

[6] Michael Tilmouth and Christopher D. S. Field, 'Consort Music II: From 1660', in *The Seventeenth Century*, ed. Ian Spink, The Blackwell History of Music in Britain, III (Oxford: Blackwell, 1993), 245–81 (272).

[7] Wilson, *Roger North on Music*, 47; see also Wood, *Purcell*, 74.

[8] Linda Phyllis Austern, 'Music and Manly Wit in Seventeenth-Century England: The Case of the Catch', in *Concepts of Creativity in Seventeenth-Century England*, ed. Rebecca Herissone and Alan Howard (Woodbridge: Boydell, 2013), 281–308.

[9] Simpson, *Compendium*, 143.

Ex. 3.1   'Of all the instruments that are' (catch in three parts)

Table 3.1 Structure of a three-part catch (numbers represent the three strains of the melody)

Voice 1:	1	2	‖: 3	1	2	:‖ 3		
Voice 2:		1	‖: 2	3	1	:‖ 2	3	
Voice 3:			‖: 1	2	3	:‖ 1	2	3

Repeat ad lib.

more than fifty catches and rounds he composed. As performed, the voices enter successively with the same melody, continuing in counterpoint with the following entries until all the parts have entered – whereupon the cycle repeats itself. The resultant structure is shown in Table 3.1.

The first sixteen bars of the second movement of Sonata III (1683) are clearly conceived in exactly the same way. The whole creative process consisted of devising the three-part passage of counterpoint shown in Ex. 3.2, after which Purcell had only to bring in the successive parts on the subject, transposing every second cycle of the complex up a fifth (/down a fourth). The resulting structure of the first platform of the canzona, shown in Table 3.2, is almost identical to that of the catch (compare Table 3.1), demonstrating clearly the strong sense of hypermetrical repetition that makes this technique so different from the *fugeing* explored in Chapter 2.

The one important difference between the canzona and the catch, however, is that the catch is written in three voices of equal range. In the

Ex. 3.2 Sonata III (1683), canzona: three-part subject complex

Table 3.2 Sonata III (1683), second movement: structure of opening 16 bars

Transposition	–	+5	–	+5	–	+5	–	+5
Vn1	S	CS I	CS II	S	CS I	CS II	S	CS I
Vn2		S	CS I	CS II	S	CS I	CS II	S
Bass			S	CS I	CS II	S	CS I	CS II

sonata movement, by contrast, the occupation of a lower range by the bass part means that in order for the rotation of the parts to work the complex must be triple-invertible, since all three of the parts must be capable of functioning as a bass. Just as he later did in his example of 'double descant' in 'The Art of Descant', Purcell uses three different permutations of the material in the second movement of Sonata III (1683) in order to demonstrate this property. Rather than deploy all six, he is concerned instead to present the subject and two countersubjects in linear succession in the bass; by running twice through this pattern he exposes each in both tonic and dominant keys, while the maintenance of the same S – CSI – CSII succession in the other parts preserves the quasi-canonic layout. As a result, from the entry of the bass (the third part to enter in this movement) the complete three-part complex is heard for a total of six iterations.[10] Most, though not all, of Purcell's canzonas and similar fugues match this design in their opening platforms; many exceed six iterations, while a few depart from the strict plan sooner.

Purcell's attachment to this technique is borne out by its extraordinary frequency in his sonatas: it pervades not only the canzonas but indeed all of the fast fugal movements, including those in dance-like triple metres. As well as using 'double descant' at the octave as in the second movement of Sonata III (1683), he incorporated invertible counterpoint at the twelfth

---

[10] Alon Schab uses the similar term 'rotations', which evocatively describes the ordered shuffling of the subjects among the parts (*Sonatas of Henry Purcell*, esp. 33–5). However, Schab includes the initial one- and two-part entries among his numbered rotations; I prefer to begin counting iterations only once all three parts are in play, hence my adoption of a different term for clarity.

Ex. 3.3   Sonata VII (1697), fourth movement: 'double descant' at the twelfth

(a)   Original complex

(b)   Rotation of parts incorporating contrapuntal inversion at the twelfth

on several occasions when it offered more melodic potential (Ex. 3.3; see also the fifth movement of Sonata III (1683), the third movement of Sonata VIII (1683), the fifth movement of Sonata II (1697), and the fifth movement of Sonata IX (1697)). 'Double descant' at intervals other than the octave seems to have been a comparatively rare phenomenon by the 1680s. Simpson, like Purcell later in 'The Art of Descant', had described only 'double descant' at the octave in his *Compendium*, and one has to go back to Morley's *Plaine and Easie Introduction* of 1597 to find a theoretical discussion of invertible counterpoint at the twelfth and at the tenth.[11]

The advantage of this promotion of invertible counterpoint for Purcell was that it provided a means of raising the intensity of contrapuntal artifice in the latest instrumental styles. Indeed, he was far from the only composer at the time to explore such compositional strategies: his examples in the sonatas are closely contemporary with the development of the so-called 'permutation fugue' in Germany, and may therefore be understood as part of a wider interest on the part of northern-European musicians in the promotion of more learned techniques in this new context.

The term 'permutation fugue' is a modern one, invented to describe a fugue constructed from between three and six melodic units in which the voices enter successively alternating between tonic and dominant, with each voice presenting the melodic units in the same order in invertible

[11] Morley, *Introduction*, 105–7.

counterpoint; in other words, the very same structural principle followed by Purcell.[12] The best-known examples are the early choral fugues of J. S. Bach, such as the opening chorus of *Himmelskönig, sei willkommen* (BWV182), but Paul Walker has traced the origins of this approach to a small group of composers working in Hamburg and Lübeck during the 1660s and 1670s, for whom Zarlino's explanation of invertible counterpoint in *Le istitutioni harmoniche* (as transmitted to them in the writings of Sweelinck) assumed paramount structural importance in the context of fugal composition.[13]

For Walker, the presence of this technique in the early choral works of J. S. Bach suggests that the very notion of fugue as a genre is in need of revision. Twentieth-century commentators, he observes, questioned the fugal status of the permutation fugue on structural grounds (particularly the lack of episodes) and because of its foundation on multiple themes, according to 'a set of requirements distilled by many generations of theorists from a small sampling of late-baroque fugal writing'.[14] By contrast, contemporary theorists would have been quick to recognize such works as fugues. If, then, the characteristics of the genre are extended to admit Bach's examples, this would also release Purcell's canzonas from the common analytical comparison with later paradigms discussed above.

Walker points out certain features of the permutation fugue (in particular the presence of a regular, invertible countersubject) in the sonatas of Johann Adam Reincken's *Hortus Musicus* of 1688, but identifies the first 'true' permutation fugues among the movements of the three sonatas at the end of Johann Theile's *Musikalisches Kunstbuch*.[15] Although this manuscript treatise is dated 1691, Carl Dahlhaus suggests that its contents were composed in the period 1675–85, placing them potentially very close indeed to the period in which Purcell must have written his sonatas.[16]

In observing how Bach's permutation fugues demonstrate an 'ability to transform Theile's dry, pedantic model into effective music', Walker also pinpoints the principal difference between Theile's examples and the canzonas by Purcell and Lonati examined above.[17] Of Theile's three sonatas, the second is the most directly comparable with Purcell's, as it adopts 'trio' scoring and contains two permutation fugues. The first of these is based on the triple-invertible complex in Ex. 3.4, and treated

---

[12] See, for example, Carl Dahlhaus, 'Zur Geschichte der Permutationsfuge', *Bach-Jahrbuch*, 46 (1959), 95–116 (95).

[13] Paul Mark Walker, 'The Origin of the Permutation Fugue', in *The Creative Process*, Studies in the History of Music, III (New York: Broude Brothers, 1992), 51–91 (esp. 56).

[14] Ibid., 91; see also 56, 90.   [15] Walker, *Theories of Fugue*, 207–8, 232–4.

[16] Johann Theile, *Musikalisches Kunstbuch*, ed. Carl Dahlhaus, Denkmäler norddeutscher Musik, I (Kassel: Bärenreiter, 1965), viii.

[17] Walker, 'Permutation Fugue', 87.

Ex. 3.4   Johann Theile, *Musikalisches Kunstbuch*, Sonata [II] *a* 3, first movement: triple-invertible complex (as in bb. 12–17)

according to exactly the same structural principle as is shown in Table 3.2; as in the fourth movement of Purcell's Sonata VII (1697), two parts are invertible at the octave, and the third (here countersubject II) inverts at the twelfth whenever it must function as a bass (bb. 23–8, 39–45). Here, however, the similarity stops. Theile uses this material to construct the whole of his fugue, without any episodes or free material until the final five bars, which he adds to provide an effective conclusion based on a more homophonic working of the motivic ideas from his subjects. By contrast, both Purcell and Lonati only use this principle to create the first platforms of their canzonas, thereafter exploring other combinations of the material, and harmonic expansion through episodes. Even more noticeably, the material itself is radically different in character: whereas Purcell uses a short passage of counterpoint with clear harmonic implications – derived, in fact, from a commonplace thoroughbass pattern, as we shall see below – Theile's triple-invertible complex is both longer and less harmonically driven.

Much of the 'dry, pedantic' character Walker perceives in this music results from the strictures of composing a three-part complex that could be melodically inverted in its entirety, an audacious feat that provides the material for a second permutation fugue in bars 63–115 of the same sonata. Notwithstanding this difference, however, the greater harmonic directness shared by Purcell's canzonas and the 'Calista' example he quoted in 'The Art of Descant' strongly suggests that it was the Italian examples that Purcell had in mind when composing his own fugues. A large collection of Italian trio sonatas is known to have been in circulation in England in the early 1680s.[18] Among these works are eleven sonatas by Colista and Lonati which between them contain no fewer than six movements with permutational expositions in triple-invertible counterpoint, and a further four that incorporate similar structural principles despite having only two fully invertible subjects.

By contrast, there is no evidence to suggest that Purcell knew Theile's *Musikalisches Kunstbuch*; no music by either Theile or Reincken survives in contemporary English copies, and there is no known connection between these composers and any of the German musicians working in England in the second half of the seventeenth century.[19] The lack of any demonstrable connection does not mask the striking similarity of purpose behind the two developments, however: Purcell's cultivation of permutational expositions as a more artificial manifestation of the Italian sonata is just one consequence of an aspect of that style that has arguably been overlooked in studies of Italian instrumental music that emphasize the dominance of Corelli from the early 1680s onwards. Indeed, similar structural principles continued to inform the fugal writing of Italian composers in this period, as shown in the Op. 1 sonatas of Tomaso Albinoni, published in Venice in 1694.[20] It seems that Bach was not the first composer to succeed in exploiting the theoretical possibilities of the permutation fugue in a practical context – and the fact that Bach composed fugues on four of the subjects from Albinoni's Op. 1 shows that Theile's cannot have been the only permutational fugues with which he was familiar.

The picture that emerges, then, is one of a widespread interest throughout Europe in the possibilities of invertible counterpoint in a fugal context. It was an identical impulse that led Purcell to recommend this particular aspect of the sonata style to readers of 'The Art of Descant' in terms so strikingly similar to Simpson's description of the fantazia in the previous generation. In so doing, he not only advocated the adoption of the Italian style, as has been read so often into his preface to the 1683 Sonatas, but proposed a strategy for the survival of strict contrapuntal artifice in its context.

---

[18] Shay and Thompson examine a group of sources related to *Lbl* Add. MS 33236, including music by Lonati and Colista as well as by G. B. Vitali, G. Legrenzi and G. B. Bassani (*Purcell Manuscripts*, 109–25 (esp. Table 3.10, 111)).

[19] On German musicians working in England see J. A. Westrup, 'Foreign Musicians in Stuart England', *MQ*, 27/1 (1941), 70–89 (81–3, 88–9). Among those with connections to Schleswig-Holstein were the viol-player Dietrich Steffkin (*d.* 1673), the violin virtuoso Thomas Baltzar (?1631–63) and another viol-player, August Kühnel (though the latter seems not to have visited London before 1682); the music of each reflects their careers as virtuoso performers, however, and is far removed from the erudite contrapuntal experiments of organists and other composers of sacred music such as Theile and Reincken, Matthias Weckmann or Christoph Bernhard.

[20] See Michael Talbot, *Tomaso Albinoni: The Venetian Composer and his World* (Oxford University Press, 1990), 86. A further sonata attributed to Albinoni, known only in a manuscript copy at Durham Cathedral, contains a movement that explores the permutations of no fewer than five subjects (ibid., 92–4).

The group of sonata movements addressed in this chapter extends beyond those that Purcell called 'canzona' to include nearly all of the fast fugal movements in the 1683 and 1697 sets. There are a few movements that Purcell labelled 'canzona' but which do not incorporate triple-invertible counterpoint at all – especially in cases where the subjects are worked in 'double fuge' from the start (see Ex. 3.5). The many dance-inspired fugues that do begin with catch-like, permutational expositions in triple-invertible counterpoint, conversely, cannot properly be called 'canzonas' owing to their triple metre. What unites all of these movements is the genre-based notion of fugue as distinct from the technique of *fugeing*, and in particular the coincidence of motivic and harmonic units that produces periodic organization such as is heard in the second movement of Sonata III (1683). Furthermore, all of these fugues share common origins in terms of the derivation of their fugal materials, an observation that leads into the role of thoroughbass in Purcell's sonata style.

THOROUGHBASS AND THE INVENTION OF FUGAL MATERIALS

The three-voice invertible complex that is the basis of the first sixteen bars of the second movement of Sonata III (1683) is an elaboration of a simple sequential progression involving a series of 7–6 suspensions over a stepwise descent in the bass. Not only, therefore, is Purcell's fugal procedure in this piece differentiated from that of the fantazias by its reliance on a permutational approach to invertible counterpoint, but it also exhibits an almost antithetical approach to the relationship between its fugal materials and the underlying harmony. In the first movement of the G minor Sonata I (1683) and the first section of Fantazia VIII, the subject material certainly had harmonic implications, but these were incipient rather than explicit; Purcell's *fugeing* manipulated the many different combinations of entries to draw upon and even generate multiple harmonic contexts. In the D minor canzona (the second movement of Sonata III (1683)), by contrast, the subject material is itself a melodic particularization of a specific underlying progression, a kind of generalized harmonic fragment that exists prior to the subject itself.

This canzona is by no means unique in this respect; indeed, the other fugue with a 'catch-like', triple-invertible opening platform cited above (the fourth movement of Sonata VII (1697); see Ex. 3.3) is founded on the very same progression. Viewed together, furthermore, Purcell's sonata fugues all rely on standard, replicable thoroughbass progressions to a greater or lesser extent. The fact that, in spite of this, Purcell is able to imbue these materials with such melodic individuality is testimony to his skilful use of the techniques of division that were so important to the English instrumental tradition, techniques that are seldom invoked in discussions of the trio sonata. While the catch provides a useful model

Ex. 3.5   Fast sonata fugues incorporating 'double fuge' from the outset (arrows indicate invertible counterpoint)

(a)   Sonata IV (1683), canzona: opening platform

(b)   Sonata V (1697), canzona: opening platform

(c)   Sonata VIII (1697), canzona: opening platform

for the structural and imitative procedures of the first platforms of these fugues, therefore, it is thoroughbass that will shed light on Purcell's process of melodic invention.

Purcell's treatment of thoroughbass in the sonatas of 1683 and 1697 has received a great deal of attention from commentators on contemporary and modern performance practice. The conventional view, as stated, for example, by Bukofzer, was that it was one of the defining differences between Purcell's fantazias and sonatas.[21] With increasing recognition that instrumental music had been accompanied at the organ throughout the seventeenth century, however, came the realization that Purcell's last-minute decision in the *Sonnata's of III Parts* 'to cause the whole Thorough Bass to be Engraven' may have been more cosmetic than practical. Since both fantazias and sonatas were apparently performed with organ accompaniment, Purcell's provision of a separate continuo part seemed little more than an Italianate affectation designed to make the sonatas seem more up to date, and was unlikely in itself to have resulted in any difference in performance practice.[22]

The addition of the continuo part as an afterthought does not imply, however, that Purcell's compositional technique was not informed by a deep familiarity with thoroughbass procedure. English musicians had long been familiar with the requisite skills to provide an improvised accompaniment to vocal and instrumental music, reading from scores, keyboard reductions or separate thoroughbass parts, very often unfigured.[23] The latter in particular requires a strong awareness of idiom and compositional technique, since the performer is essentially required to make an informed guess as to the harmonic intentions of the composer based solely on the behaviour of the bass part and his own stylistic awareness. Not surprisingly, then, it was to this skill that a large part of the advice contained in contemporary thoroughbass manuals related. Two such works by Restoration authors are extant: Matthew Locke's *Melothesia* (1673), and John Blow's unpublished 'Rules for Playing of a Through Bass, upon Organ & Harpsicon.' (thought to date from the late 1670s).[24]

---

[21] Bukofzer, *Music in the Baroque Era*, 213.

[22] Thurston Dart, 'Purcell's Chamber Music', *Proceedings of the Royal Musical Association*, 85/1 (1958–9), 81–93 (82–4); Walter Kolneder, 'Der Generalbass in der Triosonaten von Purcell', in *Heinrich Schütz e il suo Tempo [Atti del 1°Convegno Internazionale di Studi, Urbino, 26–31 Iuglio 1978]*, ed. Giancarlo Rostirolla (Rome: Società Italiana del Flauto Dolce, 1981), 281–99 (293).

[23] For a summary of the history of thoroughbass in England, see Peter Holman, '"Evenly, Softly, and Sweetly Acchording to All": The Organ Accompaniment of English Consort Music', in *John Jenkins and his Time: Studies in English Consort Music*, ed. Andrew Ashbee and Peter Holman (Oxford University Press, 1996), 353–82 (353–68).

[24] Matthew Locke, *Melothesia; or, Certain General Rules for Playing upon a Continued-Bass* (London: J. Carr, 1673). Blow's treatise is contained in *Lbl* Add. MS 34072, fols 1–5; it is transcribed in Franck Thomas Arnold, *The Art of Accompaniment from a Thorough-Bass as Practised in the XVIIth and XVIIIth Centuries*, 2 vols (Oxford University Press, 1931; repr. New York: Dover, 1965), I, 163–72.

Of the two, Locke's treatise is of particular interest given his concern to demonstrate that the skills required in order to accompany a singer or instrumentalist from a thoroughbass part at the keyboard were also extremely valuable as compositional techniques. In the concluding remarks to *Melothesia,* he observed that, by following his rules, the musically competent student would not only be able to accompany a solo or ensemble performance, but would also 'with much ease arrive to the use of the first Rudiments of *Musick*'. Indeed, the study of the final examples 'by way of transition' would take him further: 'being truly understood and applied, [they] will (in my Opinion) acquaint him with *All that's Teachable* as to matter of *Ayr*; the rest intirely depending on his Ingenuity, Observation, and Study'.[25] Hence the title of Locke's little treatise, which explicitly recalls the preface to the English translation of Descartes's *Compendium of Musick*: among the necessary attributes of the 'modern musician', the author (William, Viscount Brouncker) notes that he must be a mathematician, a geometrist, a mechanic, and 'A *Melothetic*: to lay down a demonstrative method for the Composing, or Setting, of all Tunes, and Ayres'.[26] Clearly the teaching of thoroughbass techniques formed an important part of Restoration musical pedagogy, and given that both Locke and Blow have demonstrable links to Purcell's education it seems highly likely that the contents of both of their tutors are representative of the materials he would have encountered as part of his musical training.

The idea of thoroughbass as an element of compositional technique is familiar from eighteenth-century music; indeed, Locke's comments on the relationship of thoroughbass to composition in general recall the famous words of J. S. Bach with which Joel Lester opened his chapter on 'Thoroughbass Methods' in his book *Compositional Theory in the Eighteenth Century*.[27] In the course of his survey of eighteenth-century approaches to composition through thoroughbass techniques, Lester observes that from the late seventeenth century onwards authors typically adumbrate four methods for dealing with unfigured bass parts, which in turn are representative of the kinds of procedures followed during composition:

Specific chords might be placed over a given solmization syllable or an easily identified note, such as a sharped note. Specific chords might be applied to various patterns of bass intervals. Model bass lines with chords might be learned by rote to be used wherever applicable. Or specific chords might be placed over particular scale degrees.[28]

---

[25] Locke, *Melothesia*, 8.

[26] *Renatus Des-Cartes Excellent Compendium of Musick: with Necessary and Judicious Animadversions thereupon. By a Person of Honour* (London: Thomas Harper, 1653), [viii].

[27] Joel Lester, *Compositional Theory in the Eighteenth Century* (Cambridge, MA: Harvard University Press, 1992), 49: 'Thoroughbass is the beginning of composing; indeed, it may be called an extemporaneous composition.'

[28] Ibid., 69.

In accordance with his eighteenth-century focus, Lester presents these methods as successive improvements to compositional technique rather than as complementary elements of a broader technique. Thus the first method is illustrated using examples from Lorenzo Penna's 1672 *Li Primi Albori Musicale*, which demonstrate the harmonization of the solmization syllable *mi* (the lower note of a rising semitone), or of any sharpened note, with a 6/3 rather than a 5/3.[29] The same principles inform the first part of Locke's 'second rule', the remainder of which (concerning the identification and proper harmonization of cadences) also falls within Lester's first method of handling an unfigured bass.[30] Such methods are described mainly in order to demonstrate their shortcomings, however,[31] as a preliminary to the introduction of the fourth method of treating unfigured basses – under which Lester discusses François Campion's *règle de l'octave* and its subsequent adoption and revision by almost all theorists of thoroughbass from the 1730s onwards.[32] As he acknowledges, such methods are likely to have been largely unintelligible to earlier musicians, since they rely on the association of chords with particular scale steps within a given key context. 'In all thoroughbass methods', Lester writes, 'the bass is the foundation of the harmony and chords are discrete vertical units that follow one another'.[33] And further,

Thoroughbass writers dealt with harmonies as units built above the bass. By abandoning the earlier tenor orientation and by viewing harmonies as units instead of as combinations of intervals, they came closer to the modern perspective of a chord with rearrangeable, octave-equivalent members.[34]

Such an obviously post-Rameau understanding of harmony can cause problems, however, when dealing with seventeenth-century music, and with contemporary thoroughbass treatises such as those of Penna, Locke and Blow; indeed, it is questionable whether it is representative even of later practice. Apart from anything else, it disregards the extent to which harmony can be understood as progression independently of tonal context. Such an understanding is characteristic of the second and third of Lester's identified techniques for the realization of unfigured basses – strategies frequently found in both Locke's and Blow's thoroughbass primers with their proposal of set harmonizations for particular bass patterns and recommendation of these as models for imitation.

---

[29] Ibid., 69–70; Penna's treatise is available in a facsimile of the 1684 edition (Bologna: Forni, 1969).
[30] Locke, *Melothesia*, 6.
[31] For example, in accounting poorly for minor keys, or keys with many sharps; though in fact many such observations reflect stylistic differences between seventeenth- and eighteenth-century music as much as they demonstrate any theoretical shortcomings.
[32] The *règle* was first discussed in François Campion, *Traité d'Accompagnement et de Composition selon la Règle des Octaves de la Musique* (Paris: [n. pub.], 1716; repr. Geneva: Minkoff, 1976); its influence on later thoroughbass theory is charted in Thomas Christenson, 'The "Règle de l'Octave" in Thorough-Bass Theory and Practice', *Acta Musicologica*, 64 (1992), 91–117.
[33] Lester, *Compositional Theory*, 52.   [34] Ibid., 53.

The ability of thoroughbass to account for contrapuntally driven progressions irrespective of harmonic context is demonstrated by Locke's sixth and seventh 'rules'. Here Locke proposes a number of different progressions which, as he says, can be applied whenever a bass part behaves consistently in a particular manner:

6. If many *Notes* of the same length immediately ascend one after another, the common *Descant* is a Fifth and Sixth upon every one, or most of them: And if many descend in the like manner, the *Descant* is to be a Sixth and Fifth, or a Seventh and Sixth, on each of them . . .

7. When a *Bass* moves by Thirds, the common *Descant* is a Sixth on every other Note.[35]

Although the examples Locke gives are of course notated in a particular key, his text makes it clear that these rules are to be applied whenever a bass behaves in the manner described; the resulting chords, although they must be adapted to the prevailing key, make sense only in the context of the surrounding progression, which overrides the considerations of harmony when considered as a unit above a given bass note. The result is a form of generalized counterpoint that can be imported wholesale on the recognition of these bass patterns in performance. Conceptually, if not on the same scale, this is essentially similar to the body of 'bass motions' that formed a fundamental part of the *partimento* theory first developed in Naples at around the time that Purcell was writing his Sonatas.[36]

As the *partimento* theories also emphasized, such an approach is equally applicable (and even advantageous) to composition. The progressions are both simple to produce and easily apprehended by the listener, since they involve easily recognizable patterns. Not only could they be used in any key, but they could even effect a logical modulation between different key areas by making chromatic alterations to the notes, thereby changing the key context without damaging the integrity of the progression: 'Applying the Sixes in each Introduction, as if you were really in the *Key*, you are going to', as Locke puts it.[37] Purcell uses a 7–6 progression in exactly this way in the first movement of Sonata II (1697), interrupting an expected cadence on E♭ in order to modulate to C minor (Ex. 3.6); this use of progressions at moments of harmonic and melodic digression was also common in the Italian repertoire (as we will see in Chapter 4). In Purcell's fast fugal movements, however, such 'episodic' use of basic thoroughbass progressions is less common: instead, as we have already seen in the cases of the second movement of Sonata III (1683) and the fourth movement of

---

[35] Locke, *Melothesia*, 7.

[36] See Giorgio Sanguinetti, *The Art of Partimento: History, Theory, and Practice* (Oxford University Press, 2012), esp. 135–59; also Peter van Tour, *Counterpoint and Partimento: Methods of Teaching Composition in Late Eighteenth-Century Naples* (University of Uppsala, 2015).

[37] Locke, *Melothesia*, 7.

Ex. 3.6   Sonata II (1697), first movement: use of 7–6 progression to modulate

Sonata VII (1697), Purcell used thoroughbass progressions as the very basis of his invention of fugal materials.

Although he does not say so explicitly, Locke presents the thoroughbass progressions he describes in *Melothesia* in a particular order designed to demonstrate their derivation from the most basic methods of harmonizing a scalic bass. In so doing, he demonstrates the link between successive progressions and forms a logical sequence in which the student could learn them, in order of their increasing complexity when compared with the original succession of parallel 6/3s: interpolating fifths and then sevenths over the same bass,[38] and finally dividing it into unfolded thirds and giving the consequences for the realization. In order to demonstrate the importance of these very same progressions as creative impetus for Purcell's sonata fugues I have grouped all of the fast fugue subjects together in Ex. 3.7. This example is in turn divided into six 'precepts', themselves derived from the different progressions illustrated by Locke and Blow – and presented like them in order of complexity.[39]

The sheer number of works whose materials are founded on such thoroughbass patterns makes it highly likely that Purcell was consciously using what he had learnt from his teachers as a source of ideas in the early stages of his compositional process. And indeed, in the context of his frequent use of invertible counterpoint in these works, the advantages of such a technique are even more obvious. The progression of 7–6s given in *Melothesia*, for example, is already triple-invertible, and all eight fugues that follow Precept 3 – together with a further four from Precepts 5 and 6 that incorporate 7–6 suspensions (P5b and P5d, P6a and P6c in Ex. 3.7),

---

[38] Locke limits the sequential use of 7–6 suspensions to descending basses, though as Blow notes ('Rules', 168, Ex. 20) a more complicated sequence of 7–6s over an ascending scale is possible given frequent crossing of the trebles to prepare the sevenths. Although Purcell does not use this as the basis for a fugue subject, it can be heard in the first movement of Sonata III (1697), bars 10–11, and in a remarkable passage from Sonata IV (1697) that suppresses the expected resolutions in favour of apparent retarded consecutive octaves (see bb. 24–7), or what Blow had called '7th and 8th ascending'.

[39] Unless otherwise indicated, bass figures shown in square brackets in Ex. 3.7 describe actual contrapuntal lines present in Purcell's music.

Ex. 3.7 Canzonas and other fast fugal movements from the sonatas: Purcell's subject material compared with progressions in Locke's *Melothesia* and Blow's 'Rules'

Precept 1 (Blow, 'Rules', p. 164, ex. 3)

This is Blow's example of the correct treatment of a succession of bass notes figured '6'. P1a and P1d here follow the more general principle that 'you may play as many 3ds or Sixes, ascending or descending together, as you please, they being imperfect Cords' (Blow, 'Rules', p. 163), though in P1a see bb. 74–6 for a passage in which the subject is harmonized with a sequence of eight 6/3 chords.

P1a Sonata II (1683), third movement

P1b Sonata V (1697), second movement

P1c Sonata IX (1697), third movement

P1d Sonata X (1697), fifth movement

have triple-invertible expositions like those explored above. While the other progressions are not triple-invertible in themselves, it is simple to 'correct' them in order to create triple-invertible counterpoint (as in P2b, P4b, P4d and P6h) or, failing that, to make two invertible parts that could be used in a less strict application of the same principle (P1c, P2a and P4a).

While in most cases in Ex. 3.7 the presence of the progression is obvious, a certain number of examples involve ambiguities that are worth exploring both for the integrity of the principle as a whole, and for what they can tell us about Purcell's compositional technique. To what extent must a particular progression be actually realized in a composition before one can confidently assert its role in the composition of the piece?

Ex. 3.7 (cont.)

Precept 2 (Locke, *Melothesia* (1673), 'Examples in the 6th Rule')

i 'The 5th and 6th'   ii 'The 6th and 5th'

The simplest elaboration of the basic parallel sixths from Precept 1: a straight-forward interpolation of a fifth in between each sixth. The same is advocated by Blow in his examples of 'Thoroughbass 5th & 6th ascending' and '6th & 5th descending', each given simply as a bass line with figures, and in realized form in his 'Example of 5th & 6th ascending gradually' (Blow, 'Rules', pp. 165, 168).

P2a Sonata IV (1683), second movement

P2b Sonata VIII (1683), third movement (see bb. 74–7)

P2c Sonata X (1683), fourth movement (see bb. 113–16)

P2d Sonata XII (1683), second movement

In some pieces, including the second movement of Sonata I (1683), the question only arises because the detail of the progression is not fully realized in the three written parts. Here the unfolded thirds of the second subject seem clearly to imply the kind of progression given as Precept 4, hence the figuring I have added in Ex. 3.7 (P4a). When this passage of counterpoint appears with the second subject in the bass, however, it is usually in only two parts, so that the sixths on alternate bass notes required by Locke's seventh rule are not realized in the string parts (nor

Ex. 3.7   (cont.)

Precept 3 (Locke, *Melothesia* (1673), 'Examples in the 6ᵗʰ Rule')

'The 7ᵗʰ and 6ᵗʰ'

A further elaboration of the basic parallel sixths from Precept 1; Blow gives a similar 'example of 7ᵗʰ & 6ᵗʰ, the bass descending' ('Rules', p. 165, ex. 9).

P3a Sonata II (1683), fifth movement

P3b Sonata III (1683), second movement

P3c Sonata VII (1683), second movement (see bb.54–6, 68–70)

P3d Sonata IX (1683), third movement

P3e Sonata XII (1683), sixth movement   **P3f** Sonata I (1697), second movement

P3g Sonata V (1697), fifth movement

P3h Sonata VII (1697), fourth movement

Ex. 3.7   (cont.)

Precept 4 (Locke, *Melothesia* (1673) 'Examples in the 7ᵗʰ Rule [i]')

Locke's example showing harmonization of a descending bass line in unfolded thirds. One more step away from the succession of sixths – with a 5/3 interpolated on the note above each scale step in the bass – the result is a cycle of fifths with every other chord in first inversion.

P4a Sonata I (1683), second movement (see bb. 33–6, 43–5; discussed on pp. 92–8)

P4b Sonata III (1683), fourth movement (see bb. 114–18)

P4c Sonata IV (1683), fourth movement

P4d Sonata II (1697), second movement (see bb. 51–3; compare bb. 27–9)

---

indeed in the thoroughbass part, since this movement is extremely sparsely figured; Ex. 3.8a and b). Even later in the movement, when we hear a section of three-part counterpoint with this subject in the bass, Purcell provides the expected sixth in the given parts only once, on the second crotchet of bar 51 (Ex. 3.8c). In the remainder of this passage, the overlapping entries of the first subject in the two violin parts simply produce a third and doubled octave from the bass. In such cases, the player of the thoroughbass part is left to supply the sixths according to

Ex. 3.7 (cont.)

Precept 5 (Locke, *Melothesia* (1673), 'Examples in the 4th Rule')

 i '7th and 6th with a Third Major'   ii '7th and 6th with a Third Minor'

These examples demonstrate the necessity of resolving a seventh with a major sixth, a principle that Locke says should 'generally to be observed in all passing Closes' (*Melothesia*, p. 7). The two examples given are similar in that they form cadences involving stepwise bass progression; nevertheless, the 'passing' cadence – what Blow calls the 'half cadence' ('Rules', pp. 170–71) – may occur equally on the local fifth of the key or on the key-note. Of the four fugue subjects listed here, two use this cadence to effect a modulation up a fifth; all imply fragments of the stepwise bass descent that underpinned Precepts 1–4.

P5a Sonata VI (1683), second movement

P5b Sonata VI (1683), fourth movement

P5c Sonata III (1697), fourth movement   (see bb. 101–2:)

P5d Sonata X (1697), second movement

Locke's seventh rule, as indeed does Tilmouth's suggested realization in bars 36–9 and 43–5.[40]

One passage in this movement does, however, seem to confirm that Purcell was working from the progression given as Precept 4, and

[40] PSr 5, 2–4.

Ex. 3.7   (cont.)

___

Precept 6 (subjects mixing Precepts 1–5)

___

P6a Sonata VII (1683), fourth movement

Precepts 1 & 3

P6b Sonata XI (1683), second movement

Precepts 1 & 3

P6c Sonata I (1697), fourth movement

Precepts 3 & 4

P6d Sonata IV (1697), second movement

Precepts 1 & 3

P6e Sonata IV (1697), fourth movement

Precepts 1, 3 & 4

P6f Sonata VIII (1697), second movement (opening)

Precepts 1, 3 & 4

P6g Sonata VIII (1697), fourth movement

Precepts 2 & 4

P6h Sonata IX (1697), fifth movement

Precepts 1 & 2

Ex. 3.8   Sonata I (1683), second movement

(a)   bb. 29–33

(b)   bb. 36–40

(c)   bb. 50–4

paradoxically it is a passage where the unfolded thirds are not in the bass, but in the upper parts. In Ex. 3.9a the second violin part makes a third with the bass on every other crotchet. By rotating the lower two parts (Ex. 3.9b), we can see that the passage is simply a contrapuntal inversion of the basic progression of alternating fifths and sixths over a pattern of unfolded thirds.

In terms of performance practice, such confirmation of the basic premise behind this material lends support to Tilmouth's thoroughbass realization in the passages in which he chooses to follow Locke's seventh rule and supply the sixths missing from the string parts. It even raises the question of whether they should be applied more widely, in places where Tilmouth does not follow this rule (bb. 50–54 in particular), though the need for variety and clarity of texture must also be taken into account. In terms of the analytical approach that underpins Ex. 3.7, meanwhile, this passage shows that a progression can be identified as the foundation of a movement

Ex. 3.9   Sonata I (1683), second movement: inversion of progression

(a)   Passage with unfolded thirds in violin parts

(b)   The same passage with the lower two parts rotated

even if it never appears in its original form in that movement. Its role in the derivation of materials is not undermined by its absence from the final product, especially in cases like this in which the final form of the material simply omits, rather than contradicts, elements of the precept. We might speculate as to why Purcell left out the sixths necessary to confirm the presence of Precept 4 in this movement. In some instances, such as in Ex. 3.8c, the omission will have resulted from the particular imitative combinations of material involved. In others, it might simply have been a matter of neglecting to provide figures in the thoroughbass part: perhaps Purcell considered the progression so obvious that it would be instantly recognized by its performers, or, alternatively, he may deliberately have left scope for variety in its realization.

Whereas the first movement of Sonata I (1683) differs from its contra-puntal precept only through omission, there are cases in Ex. 3.7 of direct conflict between the melodic content of subject material and its putative harmony, suggesting that the progression came later in the compositional process than the melodic content of one or more of the subjects. One such example is the last movement of the famous 'Golden' sonata, Sonata IX (1697). The passage given in Ex. 3.7 (P6h) is actually part of the three-part complex first heard in bars 132–4, and restated at the fifth, with the semiquaver countersubject in the bass (b. 135$_3$; Ex. 3.10a). It appears to be based on a progression over a descending scale in the bass, as in Ex. 3.10b: a combination of simple parallel 6/3s with the succession of 6–5s advocated in Locke's sixth rule. The two passages do not map onto one another

Ex. 3.10　Sonata IX (1697), fifth movement: disjunction between material and progression

(a)　Three-part complex as written (answer version)　　　　(b)　Possible progression

comfortably, however. The top line of Ex. 3.10a, which is actually the principal subject, contradicts the progression in Ex. 3.10b by supplying a fourth above the bass on the last quavers of bars 136 and 137, with the result that the bass notes must be heard as passing between the two adjacent notes. In other words, the true bass pattern in bars 136–8 is not a falling scale, but a succession of falling thirds on the first beat of each bar.

Attempting to make the notes 'fit' a progression in such circumstances is a futile exercise; rather, there may be considerable insight to be gained from asking questions about why such progressions are *not* present in a movement, or more generally how melodic and harmonic materials interact with or contradict one another. In the case of Example 3.10b it seems inconceivable that this progression could have been the starting-point from which the materials in Example 3.10a were derived. Rather, the melodic subject must have come first,[41] and the progression imported as inspiration for the three-part complex that formed the basis of the opening platform of this fugue. In the closing Allegro of Sonata II (1697), meanwhile, harmonization of the subject using a sequential progression only becomes possible in the closing bars: the bass subject entries in bars 185–9 and 190–94, both shadowed at the tenth above, invite 5–6s over their rising scales on the unfigured beats 2–3 of bars 186–7 and 190–91, an interpretation that is precluded in the exposition by the contours of the two countersubjects (see bb. 145–6, 157–8). A similar situation arises in the canzona of the same sonata, which will be analysed briefly in Chapter 6.

Finally, there are some movements in which the underlying similarity between each of the progressions in Precepts 1 to 4 of Ex. 3.7 is itself examined as part of the compositional process. In the third movement of Sonata VIII (1683), Purcell modifies the original progression of 6–5s over a descending bass line (P2b in Ex. 3.7) to make a succession of 7–6s

---

[41] This subject is in fact motivically related to other movements in the same sonata, and thus likely to have been conceived first on those grounds too; see Chapter 6, pp. 197–201.

Ex. 3.11   Sonata VIII (1683), third movement: intensification of progression

(a)   Three-part complex showing 6–5 progression

(b)   Later appearance of subject, incorporating 7–6 progression

(Ex. 3.11). The modification further results in a new cadence on the key-note rather than the fifth, coinciding with the return to key-note harmony for the end of the movement; thus the intensification of the progression through dissonance plays an important structural role, far from being merely cosmetic.

In the canzona of Sonata IX (1683), meanwhile, Purcell exploits the relationship between the different thoroughbass precepts as the solution to a conflict between the melodic properties of his subject and the voice-leading of the underlying progression. This fugue (P3d in Ex. 3.7) begins with a permutational exposition based on the same 7–6 pattern used in the second movement of Sonata III (1683). In this case, however, the principal subject is not an elaboration of the descending bass line but a separate, cadential theme. The implied cadence half-way through this subject brings it into direct conflict with the harmonic implications of the progression: on the second quaver of its second bar (shaded in Ex. 3.12a) the first violin makes a fourth with the bass. In order to correct this problem, Purcell altered his bass line so that it rose to an *ab* on the second quaver of the bar, providing the *c″* with consonant support as the third of the chord. He then applied a similar alteration to each of the notes in the descending scale in the bass.

Ex. 3.12b shows the complex as it appears in the canzona itself: the falling scale in the bass has become a passage of unfolded thirds filled in by passing semiquavers. Instead of revising the progression according to Locke's seventh rule, however, Purcell retained the sevenths from the

Ex. 3.12 Sonata IX (1683), third movement: 'correction' of progression

(a) Problem with relationship between subject and progression

(b) 'Corrected' complex as in canzona

(c) Different arrangement of these parts

original 7–6 progression, producing a mixture of Precepts 3 and 4 from
Ex. 3.7. This new complex demonstrates considerable subtlety, since the
modification had to retain the melodic characteristics of the original 7–6s
over a descending bass. The issue is the invertibility of the complex: when
the third subject (Vn2 in Ex. 3.12b) forms the bass part, the elaborated
descending scale of the second subject must be capable of accepting a
different harmonic context. Whereas in Ex. 3.13b, each off-beat quaver in
the second subject (bass) was interpreted as a harmony note and given a
root-position chord, in Ex. 3.12c the same notes (now in the first violin
part) must be understood as upper auxiliaries, and thus as correctly
handled dissonances. Without this recognition, the complex is not triple-
invertible, since the resultant harmony would be a series of unresolved,
parallel 6/4s over the bass. The success of Purcell's opening platform thus

Ex. 3.13   Sonata IX (1683), third movement: later treatment of thoroughbass progression

(a)   Alternating 6 and 5 over unfolded thirds in the bass

(b)   Succession of 7–6s over a descending scale in the bass

hinges on the fact that the second subject is capable of fulfilling the melodic characteristics required both by the original 7–6 progression (Ex. 3.12a) and by its modified version (Ex. 3.12b).

Purcell further demonstrates this property of the second subject by making use of both forms of the progression in the remainder of the movement. In Ex. 3.13a the simplified bass takes the form of a series of unfolded thirds, figured with a simple sixth on alternate notes according to Locke's seventh rule; the same progression as in Ex. 3.12b, but without the sevenths that resulted from the presence of the third subject. By contrast, the thoroughbass part in Ex. 3.13b ignores the upper note of the bass part, producing an alternative simplification: a simple descending scale in crotchets, figured with a series of 7–6s.

* * *

My analysis of Purcell's canzonas in relation to these thoroughbass models is not focused merely on identifying the underlying progressions, or indeed choosing between alternative interpretations, and thus situating each example within in a kind of taxonomy of the thoroughbass precepts from which Purcell drew his compositional materials. Rather, by asking such questions about the origins of his materials it is possible to arrive at more fundamental observations about the way Purcell approached the composition of this kind of movement. Given the differences between

Purcell's treatment of the material in Ex. 3.13a and b, the canzona of Sonata IX (1683) also turns out to be a useful demonstration of the importance of his treatment of the thoroughbass. Clearly this undermines any view that since the thoroughbass part was added as an afterthought, it could therefore have had no bearing on the actual composition of the works: although the part itself may affect only the performance resources, Purcell's approach to its provision illuminates the extent of his internalization of Locke's and Blow's thoroughbass techniques, and their importance throughout his composition of the sonatas.

In contrast to the *fugeing* explored in Chapter 2, the methods described here allow us to understand how Purcell constructed the opening platforms of his canzonas and related fugues, finding ideal materials for his catch-like, permutational expositions in the Italianate thoroughbass progressions that were beginning to dominate compositional technique throughout Europe at this time. With this technical foundation established, the next chapter turns to consideration of how Purcell treated these materials beyond the opening platforms of his fugues – an analytical goal that also leads back, perhaps unexpectedly, to questions of reception.

CHAPTER 4

'The power of the Italian notes':
Purcell's Sonatas as and in Reception

In recent years, the cultural background to Purcell's interest in the trio sonata has become much better understood and far more accessible. Apart from the perennial issue of his likely Italian models, we now recognize a body of 'Restoration Trio Sonatas', including works both by English composers (notably John Blow) and by Europeans active in London (among them Giovanni Battista Draghi and the elder Nicola Matteis).[1] The example of Robert King's 'Sonetta after the Italion Way',[2] apparently composed around 1680, even sits alongside Purcell's sonatas as an example of an explicitly acknowledged attempt to emulate Italian stylistic features.

In some ways it exaggerates King's significance to introduce him at the start of a chapter on Purcell's sonatas: as Peter Holman and John Cunningham note, King's diminutive effort lacks Purcell's sense of ambition in general as well as his staying-power when it comes to contrapuntal technique in particular. Alon Schab has more recently described King's grasp of the Italian sonata as somewhat superficial, primarily concerned as it is with 'surface characteristics' such as overall structure, violins in consecutive thirds, and sequential patterns. Nevertheless, as Schab observes, not only does King's sonata supply 'evidence both of the veneration of the Italian style and of the practical measures taken by English musicians of the time to imitate it', but also 'artistically there is more to this, since the very attempt to write in imitation of that foreign style shows profound awareness of style in general'.[3]

Having established in Chapter 3 the main creative strategies that set Purcell's sonata fugues apart from the *fugeing* described in Chapter 2 – the adaptation of the catch using invertible counterpoint in order to generate lengthy permutational expositions, and the systematic deployment of set sequential voice-leading progressions in order to furnish them with melodic materials – in this chapter I examine what these techniques have to tell us about the reception of Italian style in England. Most obviously, Purcell's

---

[1] See Cunningham and Holman, *Restoration Trio Sonatas*.
[2] *Ob* MSS Mus. Sch. E.443–6; edited in Cunningham and Holman, *Restoration Trio Sonatas*, 43–5.
[3] Schab, *Sonatas of Henry Purcell*, 30.

sonatas participate in that reception both through the features of Italian style that he chose to adopt and in the responses of early commentators upon his works, who in evaluating Purcell's music also reveal much concerning their attitudes towards its Italian counterparts (and in particular the near-contemporary sonatas of Arcangelo Corelli).

At the extreme, furthermore, I argue that the stylistic awareness Schab observes in Robert King, which was necessary to attempt such an emulation of Italian style, combines in Purcell with a degree of self-conscious reflexivity that ultimately surpasses – or even threatens – the 'just imitation of the most fam'd Italian Masters' promised in the Preface to the 1683 *Sonnata's*. At certain moments, that is, Purcell's sonatas cease to function as music in an Italianate style, and must instead be heard as music about the Italian style. This kind of meta-musicality, as we might call it, is another way in which Purcell's music can be understood to privilege the artificial, and alongside the contrapuntal techniques examined thus far can itself be understood as a factor in the early reception of Purcell's sonatas. At the same time, both this reflexivity and the idea of artifice in general offer clues as to the composer's own poetic goals, which I suggest were subtly distinct from the aesthetic context behind the most familiar early responses to his sonatas.

JUST IMITATION?

That Purcell alluded to the importance of the sonata at all in 'The Art of Descant' was something of a departure for English musical theorists: like Simpson, most earlier authors had resorted to fantazia as the genre of choice for illustrating fugal techniques.[4] By the early 1690s, however, when Purcell would have been writing his contribution to Playford's *Introduction*, Corelli's sonatas were approaching the height of their popularity in London, and the English fantazia was all but forgotten. It would have seemed entirely natural that Purcell should have chosen to address 'fuge' with reference to the sonata, providing examples in the trio scoring of two trebles and bass (as in all his three-part examples), and quoting from the music of an Italian composer.

What is more surprising, then, is that Purcell did not go further: of all the Italian composers of trio sonatas, he chose to quote not Corelli, whose sonatas were fast becoming the *locus classicus* of the modern style, but 'Calista' (actually Carlo Ambrogio Lonati; see Chapter 1), an older composer whose example exhibits far stricter contrapuntal working than almost any of Corelli's fugal movements.

Superficially, the two approaches are similar, especially when viewed from a modern-day vantage-point that understands the later keyboard

---

[4] Simpson, *Compendium*, 115.

fugues of J. S. Bach as the standard by which to judge all other fugal compositions.[5] If one hears Purcell's own canzonas as early examples of the mature fugal procedure of the later Baroque, his works share with the fugal movements of both Lonati (or, for that matter, Colista) and Corelli many of the defining features of that style: a clear-cut exposition with entries of subject followed by answer at the fifth, and – despite Tilmouth's statement to the contrary – a concern to avoid stretti until all the voices have entered with the principal subject(s).[6] If Purcell's fugues do not compare favourably with the apparently paradigmatic examples of Bach or Handel, or even of Corelli, so this argument would go, it is because Purcell's counterpoint lacks the expansiveness to confer variety of harmony and phrasing, relying instead on the permutational exploration of invertible counterpoint – easily dismissed as 'mere mechanistic juggling'.[7]

Yet Purcell shows himself abundantly capable of expanding and varying the harmonic and metrical qualities of a phrase elsewhere – not least, as we have seen in Chapter 2, in the first movement of Sonata I (1683). The techniques familiar from later repertoires, such as sequential expansion, evasion of cadence and the extension of voice-leading patterns, are all present in Purcell's other sonata movements (and indeed in the canzona movements, post-exposition). That he chose not to use them in favour of the strict invertible counterpoint found in movements like the D minor canzona from Sonata III (1683) should therefore be taken as a conscious decision, however one judges the success or otherwise of this decision in musical terms. The resulting regularity of phrasing and cadence may jar with modern (post-Bach) tastes, but to dismiss the movements on these grounds entirely misses the point that Purcell favoured such techniques not for their repetition or regularity, but for their artifice. While certainly less exalted than the *fugeing* of the fantazias, such a selective approach to Italian repertoire – both in 'The Art of Descant' and in his own sonatas – allowed him to stay 'on-trend' while at once buttressing his existing commitment to the poetics of artifice.

When it comes to his treatment of the sequential progressions identified in Precepts 1–4 of Ex. 3.7 (pp. 91–4), Purcell's approach was no less idiosyncratic from an Italian perspective. It is no coincidence that the thoroughbass progressions described by Locke and Blow are the very same progressions that had become increasingly common in the Italian sonata in the course of the seventeenth century. Locke may well have encountered such works through his position in the Catholic chapel of

---

[5] See, for example, Michael Talbot, *Vivaldi and Fugue* (Florence: Olschki, 2009), 8–12, 20, 42–3, 50. Talbot invokes this commonplace as the background to his aim of examining Vivaldi's fugal writing on its own merits, and studies like his go a long way towards redressing the balance in scholarly discourse; nevertheless, Bach's dominance of the popular perception of fugue is unlikely to be significantly diminished.

[6] Tilmouth, 'The Technique and Forms', 118–19.   [7] Adams, *Henry Purcell*, 35, 112.

Catherine of Braganza; *Melothesia* could certainly have been designed with the newly popular genre in mind, in order to equip his readers to accompany music in the latest styles. Peter Allsop notes that such 'stereotyping of harmonic formulas constructed over stock bass patterns' was a particular feature of the Bolognese style of chamber music.[8] It is particularly obvious in the music of Vitali, in whose works such formulas began to appear not only in slow movements, as they had in the music of Tarquinio Merula and Cazzati, but in all kinds of movements, including fugues.

It was above all in the music of Arcangelo Corelli, whose Op. 1 Trio Sonatas first appeared in 1681, that the use of thoroughbass progressions characteristic of the Bolognese sonata was refined and elevated to the position it would occupy as a key foundation of the eighteenth-century *lingua franca*. As one of the defining characteristics of Corelli's style, this feature has paradoxically garnered both praise for its simplicity and grace, and censure for its apparent lack of invention and originality.[9] Purcell almost certainly could not have heard or played any of Corelli's sonatas before he published his own first set in 1683. However, analytical comparison between the two can prove revealing in at least two senses. Firstly, both composers worked with a similar stylistic legacy when it came to the trio sonata: just as it was Purcell's encounter with the music of Legrenzi, Cazzati and Vitali, and even Lonati and Colista, that would have alerted him to the possibility of using such progressions in order to imitate the Italian style successfully, so Corelli inherited the same repertoire as a native Italian composer trained and employed inside that tradition. Hence the opportunity to deepen our understanding of the composers' respective creative strategies through analysis of their different choices in response to the same musical inheritance. Secondly, the popularity of Corelli's music when it arrived in England meant that the reception of the two bodies of music was inextricably linked; thus any analytical insight into the differing approaches of the two composers has the potential to shed greater light on the responses of early commentators to both repertoires.

As it happens, one of the more convincing passages of writing 'after the Italion way' in Robert King's sonata relies upon just such a sequential thoroughbass progression, offering a neat illustration of the way this style was conventionally interpreted by English composers. Fragments of such progressions over scalic bass lines can be heard in the second movement, notably around bars 21–5, but King best deploys this technique in the short duple-time 'close' appended to the livelier, triple-time third movement (Ex. 4.1): after striking dissonant entries from both violins, a lengthy bass pedal on the fifth of the key leads not to the expected cadence, but

[8] Allsop, *The Italian 'Trio' Sonata*, 41.
[9] See the summary of eighteenth- and nineteenth-century critical appraisals of Corelli's work in Dennis Libby, 'Interrelationships in Corelli', *JAMS*, 26/2 (1973), 263–87 (263–5).

Ex. 4.1   Robert King, 'Sonetta after the Italion way', close (bb. 63–71)

instead to a protracted rising 5–6 progression whose considerable momentum propels the harmony one step beyond the key-note on the circle of fifths (b. 69), thereby providing a stronger pre-cadential preparation for the eventual conclusion. An example of Purcell's indulgence in a similar sequential progression has already been given above (Ex. 3.6, from Sonata II (1697), first movement). The two passages share a number of key features: they are almost entirely athematic, deriving melodic features wholly from the polyphonic strands implied by their respective progressions; and the potentially open-ended nature of the process is exploited in both to generate irregular phrase lengths and comparative instability (or at least indeterminacy) of harmonic function, leading ultimately to modulation – albeit short-lived in King's case.

Corelli tended to use set thoroughbass progressions at just such moments of harmonic and melodic digression, both in slow passages and in fugal movements. Ex. 4.2 shows the exposition and two episodes from the fugue (Allegro) from his A minor Trio Sonata (Op. 1, no. 4). Although decorated with rhythmic figures from the subject, both episodic progressions (Ex. 4.2b and c) are clearly differentiated from the subject itself by the repetitive application of these figures and by their harmonic neutrality: at any one moment the key is undefined – especially in Ex. 4.2c – and each chord derives its function instead from the surrounding chords in the progression. Only when Corelli inserts a cadence does a local key area once again become clear, and in both cases he introduces a subject entry at this point in order to reinforce the new harmony.

Ex. 4.2   Arcangelo Corelli, Sonata in A minor (Op. 1, no. 4), third movement

(a)   Exposition

(b)   Episode immediately after exposition, based on 7–6 progression

(c)   Later episode based on 5–6 progression

With its comparatively strict attitude to fugal materials – extending, unusually for Corelli, to something approaching a regular counter-subject based on the suspension in the third bar of Violin 1 – this fugue makes a suitable comparison with the D minor canzona from

Purcell's Sonata III (1683). Unlike Corelli (and indeed King), rather than deploying thoroughbass progressions in order to construct episodic digressions from the subject material, Purcell takes the highly individual step of constructing the very materials for his fugue from a 7–6 progression over a complete octave descent in the bass (see Ex. 3.2, and Ex. 3.7: P3b). What is more, such a procedure was entirely typical for Purcell – as we saw in Ex. 3.7 – whereas in Corelli it is almost unheard of: as in Purcell's 'Calista' example, the subject of Corelli's A minor sonata is a simple cadential figure whose principal interest is rhythmic rather than melodic. Among the Op. 1 Sonatas, something similar could be said of the fugues in Sonatas 3, 5, 6, 7, 9 and 10. Occasionally (as in Sonatas 5 and 10) these opening gestures are extended with thoroughbass progressions of the type found in Purcell's subjects, but beyond the exposition these progressions tend to be treated as optional; they are often discarded or truncated in later appearances of the subject, or used episodically in order to modulate.

Whether Purcell's treatment of thoroughbass progressions in this way represented a deliberate creative strategy – making his canzonas a sort of critique-in-music of the Italian style – or more prosaically, a by-product of his parallel interests in 'double descant' and sequential voice-leading as markers of Italianate musical identity, it had important consequences for his own music: on the one hand in a poetic and rhetorical sense and, on the other, in more practical ways. In relation to the former, by foregrounding the sequential progressions in this way – in modern theoretical terms, quite literally, given the unusually fast harmonic rhythm applied to so many of the progressions in Ex. 3.7 – he transformed the role of such thoroughbass patterns from a means of expression to its very subject. This is one way in which Purcell's canzonas and related fugues can be understood as meta-referential. The music acquires a discursive reflexivity from the presentation of such sequential progressions as the very basis of the composer's contrapuntal invention; such passages are 'about' this aspect of Italian style, rather than inhabiting it (as did Corelli's music) or emulating it (like Robert King).

Inasmuch as this approach took Purcell's musical engagement with this technique beyond his professed attempt to imitate the 'most fam'd Italian masters', or even into conflict with this aim, it serves as a useful starting-point from which to understand the reception of Purcell's music in a context in which Corelli in particular was quickly becoming the accepted standard against whom all others were judged. Furthermore, as will become obvious later in this chapter, this form of reflexivity represents a particular kind of creative artifice that extends beyond Purcell's general approach to sequential progressions in his sonata fugues to encompass more specific examples in which he seems to be deliberately drawing attention to particular consequences of this technique.

Meanwhile, Purcell's encapsulation of his thoroughbass progressions within the closed hypermetrical units of his fugue subjects gives rise to a number of more practical consequences that further differentiate his canzonas and related fugues from their Italian counterparts. Not least among these is that by postulating sequential voice-leading as the subject of invention, he diminished the potential of such materials to provide contrast in the form of melodic and harmonic digression. As a result, he tended to resort to episodes that were conceived more melodically, and even imitatively.

Returning to the canzona from Sonata III (1683), then, after the initial exposition ending after six iterations of the triple-invertible subject complex, the subject is combined with itself in two passages exploring stretto entries of the first subject, in bars 41–2 and 50–52. In between these is an episode constructed entirely from a short motif outlining a rising fifth and its inversion. This motif is loosely related to the second countersubject of the initial triple-invertible complex (see Ex. 3.2), but of greater interest is that rather than being dictated by an abstract sequential progression, the harmonic content of this episode is the direct result of *fugeing* on this motif (Ex. 4.3): the falling fifth of the inverted motif in the bass initiates a movement around a circle of fifths, which is then reversed by two successive rising statements to return to C in bar 46. Purcell then begins the episode again much as he had in bar 43, this time turning to G minor at the end of bar 46 by simply sharpening the *f* in the bass. Like Corelli's episodes, this one ends with a subject entry but, unlike Corelli's, here the

Ex. 4.3   Sonata III (1683), second movement: episode

subject is actually used in order to cause a modulation, rather than to reinforce a key already reached by a progression.

Purcell's treatment of the subject itself beyond the exposition further demonstrates the centrality of *fugeing* to his technique once the permutational exposition had been concluded. The strong periodicity of phrasing established in these expositions exerted a considerable influence on his attitudes towards *fugeing* in these movements, however, posing different challenges from those encountered in the Fantazias. The metrical regularity of the opening platform of the D minor canzona, generated by the strict rotation and reiteration of its triple-invertible complex, builds up such a strong momentum that even potentially more artificial treatment of the subject is subordinated to its pattern of cadence. Thus when Purcell writes a pair of stretto entries on the first subject in bar 41, he alters the end of each entry in order to cadence on C at the end of a two-bar phrase, following the hypermetrical pattern established in the exposition rather than allowing the stretto – which in itself is perfectly viable – to run its course to a cadence on A (see Ex. 4.4a and b). Only after the two-bar pattern had been broken by the lengthy imitative episode in bars 43–7 (see Ex. 4.3) was the remaining three-voice stretto allowed to extend past the two-bar phrase (Ex. 4.4c), before dissolving into a passage of imitation based on a new, chromatic subject – a final rhetorical defeat for the regular phrasing that integrates the solution of this compositional problem into the structural fabric of the movement.

The almost mechanical regularity of this piece is common in canzonas built on triple-invertible counterpoint. Those fugues that have freer expositions tend to avoid it, either by working two subjects that have slightly different metrical qualities, by inserting free counterpoint between fugal entries (what would now be called a 'codetta' in a fugue by Bach) or by disguising the repetition through the introduction of additional entries. Curiously, however, Purcell almost never seeks to vary his phrasing or harmony by extending progression-based subjects sequentially in order to modulate, an obvious method of achieving variety that would exploit the transient nature of such progressions in Italian sonatas. Instead, the progressions remain trapped inside the stable metrical unit of the subject, emphasizing both the melodic integrity of the subject and the essentially stable harmonic role of the progression in many of Purcell's fugal movements. Indeed, Purcell's subject progressions are so far removed from the modulatory function of their Italian counterparts that when he does require a subject entry to modulate, this is most often achieved not by using the properties of the progression, but by reworking the cadence of the subject itself (see the analysis of triple-time fugues from Sonata VIII (1683) and Sonata I (1697) on pp. 132–5 below).

As evidence for Purcell's reception of the Italian sonata, then, his use of sequential progressions suggests that like others he associated this technique with Italian music and sought to associate himself with this style by

Ex. 4.4   Sonata III (1683), second movement: use of stretto

(a)   Stretto (bb. 41–3, BC and Vn1), altered to cadence on C after two bars

(b)   The same stretto, shown complete

(c)   Three-voice stretto (bb. 50–52) with imitative continuation

incorporating it into his own works. At the same time, his foregrounding of these materials as the source of melodic invention suggests a characteristically individual response, raising his sonatas far beyond the level of mere stylistic emulation. The technical consequences of this treatment, meanwhile, including the hypermetrical confinement of the progressions and Purcell's continued reliance on *fugeing* in order to develop his materials after the exposition of a fugue, provide ample scope for analysis in many individual movements. Furthermore, in the potential conflict between these matters of technique – the undermining of the clarity and logic of the sequential voice-leading that underpins a subject like that of the D minor canzona, when it is treated in stretto as in Ex. 4.4 – we arrive at an issue that was of key importance to the most famous early commentator on Purcell's sonatas, Roger North. Consideration of such passages can help us to understand his oft-quoted remarks with far greater nuance.

'CLOG'D WITH SOMEWHAT OF AN ENGLISH VEIN'

Roger North should not be considered an authority on Purcell's sonatas; rather, his attitude towards them is reflective of his wider views, which in turn have much to reveal about why Purcell's sonatas suffered so much in the face of competition from Corelli's and those of his imitators. It is no exaggeration, I would suggest, to view the almost simultaneous appearance of Purcell's and Corelli's sonatas as something of a crossroads in English attitudes towards music. Responding in their different ways to the challenges posed by instrumental music in the intellectual climate of the late seventeenth century, the two composers' works embody equally valid but very different poetic attitudes, either of which could have prevailed.

North's few but familiar surviving comments on Purcell's sonatas should be interpreted in exactly this context: North was an ardent Corellian. And indeed, given this observation, he is remarkably well disposed towards Purcell's sonatas. Having played the sonatas through with the composer, North evidently admired them: he described them as 'very artificiall and good musick', and 'his noble set of sonnatas'.[10] Nevertheless, his comments contained some pointed qualifications. '[Purcell] imitated the Itallian sonnata', North writes, 'and (bating a little too much of the labour) outdid them'; his sonatas were 'clog'd with somewhat of an English vein, for which they are unworthily despised'.[11]

Exactly what North meant by this has been the subject of some speculation (as discussed in the Introduction), and no doubt it could potentially apply at once to several parameters within the music. When read alongside some of his remarks concerning Italian music, however, it becomes clear that one of the features of Purcell's sonatas that North was likely to have found 'laboured' or even 'clog'd' was exactly the reliance on *fugeing* described in the previous section. Consider, for example, the following remark on fugal technique, illustrated with an admiring recommendation of the Corellian approach to such matters that contrasts strongly with his remarks concerning Purcell's sonatas:

The great danger in conducting fuges, is the going too farr for variety, and so by tossing the point from to [*sic*] key to key the ayre of the genuine key is lost, which is unwholesome for the musick; and in that respect Corelli's fuges are admirable, for tho' driven thro' variety enough, yet the air of the key is preserved.[12]

In other words, for North, the presentation of the subject at several different transpositions risks obscuring the sense of key. He recognizes that the melodic aspect of an imitative point does not exist in isolation; even at the beginning of the fugue, when it is heard unaccompanied, the listener understands it in the context of certain implied harmonies. If the subject is subsequently transposed and combined with itself, as is the case in Purcell's fugues, the listener is forced to reinterpret its harmonic implications in order to make sense of the tonality of the passage in question.

These comments concerning the careful handling of fugal technique and its exemplary treatment in the music of Corelli provide a level of technical detail that is missing from North's more enigmatic remarks upon Purcell's

---

[10] Quoted in Burden, *Purcell Remembered*, 35.   [11] Ibid., 35.
[12] Wilson, *Roger North on Music*, 180.

sonatas. As such, they might serve as the starting-point for a more systematic analytical investigation of the contrast between the approaches of the two composers: to what extent, we might ask, can North's contrasting reception of Corelli's and Purcell's sonatas be substantiated at an analytical level?

One scholar who has attempted to develop a systematic approach to the relationship between fugal materials and tonal procedures in this repertoire is Christopher Wintle, in his analysis of the second movement of Corelli's Sonata in F major (Op. 3, no. 1).[13] This fugue is a considerably more substantial movement than the A minor one quoted above. In the eight years between the publication of Corelli's Op. 1 and his Op. 3, his music became considerably more expansive: commenting on the first movement of the same sonata, Dennis Libby noted that although Corelli's music always 'sticks close to sequences as the main means of extension and movement between one harmonic goal and the next', by Op. 3 'he is beginning to get away from relying so much on the simplest and most straightforward sequential and cadential progressions, learning to reach the final goal of a passage less directly, putting it off by decorations of the basic motion'.[14] Nevertheless, the same techniques are important here as were observed in the A minor fugue: episodes are built on progressions (as in bb. 17–18) and the subject returns to provide harmonic stability (bb. 24, 35). There is greater integration between the two types of material than before, since progressions interrupt subject entries in order to delay cadences (bb. 13, 26), but the essential contrast between the stability of the subject and the transitory harmonies of the progressions remains intact.

Wintle's analysis of this movement begins from the premise that its subject is derived from a particular 'tonal model'. This is demonstrated not through a hierarchical reduction as in orthodox Schenkerian studies, but on a series of staves designed to show successive stages of elaboration from the basic model (Ex. 4.5). As the labelling across the top of the example shows, the tonal model in question here is in fact a conventional Schenkerian interrupted '5-line', compressed at stage (b) to avoid the return to tonic harmony at the resumption of scale-degree 5 in the treble. The subject of the fugue (c) is derived from the bass arpeggiation, and towards the end leaps up to outline the implied 7–6 suspension in the inner voice.[15] Wintle accounts for appearances of the subject in other voices in terms of changes in registration.[16] Since both this movement and the fourth movement of the same sonata have fugal expositions in which the subject is presented throughout in the tonic, he avoids the often difficult question in Schenker-influenced approaches to fugue of how the transposition of the subject to the dominant affects its relationship to the

---

[13] Wintle, 'Corelli's Tonal Models', 55–9.   [14] Libby, 'Interrelationships in Corelli', 270.
[15] Wintle, 'Corelli's Tonal Models', 57.   [16] Ibid., 55.

Ex. 4.5   Corelli, Sonata in F major (Op. 3, no. 1), second movement: derivation of fugal materials from tonal model

underlying voice-leading. Given, however, that his tonal models exist at the middleground rather than deep background level, and are themselves tonally complete, we may assume that the transposition of the subject implies a transposition of the corresponding tonal model.

Wintle understands the motivic aspects of Corelli's music as essentially ornamental, as he acknowledges at the beginning of his treatment of the fourth movement:

Seen from a thematic perspective, the fugal movements of Italian Baroque music are often considered to be less to the point, less consistently sustained, than their counterparts in German Baroque music. Although there is truth in the observation, censure of the Italian works rests on the assumption that that these movements are primarily 'about' themes and their motives. This, however, is not an assumption that may necessarily be upheld in the face of Corelli's music. On the contrary, the thematicism here is essentially decorative. The fugal themes are designed to examine selected aspects of the fundamental models that make up his musical rhetoric. To describe the themes is necessarily to invoke the models, and, indeed, a fugal theme may be related to (or 'discovered in') more than one of these.[17]

---

[17] Ibid., 49.

Although he does not demonstrate this in relation to the second movement, it is relatively easy to find instances of the tonal models being 'examined' in different ways in the course of the movement. In bars 6 to 10, for example, a cadence in the dominant is reached by transposing the entire model up a fifth. Ex. 4.6 (my own analysis, adapting Wintle's notation) starts from exactly the same tonal model (a), and proceeds to show (b) how the initial 5–2 descent is transferred to the bass and used as a modulatory progression from the tonic. The remainder of the model is unaltered, except for the decoration of the bass V which adds consonant support to the treble *e″* and inner voice *c″* in bar 9. Despite this reliance on the same tonal model, however, the musical foreground (c) shows very little melodic resemblance to the subject of the fugue: in Wintle's terms, the movement is 'about' the underlying model. The subject is simply an ornamentation of this model, and may or may not appear in conjunction with its every occurrence.

According to this approach to Corelli's music, it should be no surprise that the subject entries, when they are heard, maintain an essentially constant relationship with the underlying tonal model (see, for example, bb. 23–4, 24–5 and 34–5). The subject is designed to ornament or 'examine' the model by drawing attention to its characteristic voice-leading; any change in the relationship between the two would

Ex. 4.6   Corelli, Sonata in F major (Op. 3, no. 1), second movement, bb. 6–10: appearance of tonal model

undermine this function, obscuring the statement of the model. This observation also accounts for what at first seems to be an exception to the rule, what Wintle calls the 'radical alteration and limitation upon extent undergone by the modally adjusted form of the subject at mm. 10–12'.[18] This alteration serves to maintain the relationship of subject to model by acting as a bridge between the key-note and relative minor harmonies. This is shown in Ex. 4.7, again adopting Wintle's notation: what is apparently a strange corruption of a tonal answer in the bass can be explained by the modulation, since the alteration of the subject's fourth note to a B♭ makes it an upper neighbour to A, the new scale-degree 5. (The progression in bb. 13–15 simply delays the expected cadence, by prolonging the local fifth reached in the bass at b. 13$_3$.)

Ex. 4.7   Corelli, Sonata in F major (Op. 3, no. 1), second movement, bb. 12–15: treatment of tonal model

18 Ibid., 56–7.

Three important characteristics emerge from this approach to Corelli's 'tonal models'. Firstly, the essential point of Corelli's compositional technique is to examine the qualities of the particular model on which the movement is based; this offers a strong explanation for the musical coherence of whole movements despite the fact that they appear to be less well argued in thematic and motivic terms. Secondly, the subject of a Corelli fugue exists as an ornamentation of the underlying model, designed in order to accentuate its most important features and to draw attention to its recurrence. Finally, and as a consequence of these two characteristics, the relationship between subject and model remains to all intents and purposes the same in the course of a movement. The subject is a melodic expression of the underlying stability of the tonal model, and thus its function is diametrically opposed to the progression-based episodes, which are unstable and introduce harmonic contrast.

A simple comparison with Corelli's F major fugue can be heard in the second movement of Purcell's Sonata IV (1683), in which – as in the D minor canzona analysed above – the distinction between subject (stable harmony based on tonal model) and progression (harmonic contrast and digression) found in Corelli's music is fundamentally undermined. As was shown in Chapter 3 (Ex. 3.7, P2a), this double fugue is based on a simple 5–6 progression realized in its two subjects and followed by a cadence (Ex. 4.8). Although superficially similar, such a progression is very different from the kind of 'tonal model' Wintle identifies in Corelli's music: the much faster harmonic rhythm of Purcell's progression makes it a foreground, not a deep middleground phenomenon, and the relationship between the melodic elements and the harmonic function of the phrase is too ill defined. Whereas each successive element of Corelli's 'model' could be related to its specific function in outlining the descent to the keynote, in Purcell's subject material the progression could continue indefinitely: it is only the interruption of a cadential suspension that creates the illusion of a goal-directed model. As such, the difference in the technique of the two composers is akin to the difference between the key-specific *règles de l'octave* that Lester examines in relation to the realization of an unfigured bass, and the rules that Locke proposed for the same purpose which rely on the melodic behaviour of the bass irrespective of harmonic context (see Chapter 3).

Ex. 4.8   Sonata IV (1683), second movement: subjects and progression

The proposal of an alternative tonal model for Purcell's fugue only underlines the problem of understanding Purcell's compositional technique in this way. The suggested model in Ex. 4.9a seems accurately to represent the harmonic trajectory of the subject at the opening, and at certain later points in the movement when, as in the Corelli fugue, the subject returns in exactly the same harmonic context (twice between bb. 44₄ and 49, for example). The idea that such a model could have formed part of Purcell's 'workbench methods' seems unlikely, though: the descent from the fifth scale-degree to the key-note directly contradicts the prevailing melodic *ascents* throughout the movement, and the bass line of the model is contrapuntally incompatible with the second subject (owing to parallel fifths) except in very limited circumstances. Purcell's subjects are clearly derived from the 5–6 progression, undermining any sense that they could be designed either in order to 'examine', or as an ornamentation of, this model.

Since, then, the fugal materials of Purcell's canzona take precedence over, rather than having been derived from, the harmonic context in which they are heard, the movement cannot be 'about' the manipulation of a tonal model, as was the case in the Corelli fugue. When we turn to Purcell's treatment of the melodic aspects of his subjects this becomes even clearer: embedded within the two-subject complex that begins the canzona is an imitative working of the first subject alone (Ex. 4.9b) – effectively an interlock concealed by the melodic ornamentation of the second entry. This two-part subject complex must therefore be understood in melodic

Ex. 4.9 Sonata IV (1683), second movement: derivation of materials

(a)   Possible tonal model

(b)   Derivation of subject material from *fugeing*

terms; the result may be similar in harmonic effect to the tonal model in Ex. 4.9a, but its incorporation of two statements of an identical point further undermines the notion of the subject as an ornamentation of such a model.

The treatment of the subject later in the movement further confirms this melodic and imitative emphasis in Purcell's technique. In bars 36–8 he introduces a second combination, a minim apart at the interval of a fifth (facilitated by shortening the first note of the subject to a crotchet) – the only other two-part interlock that works at a distance of less than one bar. He then uses these two inventions several times, interchanging the plain and ornamented versions of the point (first and second subjects) in order to achieve variety. On the last page of the fugue, there is even evidence of attempts to build larger, three-part complexes from these two combinations. In bars 50 to 53, for example, Purcell attempts to combine the original two-voice complex with a new stretto (Ex. 4.10), requiring a number of alterations to the second subject (violin 1) in order to avoid simultaneous parallel fifths and octaves with the bass. An even more complicated passage arises in the closing bars from an attempt to overlay two statements of the opening two-voice complex of the movement; in this case, the entry in the bass is interrupted with a pedal on the fifth degree in order to avoid parallel fifths with the first violin.

Taking stock, then, Wintle's theory of 'tonal models' has much to offer as a potential means of corroborating analytically North's comparative responses to the sonatas of Corelli and Purcell. Its attempted application to

Ex. 4.10   Sonata IV (1683), second movement, bb. 50–53: combination of two interlocks

Purcell's F major canzona broadly confirms the observations made in connection with the D minor canzona examined above: Purcell's compositional process begins not with a harmonic unit like the 'tonal model', but with subjects derived from melodic sources. The remainder of a movement consists of the interrogation of this subject material from an imitative and motivic point of view, rather than the examination of underlying harmonic processes. Indeed, whereas in Corelli's music the subject, with its ornamental role, can be used to draw attention to the affinity between different forms of the tonal model, in Purcell's canzona the imitative combinations are themselves used to create varied harmonic contexts.

In one sense this is evident from Ex. 4.9b alone: since this opening complex incorporates two entries of the subject, it follows that the two are heard differently against the same harmonic progression, rather than being themselves designed to elucidate it. Similarly, when a different combination is used we can see that the relationships change yet again. This is true of the second-subject combination in bars 36–9, and of the passage in bars 49–50 in which the first combination (that in Ex. 4.9b), here with both entries given in the decorated form of the second subject, begins in C and ends with a cadence in B♭. Both of the examples of larger, three-part complexes cited above also introduce new harmonic contexts. In a texture like this, the tonal implications of the subject simply cannot remain constant as they do in the Corelli, and a listener who is unable to assimilate the new harmonic contexts in which the subject is heard will be left tonally disorientated – as North put it, 'the ayre of the genuine key is lost'.

ORNAMENT OR ARTIFICE?

How was it that having performed Purcell's Sonatas with the composer in the 1680s, North could have arrived some forty years later at an aesthetic position so fundamentally opposed to the advocacy of compositional artifice that I associated with Purcell in Chapter 2? A closer look at the evolving artistic theories of North's lifetime should permit the reconstruction of an alternative critical response that, for all the eventual dominance of North's views – not to mention that of Corelli's version of the Italian style – remained for a short period at the start of the eighteenth century a valid alternative critical starting-point from which Purcell's sonatas could be appraised. This will serve as the basis for the remaining analytical studies to be presented in the final section of this chapter.

At a superficial level, North's concern for the primacy of 'ayre' anticipates the status of the 'tonal model' in Wintle's theory: just as Wintle understands fugal thematicism in Corelli to be fundamentally decorative, so North seems to consider fugue an 'ornament'.[19] And like any other

---

[19] Wilson, *Roger North on Music*, 180.

ornament, it was thus to be used in moderation – as can be seen, for instance, in Christopher Wren's use of a musical analogy in the course of an uncharacteristically generous assessment of the Gothic architecture of Salisbury cathedral from 1668:

The Mouldings are decently Mixed with large planes, without an affectation of filling every corner with ornaments, which (unless they are admirably good) glut the eye, as much in Music too much division cloyes the eare.[20]

For Dryden in 'A Parallel of Poetry and Painting', meanwhile, similar concerns led to an injunction at least for propriety and decorum where ornaments are unavoidable: 'they must at least be decent: that is, in their due place, and but moderately us'd.'[21]

The separation of 'ayre' and fugue as ornamentation in North's mind is nowhere better illustrated than in the fact that even in illustrating the 'admirable' fugues of Corelli he remarks 'I cannot say that either the melody or the harmony of this passage is exalted by the fuge', continuing that 'both might be as well, or rather better, in plain consort notes'.[22] From such a perspective, Purcell's densely motivic fugal textures might well seem 'clog'd' (or indeed 'cloyed'). Yet such a separation of fugal surface from underlying 'ayre' is impossible to maintain in the face of Purcell's approach to *fugeing* in which, as we have seen, melodic and harmonic events are to a large extent subordinated to a process of invention and disposition guided from the start by artificial conceits.

Some of North's other remarks on fugal technique suggest that he may have been alive to this more fundamental marker of aesthetic difference in Purcell's music:

There have been many industrious treatments of fuges, as reverting, retorting, &c, all which may be seen in Mr Morley, but without any real vertue in the musick, but rather to dull it; for what signifies tricks against sound and free harmony? For that is to flow, and be full, and will not be tyed up to shapes and formallitys. They are like poetry wrote in the shape of an altar, or of an heart or the like, which may contain very good witt, but never the better for the confinement.[23]

At first glance, one might imagine that here again North views fugue not as integral to the invention, but as something ornamental and separate from the essentially harmonic content of the work. Yet the specific reference to poetry in the shape of an altar suggests (as Wilson hints) that North may have been thinking here of the famous poem by George Herbert, and more pertinently its appraisal by Joseph Addison in *The Spectator*, issue 58. Addison's acerbic commentary in this essay on what he calls 'false Wit' makes clear that the outward presentation of such

[20] Soo, *Wren's 'Tracts'*, 63.   [21] Dryden, 'Parallel', xxxvi.
[22] Wilson, *Roger North on Music*, 181. (The notated 'passage' in question here is for three violins and bass, and apparently of North's own invention – though 'hinted from Corelli'.)
[23] Wilson, *Roger North on Music*, 139.

'Poems in Picture' is far more than simply an issue of ornament; rather, syntactic and semantic content alike are profoundly altered by the need to conform to the intended shape: 'the Poetry was to contract or dilate itself according to the Mould in which it was cast … the Verses were to be cramped or extended to the Dimensions of the Frame that was prepared for them.' In proving himself 'more intent upon the Figure of his Poem, than upon the Sense of it', Addison argues, 'a Writer does not shew himself a Man of a beautiful Genius, but of great Industry'.[24] North's remark that such poems are 'never the better for the confinement', meanwhile, strongly recalls Purcell's own remark about the combination of fugue and ground bass being 'confined[,] like a *Canon* to a *Plain Song*' (see Introduction).

Far from misidentifying *fugeing* as an over-elaborate surface phenomenon, this suggests that North would have understood the compositional priority of fugal invention in Purcell's sonatas perfectly well. The difference was that where Purcell argued for the symbiosis of 'Art mixed with good Air', according to North the former was explicitly detrimental to the latter. By 1750, Charles Avison could essentially remove artifice from this equation altogether, focusing instead on the balance between melody (called 'air') and harmony as the deciding factors in the quality of musical expression. His *Essay on Musical Expression* devotes much attention to 'the too close attachment to harmony, and neglect of air', while expressing distaste for anything over-intellectualized:

The learned contrapuntist may exercise his talent in many wonderful contrivances, as in fugues and canons of various subjects and parts, &c. But, where the master is thus severely intent in shewing his art, he may, indeed, amuse the understanding, and amaze the eye, but can never touch the heart, or delight the ear.[25]

The word 'learned' has acquired faintly pejorative tones, while fugue and canon are caricatured as the mere 'amusing' of the understanding. One is reminded of J. A. Scheibe's trenchant criticism of J. S. Bach in the late 1730s, in which he described the composer's music as 'turgid'.[26]

Avison's insistence that music should 'touch the heart' and 'delight the ear' arguably brings into focus a broader issue that is already fundamental to the attitude to fugue and counterpoint encountered above in the writings of North: above all, his concern is to demonstrate the primacy of 'ayre', since it is this quality that carries the very ability of instrumental music to function as expressive. This idea resurfaces again and again in his writings. In a negative sense, it informs his trenchant criticism of the style of the old In nomine:

---

[24] *The Spectator*, 58 (Monday 7 May 1711).
[25] Charles Avison, *An Essay on Musical Expression*, 3rd edn (London: L. Davis, 1775), 39.
[26] See Malcom Boyd, *Bach* (London: Dent, 1983), 160–61.

That which is properly termed Ayre was an intire stranger to this sort of harmony, and the audience might sit with all the tranquillity in the world . . . and not be in the least moved.[27]

The final clause here seems fundamentally at odds with Thomas Mace's description of the qualities of the old consort music (for example), which represented for him so many '*Divine Raptures, Powerfully Captivating all our unruly Faculties, and Affections . . . and disposing us to Solidity, Gravity, and a Good Temper, making us capable of Heavenly, and Divine Influence*'.[28]

Perhaps, however, Mace's flurry of adjectives suggests a more generalized notion of the power of music to influence the passions, without attributing particular sounds to particular affects. In his second *Musicall Grammarian* essay (1728), North seems to suggest something rather more specific: 'a composer should reflect which . . . humours he is to represent', and then 'forme the style of his ayre accordingly.'[29] Even more revealingly, North's essay 'What is Ayre?', and the notes he wrote for its preparation, repeatedly draw the comparison between 'ayre' in music and 'wit' in poetry. In one sense this is a way of accounting for (or, more cynically, glossing over) the rather vague, ineffable nature of 'ayre' as a concept: 'Ayre in Musick, is like witt in poetry, not fixt upon any one quallity, but being taken all-together gives the recommendation.'[30] Recalling the use of the word 'wit' by Dryden, however, North's analogy takes on a new level of meaning. In his preface to *Annus Mirabilis* (1667), Dryden had defined 'wit' in poetry as the product of 'some lively and apt description, dress'd in such colours of speech, that it sets before your eyes the absent object, as perfectly and more delightfully then nature'.[31] Given that 'ayre' and 'wit' were so closely associated in North's mind, Dryden's definition of 'wit' can be used to infer that it was 'ayre' that North understood to endow music with its power to influence the passions.

North's most detailed description of the expressive power of instrumental music draws heavily on a comparison with painting to demonstrate the mimetic potential of music alongside that of its 'sister arts':

If a painter takes upon him to present the various conditions of adult manhood he will first produce the pourtrait of a person in a garb and posture that speaks him full of thought and design; then of one in action as very buisy about divers important concernes . . . ; [North gives several more stages of the daily activity of contemporary life, concluding with:] one dauncing and capering in the midst of good company. How near these are paralell with the various scenes of musick, now used in our comon Sonnatas a little reflection will shew . . .

27 Wilson, *Roger North on Music*, 287.
28 Thomas Mace, *Musick's Monument* (London: the author, 1676), 234. Mace uses italic type to draw attention to important words and phrases; the length of this passage in italics surely underlines the depth of his enthusiasm for the old consort music. Note, too, Mace's use of the word 'gravity' here.
29 Wilson, *Roger North on Music*, 123.   30 Ibid., 70.
31 John Dryden, *Annus Mirabilis: The Year of Wonders, 1666* (London: Henry Herringman, 1667), sig. A7v.

Now our composer wants intirely the helps a painter hath, being furnisht onely with sound and time. But yet with these he is inabled to shew caracters as the painter doth, and to make his measures and harmony to resemble thoughtlyness of others so much that by a reciprocation of effects, the musick shall excite in the hearers a similar course of thinking, be it serious, executive, grave, in haste, or merry, &c; and by these varietys obviate tedium, and at least leave the hearer in such humour as the composer is pleased the musick shall conclude with.[32]

This formulation of the medium of musical expression resembles older descriptions of the nature of musical 'ayre' that go back at least as far as Thomas Hobbes (the '*Consequence of one Note after another, diversified* both by *Accent* and Measure'); and North's reference to the 'reciprocation of effects' similarly resembles Hobbes' notion of the ability of 'ayre' to arouse the passions of musical listeners.[33] But in the specificity of his analogy with the mimetic ability of painting to represent 'the various conditions of adult manhood', North's formulation is strongly redolent of Addison's description of the place of music among the 'Pleasures of the Imagination':

Among the different Kinds of Representation, *Statuary* is the most natural, and shews us something *likest* the object that is represented. . . . but should [one who is born Blind] draw his Hand over a *Picture* . . . he would never be able to imagine how the several Prominencies and Depressions of a Human Body could be shewn on a plain Piece of Canvas . . . *Description* runs yet further from the things it represents than Painting; for a Picture bears a real Resemblance to its Original, which Letters and Syllables are wholly void of. Colours speak all Languages, but Words are understood only by such a People or Nation . . . It would be yet more strange, to represent visible Objects by Sounds that have no Ideas annexed to them, and to make something like Description in *Musick*. Yet it is certain, that there may be confused, imperfect Notions of this Nature raised in the Imagination by an Artificial Composition of Notes; and we find that great Masters in the Art are able, sometimes, to set their Hearers in the heat and Hurry of a Battel, to overcast their minds with melancholy Scenes and Apprehensions of Deaths and Funerals, or to lull them into pleasing Dreams of Groves and Elisiums.[34]

Addison's formulation of the problem of musical expression in this passage is very similar to that of Dryden, though the poetic system he would develop was to be quite different.[35] In this passage he demonstrates the common origins of all of what he calls the 'Secondary pleasures of the Imagination' in the actions of the mind in comparing the sensory information it receives from contemplation of a statue, painting, poem or piece of music, with its own internal ideas arising from 'Original Objects'. Hence his organization of the 'sister arts' on a continuum derived from their proximity to 'natural' imitation, beginning with statuary, which is closest,

---

[32] Wilson, *Roger North on Music*, 116.   [33] See Hobbes, *Humane Nature*, 81–2.
[34] *The Spectator*, 29 (3 April 1711).
[35] On Addison's relationship with Locke and Dryden see William H. Youngren, 'Addison and the Birth of Eighteenth-Century Aesthetics', *Modern Philology*, 79/3 (1982), 267–83 (269, 272–6).

and then painting. He thus couches the mimetic ability of verbal description, which requires a common language, and by extension, music, whose sounds 'have no Ideas annexed to them', within a Lockean model of language in which the meanings of words are contractually understood by members of a culture as a means to facilitate communication:

[Words] came to be made use of by men as *the signs of* their *ideas*: not by any natural connexion that there is between particular articulate sounds and certain *ideas*, for then there would be but one language amongst all men; but by a voluntary imposition whereby such a word is made arbitrarily the mark of such an *idea*.[36]

The most revealing phrase in Addison's discussion of musical 'Description', however, is his assertion that music's mimetic capabilities result from an 'Artificial Composition of Notes' on the part of the composer. As a measure of North's Addison-inspired reception of Purcell's sonatas, Addison's use of this word to refer to the descriptive power of music rather than its contrapuntal ingenuity shows just how far we have come from the promotion of contrapuntal artifice I associated earlier with Purcell himself. Indeed, the kind of 'artifice' imagined by Addison implies a far more literal ideal of 'imitation', whereby specific moods are invoked – the sort of model that would ultimately (and much later) give rise to the rather over-inflated idea of the 'doctrine of the affections'. Even though such a formalized set of mimetic principles in the music of the seventeenth and eighteenth centuries has long been discredited, many of its basic tenets were clearly familiar to contemporaries and remain important to an understanding of Purcell's sonatas and of instrumental music in general at this time.

'OF NEARER KINDRED TO THE SOULE'

An alternative view of the success of Purcell's sonatas in the early eighteenth century can be reconstructed from a slightly surprising source: the polemical tract *The Great Abuse of Musick* (1711) by the clergyman and reformist of manners, Arthur Bedford. An ardent Purcellian, Bedford peppered his recommendations for the reform of music (and church music in particular) with numerous references to the music of Purcell and Blow. Of particular interest in the present context are two observations relating, respectively, to the deployment of dissonance and the desirability of 'fuges':

The *Italian Compositions* (especially their *Sonatas*) is [*sic*] very eminent in this Respect. From thence Mr. *Purcel* seems to have taken this his *Master-piece*, in which he hath since been inimitable.[37]

---

[36] John Locke, *Essay Concerning Humane Understanding*, ed. John W. Yolton, 2 vols (London: Dent, 1961), ii, Book 3: 'Of Words', 12.
[37] Arthur Bedford, *The Great Abuse of Musick* (London: John Wyatt, 1711), 224.

Another *Improvement* of *Musick* is by *Fuges*, when one *Part* leads, and another follows in Imitation of it. We have wonderful *Varieties* hereof in our *Instrumental Musick*, especially of many *Parts*.[38]

That the second of these excerpts also refers to works such as Purcell's sonatas can be inferred from a later comment, that 'Our *Sonatas* are reckon'd the greatest Perfection of *Instrumental Musick*, wherein the *Composer* useth all the skill which *Art* and *Fancy* can invent, to affect the *Passions*'.[39]

Without wishing to elevate Bedford's brief remarks to the level of North's more considered reception of Purcell's sonatas, it is revealing that he singles out for praise some of the very characteristics that caused problems for North's Addison-influenced insistence on the necessity of a mimetic 'ayre' unfettered by contrapuntally inspired creative preconditions. It should also be borne in mind that Bedford's views on 'The Corruption of Modern Musick by Mean Composures'[40] were already somewhat reactionary, at least inasmuch as they applied to secular music (though they would find greater resonance in the music of the church). As such, they arguably bear witness to a poetic stance that to some extent had already lost out; that said, they still offer valuable confirmation that at least some near-contemporaries might have been much more in sympathy with Purcell's creative goals than might be suggested by the emerging main-stream position represented by North.

Bedford's tract is almost exactly contemporary with Addison's 'Pleasures of the Imagination' essays, and indeed the polemicist's acknowledgement of the ability of the sonata to 'affect the Passions' seems very much in keeping with the attitudes of North and Addison towards musical expression. For Addison, however, the 'pleasures of the imagination' lay midway between sense and understanding – 'not so gross' as the former, yet 'not so refined' as the latter.[41] This had the advantage of acknowledging that the exigencies of taste were not subject to the logic of reason, yet avoiding the disparaging attitude towards mere sensual pleasure already evident in the writings of Dryden. With Bedford, and other controversialists of a similar persuasion, this same sensuality, and the power of music to 'move' the listener to particular moods and emotions, takes on an almost threatening dimension:

the Force of *Musick* is more wonderful than the Conveyance, especially of a consort. It strangely awakens the Mind. It infuses an unexpected Vigour. It makes the Impression agreeable and sprightly, and seems to furnish a new Capacity, as well as a new Opportunity of Satisfaction. It raises and falls and Counterchanges the Passions at an unaccountable rate. It changes and transports, ruffles and becalms, and almost governs with an Arbitrary Authority, and there is hardly any Constitution so heavy, or any Reason so well fortified as to be absolute proof against it.[42]

---

[38] Ibid., 225.   [39] Ibid., 238.   [40] Ibid., 196.

[41] Youngren, 'Addison and the Birth of Eighteenth-Century Aesthetics', 281.

[42] Jeremy Collier, 'Essay on Musick', in *Essays upon Several Moral Subjects in Two Parts* (London: R. Sare and H. Hindmarsh, 1697), II, 20–21.

This passage, which Bedford quotes in full, is taken wholesale from Jeremy Collier's even more extreme 'Essay on Musick', which begins with a long survey of the evidence for the power of music in classical mythology, and ends with a diatribe against the modern misuse of these powers to licentious and immoral ends. Irrespective of his ideological intent – Collier is better known for the infamous *Short View of the Immorality and Profaneness of the English Stage* (1698) – his remarkable figurative descriptions of musical expression, and the particular cultural phenomena on which they draw, show just how powerful this aspect of musical experience could be. Firstly, the power of music to 'raise and fall and counterchange the passions' is understood in an almost Newtonian sense as an exertion of forces in different directions on a passive body (the listening subject), which is thereby set in motion or 'moved' to a particular state of mind. This coercive aspect of musical experience is then further emphasized by applying the notion of 'arbitrary authority' to the action of music upon the listener's consciousness, effectively inverting the common early-modern trope of the 'body politic':[43] here it is the nation-state that stands in for the human body, the spectre of illegitimate rule a particularly powerful image for Collier as a prominent non-juror.

Ever keen to observe the power of music in its modern practice, rather than in more abstract terms as Collier had done, Bedford follows up his quotation from Collier with the observation that

There are some swift *Notes* and *Leaps* in a *Sonata,* especially in the upper Part, which shall almost command a Laughter. There are also slow Movements, with Variety of *Discords,* which shall bring down the Mind again into a pleasing *Melancholy,* and all this shall happen frequently in the playing over of the same *Tune.*[44]

What, he implies, could be more unaccountable or unpredictable than that musical sounds, which (as Addison had it) 'have no Ideas annexed to them', should nevertheless 'command a Laughter' in the listener? And furthermore, even familiarity does not diminish the power of the notes to influence the passions.

While often pleasurable or beneficial, for Collier it is the element of coercion – the unpredictable, capricious and unaccountable quality of music – that makes it particularly suspect:

Though the Entertainments of Musick are very Engaging; though they make a great Discovery of the Soul; and shew it capable of strange Diversities of Pleasure: Yet to have our Passions lye at the Mercy of a little Minstrelsy; to be Fiddled out of

---

[43] The most famous example of the application of this metaphor is of course Thomas Hobbes's *Leviathan, or the Matter, Forme, & Power of a Commonwealth Ecclesiasticall and Civil* (London: A. Crooke, 1651), ed. John C. A. Gaskin, Oxford University Press, 1998). On arbitrary rule see John Locke, *Second Treatise of Government* (1690), ed. C. B. MacPherson (Indianapolis, IN: Hackett, 1980), 79.

[44] Bedford, *The Great Abuse of Musick,* 169.

our Reason and Sobriety; to have our Courage depend on a *Drum*, or our Devotions on an *Organ*, is a sign we are not so great as we might be. If we were proof against the charming of Sounds; or could we have the Satisfaction without the Danger, or raise our Minds to what Pitch we pleas'd by the Strength of *Thinking*, it would be a nobler Instance of Power and Perfection.[45]

In this last passage we get a clear indication of the importance Collier attaches to reason as a fortification of the mind. The power and unpredictability of music is associated with purely sensual pleasure ('the charming of Sounds'), and identified as a sign of human weakness; a stronger constitution is one capable of controlling the passions 'by the Strength of *Thinking*'.

Given Bedford's familiarity with Collier's essay, it is surely significant that Bedford places such emphasis, among the qualities he ascribes to 'a *good Composer*', on what he calls '*Intention of Mind*':

Musick is a *Mathematical Study*, and he who would place the *Notes* aright, ought to be as thoughtful as if he was finding out and demonstrating a new *Problem* in *Geometry*.

The *Playhouse*, and the *Musick* compos'd for it are design'd to lay all *Thinking* and *Reflection* asleep. And as our *Masters* are wholly become their *Servants*, so they are debased into the Bargain, and seldom use that *Freedom* of *Thought* which is necessary for the *Professor* of a *Liberal Science*.[46]

Reading Collier and Bedford together here, a context emerges for the celebration of compositional artifice that is in stark contrast with the suspicion it engendered in North and later in Avison. Even if it does not compensate for the dangerous sensuality inherent to music – much as Bedford is at pains to disavow any notion that 'the Excellency of [Purcell's] *Tunes*' might vindicate his songs from 'the *Wantonness* or *Profaneness* of the Words'[47] – such '*Thinking* and *Reflection*' is nevertheless to be valued precisely for its ability to appeal to the intellectual faculties of the mind. Although Bedford's chosen analogy between music and mathematics is well-worn, its specific application here to the mindset of the preoccupied geometrician seems a particularly apt comparison with the compositional concerns I attribute to Purcell. And when Bedford introduces another admiring reference to 'a fine *Sonata*, set only for *Instruments*' with the wish 'that we were as well acquainted with the solid as we are with the frothy Part of *Musick*'[48] it is easy to imagine that he might have in front of him Purcell's 1683 Sonatas, with their prefatory appeal to the 'seriousness and gravity' of Italian music as contrasted with the 'levity, and balladry of our neighbours'.

Although Purcell seems unlikely to have shared Bedford's distrust of the affective powers of instrumental music, at least one source with which he

---

[45] Collier, 'Essay on Musick', 24–5.   [46] Bedford, *The Great Abuse of Musick*, 200.
[47] Ibid., 201.   [48] Ibid., 171.

was intimately familiar enables us to speculate that he would have recognized just why Bedford attached so much importance to what he called *'Intention of Mind'*. Here is Dryden, picking up from the point at which we left his draft for the Preface to *The Prophetess, or the History of Dioclesian* in Chapter 2:

Painting is indeed, another sister, being like [music and poetry], an imitation of Nature: but I may venture to say she is a dumb Lady, whose charmes are onely to the eye: a Mute actour upon the stage, who can neither be heard there, nor read afterwards. Besides that she is a single piece; to be seen onely in one place, at once, ... This is not sayd in disparagement of that noble Art; but onely to give the due precedence, to the others, which are more noble; and which are of nearer kindred to the soule; have less of the matter, & more of the forme; less of the manuall operation, and more of the rationall spirituall part, in our humane nature.[49]

Such a formulation neatly illustrates how both the North/Addison and Collier/Bedford positions I have described could have developed from similar origins at the end of the previous century: Dryden's hierarchy, to some extent stripped of its assumptions concerning the relative value of the 'sister arts', survives recognizably in Addison's continuum from the naturalness of statuary to the mysterious artifice of music among the 'Pleasures of the Imagination'; meanwhile, suspicion and mistrust towards the sensual – whether born of moral considerations alone or together with the influence of rationalist modes of thought – led Bedford to place a premium on the qualities of 'thinking and reflection'.

As a potential framework in which to understand Purcell's own promotion of musical artifice, meanwhile, Dryden's descriptions of painting, poetry and music can be read through a Lockean differentiation between sensation and reflection: if painting relies principally on the former, poetry and music draw on the latter. Music can be considered a 'just and lively image of human nature' in that its organization resembles just the kind of internal contemplation that Locke describes as the mind 'reflecting on its own Operations within it self'.[50] Moreover, we might suggest, the greater the musical artifice, the more the music could aspire to Dryden's 'rationall' and 'spirituall' condition. The more overt forms of musical representation described by Addison and North, which rely on onomatopoeic or affective devices, belong more to the sensational realm of music, in that their effect relies on the direct imitation of sounds or invocation of affects. Purcell's most artificial music, by contrast, comes closer to Locke's idea of reflection as the *'Perception of the Operations of our own Minds* within us'.[51]

The self-consciously reflexive nature of this process offers a valuable seventeenth-century framework within which to situate the kind of 'meta-referential' characteristics I attributed to Purcell's music earlier in this

---

[49] Quoted in Burden, *Purcell Remembered*, 89.   [50] Locke, *Essay*, I, 77–8.   [51] Ibid., 77.

chapter. Already, the intricate *fugeing* of the Fantazias closely resembles the kind of thinking and reflection with which Bedford would characterize his quality of '*Intention of Mind*': my analysis of Fantazia VIII in Chapter 2 shows Purcell taking an idea and viewing it from different angles, combining it in different ways, making judgements about its validity in different contexts, and attempting to reach new conclusions by combining the results of previous experiments. And while such processes continue to dominate many movements of the Sonatas, including large sections of canzona movements post-exposition, the canzonas as a group further raise the level of artifice by taking one characteristic of Italian style (the use of sequential voice-leading progressions) and re-framing it as the very subject of contrapuntal discourse.

The remainder of this chapter returns to more analytical concerns, in order to flesh out how Purcell's compositional strategies allowed him to create such music 'about' music: first, in two examples designed to show him grappling with the sense of metrical regularity established by the periodic organization of his permutational first platforms, and then, finally, in one extremely ingenious, if idiosyncratic case that provides the exception to the rule that Purcell typically deployed his thoroughbass progressions as the basis of his fugal materials.

From the above analyses of the second movements of Sonata III (1683) and Sonata IV (1683) it is apparent that many of the techniques Purcell exercised in the latter portions of his sonata fugues relied on the same principles of *fugeing* that he explored in the fantazias and that remained important in pieces such as the first movement of Sonata I (1683). There are movements which incorporate exhaustive imitative research and adapting of failed complexes (Sonata I (1697), second movement, and Sonata VIII (1697), first movement), inversion of subjects (Sonata I (1697), second movement) and even augmentation (Sonata X (1683), fourth movement). Such techniques have already been examined in Chapter 2, however; it is where they come into contact with the more specific characteristics of the sonata fugues that they can offer additional insights into Purcell's compositional approaches.

This is particularly obvious in some of the many dance-inspired, triple-time fugues across the two books of sonatas. Perhaps unsurprisingly, such movements tend to exhibit even more hypermetrical regularity than the canzonas and other duple-time fugues, frequently retaining the phrasing patterns of the subject throughout. At the same time, many of these dance fugues show a concern for compositional artifice that is just as strong as in Purcell's other fugal movements, and certainly more strict than one would expect to find in music that was truly intended for dancing. A good example is the third movement of Sonata VIII (1683), in G major. This fugue has a subject built on a descending 6–5 progression (see P2b in Ex. 3.7, and the brief discussion on pp. 99–100), and consists entirely of four-bar phrases until the very end, when a series of stretto entries causes the last two phrases to be telescoped into seven bars.

Within this restrictive framework, Purcell nevertheless shows a characteristic interest in the imitative properties of his materials. The second countersubject is derived from an aborted two-voice interlock using the main subject, and later in the movement we hear more complete – and more conspicuously worked – stretti at the fifth, a bar apart (bb. 90–93 and 120–23) and at the octave, two bars apart (bb. 118–20). The subject is also inverted at bar 98, and a subsequent inverted entry is accompanied by stretto at the unison, a minim apart (bb. 106–9). Even more interesting, however, is the way that Purcell manages to achieve harmonic variety and even a logical harmonic trajectory, in a scheme that allowed for no variation of phrase length or introduction of additional, modulatory material. After a long permutational exposition incorporating five complete iterations of the original three-part complex, and the expected alternation of cadences on the key note and fifth of the scale, he sets about reworking the end of the subject and its melodic inversion into an impressive array of alternative cadences (Ex. 4.11a and b).

Such variety of cadence did nothing, however, to alter the overriding effect of metrical regularity in this fugue. In the fourth movement of Sonata I (1697), by contrast, Purcell uses *fugeing* actively to subvert the expected regularity. This movement is almost identical in organization to the third movement of Sonata VIII (1683): it begins with a permutational exposition incorporating five iterations of the complex in Ex. 4.12a, and maintains four-bar phrasing until well after the end of the first platform. Instead of allowing this regularity to dominate the sound of the music, though, Purcell upsets the listener's perception of the periodicity by introducing a close stretto, at the distance of a minim, immediately after the end of the exposition (Ex. 4.12b). While the music still cadences after four bars, the stretto is sufficiently disorientating that the cadence sounds as if it has been displaced. In the following two phrases Purcell then intensifies this ambiguity, first by extending an idea taken from the second subject (Ex. 4.12a, Vn2) into a succession of four crotchets falling by thirds (bb. 128–31), and then by transferring this idea to the bass and using the sighing suspensions from the third subject in the violins to create a hemiola effect.

The four-bar phrasing is finally defeated in the phrase from bar 140, in which Purcell essays another stretto at the distance of a minim, this time at the lower fifth. In order to make this work, he shortens each bar of the subject to just two minim beats, such that the metre is once again disrupted (Ex. 4.12c). At the same time, the sequential part of the subject finishes a bar earlier than it would have done in its original form, with the result that

Ex. 4.11   Sonata VIII (1683), third movement: cadential alterations to subject

(a)   Subject in prime form

(b)   Subject inverted

Purcell has to compose additional material to complete the four-bar phrase. The effect is that the sense of regularity is almost completely removed: the basic alteration to the subject is apprehended easily, but the progression, despite the fact that it has been compressed, seems to reinforce its integrity. The extension to the cadence therefore sounds like an added bar, creating the impression of a longer phrase even though the cadence falls after four bars as had been the pattern throughout the movement. After this cadence, the four-bar phrasing suddenly dissolves. A six-bar phrase reworks the metrically unstable bars 128–35, and then the groups of crotchets from bar 128 take over. The *Grave* that closes the sonata (Ex. 4.12d) is doubly effective since it recasts this four-crotchet idea in duple time: by drawing on the conflict of metres in the preceding bars, it

Ex. 4.12   Sonata I (1697), fourth movement: manipulation of metre

(a)   Triple-invertible subject complex

(b)   Passage immediately after opening platform

(c)   Shortening of subject in order to accommodate stretto

(d)   Closing bars

completes the process of metrical dissolution that has characterized the movement since the end of the opening platform.

The most impressive instance among Purcell's canzonas of the kind of reflexivity I propose above is undoubtedly the second movement of Sonata X (1697), which offers a detailed commentary in music both on the Italian style as Purcell heard it, and on its potential for compositional artifice according to his wider poetic goals. If the canzonas as a group can be understood to be 'about' the Italian style inasmuch as they take the sequential progressions typical of moments of episodic digression in Italian sonatas and frame them as the very subject of contrapuntal discourse, in the canzona of this D major sonata Purcell upends this whole concept by exceptionally allowing the progressions to retain their episodic function, yet bringing to bear upon them the full ingenuity of his contrapuntal technique – manipulating the episodes as though they were subject materials, and arranging the results in order to display the resulting relationships to their full advantage.

This sonata is often cited as Purcell's most modern and Italianate example, and in the canzona the trumpet-like contours of the subject together with extensive use of 5–6 and 6–5 progressions appear to support this hypothesis. The fugue opens with a permutational exposition based on the three-part complex in Ex. 4.13, after which comes a long passage of progressions (Ex. 4.14). The first (P1) is a 5–6 progression incorporating sequential repetition of a new motif in the violins over a rising scale in the bass; Purcell then rotates and inverts this, producing falling scales in the upper voices over a sequential bass (P2), which are then followed by a further passage based on P1. Already, then, Purcell is treating his progressions not just as simple harmonic patterns to be imported as 'stock' sonata material, but as thematic content to be manipulated and examined.

After a series of entries of the original subject in bars 43–50, Purcell again returns to these progressions. This time, however, P1 is simply rotated, placing the sequential repetition in the bass and the rising scales in the upper parts to generate P3 (Ex. 4.14). The same process is applied to P2 in bars 54–6, resulting in a simple succession of 6–5s over a falling bass.

Ex. 4.13   Sonata X (1697), second movement: triple-invertible subject complex

Ex. 4.14   Sonata X (1697), second movement: manipulation of thoroughbass progressions

This final transformation results in the harmonic retrograde of $\boxed{\text{P1}}$; thus the two passages of progressions effectively mirror one another.

It was this 'mirror' effect that allowed Purcell to dispose these inventions in such a way as to draw attention to their origins in the strict manipulation of the supposedly episodic materials, thereby giving rise to a structural plan reminiscent of some fantazia sections in its reliance on artifice as the controlling factor. Purcell's manipulation of the thoroughbass patterns is superbly subtle: not only are progressions $\boxed{\text{P1}}$ and $\boxed{\text{P4}}$ harmonic retrogrades of one another, but also the sequences built on them are constructed in such a way as to achieve this retrograde by the melodic inversion of the material. Thus the moments at which the progressions change, at bars 38_3, 40_3, 54 and 57_3, are points at which melodic inversion *causes* harmonic retrogression. Furthermore, the mirroring of the two progressions at each of these moments is replicated on a large scale by the rotation of the parts the second time the passage of progressions is heard, in bars 51–59. Purcell even draws attention to this large-scale mirroring by inverting the original fugue subject in bar 45, thereby repeating at the level of the movement the causal relationship between inversion and retrogression. Everything that happens between the end of the opening platform (b. 33) and the end of this inverted entry (b. 47_1) is repeated in reverse order from bar 47 to the end, creating a large-scale palindrome (see Table 4.1; the palindrome can be followed in the sequence of 'events', from A to F and back from F′ to A′).

Purcell's ability in this canzona to bring his *fugeing* to bear on the very characteristic materials that he identified with the Italian sonata, and which elsewhere were treated as almost antithetical to the kind of self-conscious ingenuity he so favoured, shows just how highly developed were his techniques by the mid 1680s not only in terms of contrapuntal artifice *per se*, but also as a language in which he could offer a musical critique of the very stylistic features he professed to imitate. In offering a glimpse of Purcell's own reception of the Italian style, his canzonas and related fugues also take their place in the history of English reception of the Italian sonata, which – as the writings of North show – was ultimately to leave behind Purcell's brand of conscious elevation of the 'rationall' qualities of music in favour of a more directly mimetic aesthetic, together with a suspicion of contrapuntal artifice that carried about it more than a whiff of the anti-intellectualism that was to become characteristic of much English commentary on the arts.

* * *

Whatever the implications for future studies of reception, it is clear that Purcell's relationship with the Italian style was a far more active and reflexive process than is suggested by the commonplace notion of 'influence' between composers. In the present context, meanwhile, the

Table 4.1 Sonata X (1697), second movement: large-scale palindrome

	Bar nos.	Event		Remark
	21–33			Permutational exposition
Progressions	34–35	A		*Fugeing* on subject cadence
	36–38$_2$	B		P1
	38$_3$–40$_2$	C		P2
	40$_3$–42$_1$	D		P1
Subject	43–4	E		Middle entry in A
	45–6	F		Middle entry in E, inverted
Subject	47–8	F′	Order of events reversed	Middle entry in A, inverted
	49–50	E′		Middle entry in D
Progressions	51$_3$–53	D′		P3
	54–56$_3$	C′		P4
	57$_3$–59	B′		P3
	60–63	A′		*Fugeing* on subject cadence

remarkably individual assimilation and transformation of stylistic phenomena explored in this chapter offer an equally productive point of
departure for analysis as did the process of *fugeing* in the fantazias, greatly
adding to the overall picture of a composer who sought at this stage in his
career to promote more artificial and 'serious' forms of musical expression
over what he saw as the superficial preoccupations of his contemporaries.
Armed with these multiple tools for the analysis of his creative strategies,
the second part of this study now turns to some of Purcell's most famous
later works.

'Thou dost thy former skill improve'

CHAPTER 5

'Celestial art[ifice]' in Hail, bright Cecilia

Having laid out in Part I some of the ways in which Purcell's instrumental music can be better understood through a historically sensitive approach to analysis, learning from contemporary theoretical discussions – both their contents and their omissions – I turn in Part II of this study to a broader consideration of what the same methods can reveal about some of the best known of the composer's later works, while at the same time developing tools where necessary to explain the phenomena to be found there. This shorter chapter uses Purcell's 1692 Ode on St Cecilia's Day as a case study in the relevance of these analytical insights in this context. *Hail, bright Cecilia* is an ideal illustration of how the approach suggested for the instrumental music can explain not only the technical underpinning of Purcell's later style, but also its very success as vocal music – that is to say, Purcell's ability to use the techniques of his artificial style in order to engage with the verbal content of his texts, thereby enhancing and amplifying both their delivery and in some cases even the very concepts that they convey.

Even when considered from a purely technical viewpoint, the choruses of *Hail, bright Cecilia* mine the resources of Purcell's contrapuntal artifice to a depth not reached since the fantazias and sonatas of a decade and more before. The four choral movements are dispersed throughout the work and act as structural pillars; after two with extensive contrapuntal workings ('Hail, bright Cecilia' and 'Soul of the world') and a third in tuneful, dancing homophony ('Thou tun'dst this world'), a climax is reached in the final chorus with its double exposition on 'Who whilst among the choir above/Thou dost thy former skill improve' (Ex. 5.1). Purcell sets these two ideas in the first of the two vocal expositions to a passage of double *fugeing* (Ex. 5.1a), with the first subject treated *per arsin et thesin* as more instruments are added to the ensemble; then in the second vocal exposition, as if this level of 'skill' were not already impressive, he explicitly 'improves' upon the first by incorporating a bass entry of the first subject, *arsin*, in augmentation to four times the note-values of the original (Ex. 5.1b).

As Bryan White points out in his recent book on the celebration of St. Cecilia in Restoration London, Purcell's elaboration of the verbal concept of 'skill' in this passage works on multiple levels: the self-conscious exercise

143

Ex. 5.1   *Hail, bright Cecilia* (1692), 'Who whilst among the choir above'

(a)   Beginning of first setting

(b)   Beginning of second setting

of all aspects of compositional skill throughout the ode, and not limited to counterpoint – the famous arioso for countertenor, "'Tis Nature's voice', uses a whole different set of 'skills' – is already entirely appropriate for a work addressed to the patron saint of Music.[1] And as the most ambitious contrapuntal movement, this final chorus also enacts in a literal sense the improvement of skill invoked in the text. The way in which Purcell transforms this general principle into a specific 'improvement' to the second of two otherwise comparable expositions raises the interaction between text and music here to an altogether higher plane. Furthermore, this final chorus also completes a much larger-scale symmetry with the opening chorus of the work, which similarly began with a more homophonic setting of the words 'Hail, bright Cecilia', and continued with a section comprising two contrapuntal expositions – setting the words 'Fill ev'ry heart with love of thee and thy celestial Art' – separated by orchestral *fugeing*. And in this earlier chorus, too, the second choral section incorporates augmentation: but only to double the note-values, and in a much less strict working that involves considerable melodic compromise. As well as enshrining within itself a sense of 'improvement' in the course of the movement, then, the final chorus also improves upon the level of artifice displayed in the opening chorus of the work.

The difference between these two choruses, and the reasons why the augmentation is more successful in the latter than the former, raises an important question concerning the technical demands of contrapuntal augmentation. Indeed, the consideration of exactly how Purcell devised such passages can provide further paradigms for analytical insight to place alongside those available from the simpler kinds of *fugeing* examined in Chapter 2. This, then, is the subject of the second main chapter in this section, Chapter 7, which tackles the methods by which Purcell might have devised passages involving compositional augmentation in his earlier music before examining later instances against this background. While the technical demands of augmentation are themselves a fascinating analytical starting-point, the idea of the rhetorical augmentation of verbal concepts through artifice, including (but not limited to) *fugeing* 'per augmentation', also emerges in this chapter as an important component of Purcell's compositional style.

White is not the only writer to observe that the idea of improvement of skill enshrined in Brady's final stanza of *Hail, bright Cecilia* is enacted by Purcell in the details of his musical setting; Martin Adams even points out another material reference: the similarity between the vocal line setting 'Thou dost thy former skill improve' in Example 5.1a and the second of

---

[1] Bryan White, *Music for St Cecilia's Day from Purcell to Handel* (Woodbridge: Boydell & Brewer, 2019), 126–34. I am grateful to Bryan White for sharing material from his book before it was published.

three subjects worked in the canzona section of the opening symphony from the same work.[2] Given the multi-layered nature of these relationships between sections there is no need to insist upon one passage or another as the source of this material; the verbal meaning is only enhanced by the existence of further references both within and, as we shall see, beyond the ode itself. However, the connection with the symphony is relevant in the present context since it draws attention to Purcell's revival of the canzona in the 1690s in the context of the large-scale instrumental symphonies of his odes and theatre music. Michael Tilmouth termed these symphonies 'Italian sonatas in orchestral garb' – hence the title of my Chapter 8 – and indeed in these later canzonas we can hear Purcell revisiting many of the compositional strategies and choices explored above (Chapters 3 and 4) in the fugal movements of the Sonatas, albeit in a much altered stylistic context and with the possibilities for artificial display greatly expanded by the increased scale.

The canzona in *Hail, bright Cecilia* at first seems much looser in construction than those of the sonatas, but when one looks for repeated imitative modules it soon becomes clear that many of the same principles are in operation (Ex. 5.2a). The principal differences are in the conception of the subjects *x* and *y* themselves (shown, respectively, in conventional and diamond-shaped noteheads on the main stave of Ex. 5.2a): unlike those of most Sonata canzonas, these are of different lengths (and, in the case of *y*, variable length), beginning and ending at different times and thereby already introducing greater flexibility of phrasing than is found in the strict permutational expositions of the Sonatas. Perhaps as a result of this feature, Purcell does not introduce the two subjects successively in the same part but instead positions the entry of *y* in the first violin (b. 2_3) as an 'answer' to *x* in the second violin. The continuation of the second violin in bars 2–4 provides an alternative counterpoint to *y* which in a Sonata canzona might have been treated as a strict countersubject, but here only provides snippets of cadential voice-leading where convenient (bb. 4–5 and 10–11, Vn1; bb. 8–9, Va). As Adams observes of several of these later canzonas, the result is a much less rigid or mechanistic effect, but against that background it is fascinating to see just how much of Purcell's earlier technique remains intact: after the initial entries of both subjects, the first fifteen bars of this canzona are still founded on five iterations of the same two-subject complex.

Although these iterations have been distributed among the larger ensemble available here, their structural role is made more obvious when notated in succession as on the main stave of Ex. 5.2a: iterations $\boxed{\text{i}}$ and $\boxed{\text{ii}}$ present the subjects in the same configuration (with tonal answer-like flexing of *x*), while iteration $\boxed{\text{iii}}$ demonstrates their invertibility at the

---

[2] See Adams, *Henry Purcell*, 82, 264.

Ex. 5.2   *Hail, bright Cecilia* (1692), canzona: iterations of two-subject complex

(a)   Opening

(b)   bb. 13–16

octave. All the other entries of either subject (those notated on the smaller staves in Ex. 5.2a) have been added to this basic framework according to more general principles of *fugeing* – a task made easier by the fact that both subjects essentially elaborate descending scale fragments, and are thus capable of treatment in two-part stretto *fuga*. In bars 11–13 and 16–21 Purcell additionally explores stretto treatment of the second subject *per arsin et thesin*, but in between there is a neat return to the permutational principle further modified by the overlapping of two entire iterations (iterations iv and v) by a whole bar (Ex. 5.2b). In this and even more so in the three examples treated at greater length in Chapter 7, Purcell is quite clearly 'improving his former skill', not only in his ability to assimilate his earlier concerns into the Italianate stylistic context – which is itself impressive – but also in terms of contrapuntal artifice itself.

To return to the final chorus of *Hail, bright Cecilia*, there is one more sense in which Purcell's setting of 'Thou dost thy former skill improve' offers insight into Purcell's creative strategies in the ambitious vocal works of the 1690s. As far as I am aware it has not previously been noted that the first subject in this passage, to 'Who whilst among the choir above', repurposes a subject Purcell originally used to open his second In nomine (Ex. 5.3; compare Ex. 5.1). Notwithstanding the change of mode from minor to major, the similarities are unmistakeable: the subjects share an identical contour, and are treated *per arsin et thesin* in both works. Thus in this case we can see Purcell returning not only to the general principles of his earlier preoccupation with artificial techniques, as in the Canzona, but also to the specific materials on which that preoccupation was exercised.

There are several reasons why Purcell might have alighted upon this particular contrapuntal subject in composing the final chorus of *Hail, bright Cecilia*. In the first place, as a passage of *fugeing* on a *cantus firmus*, the opening of the In nomine offered a ready-made technical solution to the premise of the second exposition of these materials in the later chorus, with its greatly augmented subject entry in the bass. As we shall see in Chapter 7, such augmentations can often be understood as *cantus firmus* parts themselves; thus in *Hail, bright Cecilia* Purcell could well have consciously selected the subject from the second In nomine for its known suitability for such treatment. Secondly, however, in the light of the observation above about Purcell's self-consciously artificial setting of the text 'Thou dost thy former skill improve', it is hard to ignore the fact that for anyone with knowledge of Purcell's consort music, the connection between the two passages adds yet another layer to the musical enactment of this verbal concept; a 'former skill' of some twelve years previously to add to those earlier in the same work and in the same movement. It is a moot point whether any of Purcell's contemporaries are likely to have grasped the link, but in terms of his own approach to the music the reality of the connection would be no less profound even if only the composer himself had been able to enjoy the reference at the time.

Finally, this specific self-quotation from a much earlier work brings to the foreground the more general transformation of Purcell's youthful contrapuntal experiments in this new stylistic context. In fact intertextuality of various sorts, from the borrowing of contrapuntal commonplaces, through the almost obsessive probing of the contrapuntal potential of a given set of materials across multiple works, to the modelling of some passages on the music of other composers, is more common in Purcell's music than has often been allowed. Not only does this add to the methods

Ex 5.3   In nomine II, opening

at the composer's disposal for the deployment of artifice to rhetorical ends in the setting of texts, but it also opens up further analytical potential in offering an alternative known starting-point for the contrapuntal methods already explored in Part I of this study. It is this aspect of Purcell's creative process that forms the core of Chapter 6, which aims both to demonstrate the importance of ideas of borrowing, *imitatio* and musical modelling more generally to Purcell's compositional technique, and to show how this can be usefully harnessed in an analytical context.

CHAPTER 6

Artifice and Musical Modelling

At the climax of his last great choral work, the orchestral Te Deum and Jubilate in D major for the St Cecilia's Day celebrations of 1694, Purcell dusted off a contrapuntal motif familiar from the end of his much earlier Fantazia XII (Ex. 6.1). Moreover, he also used exactly the same compositional conceit in his working of this motif – no doubt, in fact, his very choice of materials was motivated by the desire to select an idea suitable for subjection to the extreme contrapuntal augmentation of bars 201–8, an illustration of the words 'world without end'. This kind of artificial word-painting, and indeed the particular role of the technique of augmentation in relation to such procedures, will form the subject of Chapter 7, but for now I am concerned with the remarkable extent to which Purcell returned in this late music not merely to the techniques of his earlier fascination with abstruse contrapuntal workings, but to the very building-blocks of his earlier successful exploration of this way of composing. It is as if the re-conception of his artificial manner in the new stylistic context of the 1690s required an almost systematic revisiting and reworking of these familiar contrapuntal fragments, and their associated compositional strategies, in order that he could be satisfied as to their full assimilation into his later style.

We have already seen in Chapter 5 that Purcell repurposed materials from his seven-part In nomine II for the setting of the words 'thou dost thy former skill improve' in the final chorus of *Hail, bright Cecilia*, and in Chapter 8 we will examine more closely a much-noted instance of the reworking of an earlier canzona in Purcell's last 'dramatick opera', *The Indian Queen*. The present chapter will first examine the role of pre-existing materials and their reworking in the Fantazias, before leading ultimately to an examination of the extension of these principles in Purcell's later vocal music – specifically, the 1694 Te Deum and Jubilate. As we shall see, the passage at 'world without end' is far from the only such instance. In fact, like the central chorus of *Hail, bright Cecilia*, the whole of the doxology from the 1694 Jubilate forms a kind of choral reimagining of the fantazia genre. In the later work, each of the contrapuntal sections of this reinvention – and indeed many of the imitative sections from elsewhere in both the Te Deum and Jubilate – can be shown to derive closely from the specific techniques and

Ex. 6.1   Purcell's re-use of earlier subject materials

(a)   Jubilate Deo in D, bb. 196–209

Ex. 6.1(b) Fantazia XII, conclusion

materials of earlier consort pieces. From this perspective, I shall argue, the file copies of Purcell's instrumental music in *Lbl* Add. MS 30930 functioned as a useful store of contrapuntal ideas and procedures, which Purcell later plundered when he required impressively artificial music for the Service in D.

It would be tempting to use this observation to bolster Bruce Wood's speculation that Purcell completed his work on this Te Deum and Jubilate in a hurry,[1] and to propose that this act of self-borrowing was a matter of simple expediency in the face of intractable time pressures. Yet Purcell's efforts to harness and intensify these contrapuntal inventions in this late work are wholly in line with his earlier attitudes towards the identification and treatment of pre-existing materials. In order to understand Purcell's creative strategies in the choral sections of this work, then, we will also need to consider two more, closely intertwined phenomena: firstly, the rhetorical concept of *imitatio* – and its close cousin, *emulatio* – and their roles in the earliest stages of the creative process (the 'finding of the thought'[2]); secondly, the extent to which Purcell's creative engagement with the contrapuntal potential of his materials in his early instrumental music crossed the boundaries between specific works, resulting in a large amount of shared materials

---

[1] Wood, *Purcell*, 162; see also Henry Purcell, *Services*, ed. Bruce Wood and Margaret Laurie, PSr 23, xv.

[2] This is Dryden's description of 'Invention' in the preface to *Annus Mirabilis*, [xii].

among different Fantazias. Throughout the creative process, we will find Purcell grappling with the implications of the existing materials and the transformations to which they are subjected, opening up a window, as in the cases explored in Part I, onto his compositional priorities in general, and into the more specific creative problems he would have encountered – not to mention the solutions at which he arrived – as he worked.

In Chapter 2 we saw that the overt quotation of two bars from Fantazia VII at the climax of the first section in Fantazia VIII provided a key to identifying a material connection between these works that was otherwise obscured by a process of contrapuntal experimentation, during which the imitative materials of Fantazia VII were transformed in order to facilitate a working of *arsin* and *thesin* versions (that is, prime and inverted) of the same point simultaneously. This particular instance proves the exception rather than the rule, however, in terms of the kinds of connections among different fantazias in which I am interested in this chapter. Ex. 6.2 demonstrates something more typical: the re-use of the same point of imitation towards the end of the first section of Fantazia IV (a), and again in both the Fantazia upon One Note (b) and the six-part In nomine I (c).

Such interrelationships seem unremarkable when they arise between movements or sections of the same piece; Ex. 6.2d, for example, shows the appearance of the same imitative point in the first and last movements of Sonata VIII (1683). Both Michael Tilmouth and Martin Adams examine the similar procedure of Sonata V (1683) in A minor, linking the return of the opening theme of the sonata in the last movement to Italian interests in *da capo* forms and thematic relationships between movements, and drawing attention to the ingenuity with which Purcell presents the 'recap-

Ex. 6.2   Similarity of subject material among four instrumental works

(a)   Fantazia IV, bb. 17–21

(b)   Fantazia upon One Note, bb. 19–25

(c)   In nomine I, bb. 18–30

(d)   Sonata VIII (1683), first and last movements

'itulated' material in counterpoint with new melodic ideas.[3] Such observations fit well with the more general notions of large-scale integration through motivic resemblance between sections which Adams finds in both the sonatas and the fantazias, and it seems plausible that at least in these two sonatas Purcell was deliberately recalling his opening materials towards the end in order to imbue the whole with a sense of coherence.

The strong similarity of materials between the four different works represented in Ex. 6.2a–d, however, cannot be understood in the same way; neither can the quotation from Fantazia VII in Fantazia VIII noted above, nor the equally close correspondences between otherwise unrelated sections of five fantazias shown in Ex. 6.3. According to the same post-Romantic aesthetic that prizes motivic coherence as a measure of the unity and integrity of the individual work, such strong resemblances between different works can seem to undermine their status as independent entities – especially when we look beyond the concentrated studiousness of Purcell's 'Fantazia Project' of 1680 and discover that the same motif shown in Ex. 6.3 continues to crop up in Purcell's later music, right down to the doxology of the D major Jubilate with which this chapter began (see Ex. 6.4, though this is not intended as an exhaustive survey).

Ex. 6.3 Similarity of subject material among five other instrumental works

(a) Fantazia II, bb. 30–52

(b) Fantazia VII, bb. 43–6

(c) Fantazia IX, bb. 28–33

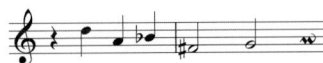

(d) Fantazia XII, conclusion

(e) 'Three Parts upon a Ground', ground bass

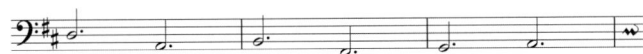

[3] Adams, *Henry Purcell*, 110–11; Tilmouth, 'The Technique and Forms', 113–15.

Ex. 6.4   Later works sharing the same subject (the same as that in Ex. 6.3)

(a)   'Golden' Sonata (1697, no. IX), first and last movements

(b)   *Dido and Aeneas*, 'Ah! Belinda': ground bass

(c)   *Dido and Aeneas*, 'Great minds against themselves conspire', second section

And   shun   the   cure   they   most   de - sire,

(d)   *The Prophetess*, 'Triumph victorious Love': ground bass

(e)   Jubilee Deo in D, 'World without end'

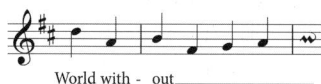

World with - out

We cannot really understand these instances of Purcell's re-use of materials from his own earlier works, I would argue, without considering them alongside the role of pre-existing materials taken from other composers in his creative process – a question, of course, that itself raises further issues around the concept of originality and which has been of considerable interest to scholars of early music in recent years.[4] Elsewhere I have shown that Purcell based the first section of his three-part Fantazia III on a reworking of the opening of Orlando Gibbons's part-song 'What is our life',[5] and in Chapter 8 we will see that one of the most artificial of Purcell's late canzonas resulted from a creative process that set out from a specific set of materials taken directly from Italian models. If the former case can plausibly be construed in the context of the ubiquity of notions of *imitatio* as a pedagogical principle observed by Rebecca Herissone, the latter instance demonstrates clearly (again in line with Herissone's conclusions) that, far from being confined to his compositional apprenticeship, such creative practices stretched across

---

[4] For an excellent summary of the issues specifically tailored to Restoration England, see Herissone, *Musical Creativity*, Chapter 1: 'Imitation, Originality and Authorship'.

[5] Alan Howard, 'A New Purcell "Borrowing" from Orlando Gibbons', paper delivered at the 2014 Biennial Conference on Baroque Music (Queen's University, Belfast, 30 June–4 July 2010; an extended version of this paper will appear as '"Of great value to a Composer": Henry Purcell's Youthful Encounter with the Music of Orlando Gibbons' (in preparation).

Purcell's career. Yet both of these represent comparatively rare instances in Restoration music in which a composer appropriates and re-works substantial portions of an identifiable model work by another individual.

More common is the kind of process by which commonplace materials are adopted and freshly examined in Purcell's music. The sequential pattern of fourths linked by a stepwise interval in the opposite direction (Exx. 6.3 and 6.4), for example, must have been familiar from the traditional bass line of the chaconne, a context that feeds directly into its presence both in 'Three Parts upon a Ground' and 'Triumph victorious Love', as well as in Dido's 'Ah! Belinda'; in a melodic context its lineage encompasses Dowland's setting of the words 'Till death, till death do come' in his song 'In darkness let me dwell',[6] whose use of a diminished fourth is echoed by Purcell in each of the fantazia sections to use this motif and in the setting of the words 'And shun the cure' in the penultimate chorus of *Dido and Aeneas* (Ex. 6.4c).[7] Rather than active imitation of a given model, such resemblances imply the existence of a repertoire of common materials drawn on by numerous composers,[8] though no less consciously probed by Purcell, as we shall see. Indeed, albeit not given in this specific form, this subject clearly belongs to the category of sequential imitative subjects identified by Julian Grimshaw as common to sixteenth-century English *fuga*.[9] In a similar vein, several sections of the fantazias, including the opening of Fantazia III, via Gibbons's 'What is our life?', recall the opening of Dowland's *Lachrimae* Pavan.[10] The subject shared by the sections identified above in Ex. 6.2, meanwhile, seems – despite its coincidental resemblance to the first line of Martin Luther's chorale melody 'Vom Himmel hoch, da komm ich her' – to be based on the elaboration of a cadential suspension.

Purcell's 'self-borrowing', then, is closely akin to the process of creative imitation that is widely discussed in the music of other Baroque composers; as Herissone observes, it most often draws upon the musical common property of Purcell's time, rather than attempting to re-shape specific models to form complete pieces. Inasmuch as both his appropriation of existing materials and his 'self-borrowing' can be shown, as we shall see, to be based on a principle of 'added value', we might view them together as

---

[6] This song was published by Dowland's son Robert in *A Musicall Banquet* (1610); see Ex. 7.13b and related discussion in Chapter 7 below.

[7] In fact the same motif can be found in several other places throughout *Dido and Aeneas*; to give just two telling examples, see the end of the first chorus (at 'Grief should ne'er approach the fair'), and – in a major key – the last chorus of Act I (at 'Go revel, ye Cupids').

[8] See Herissone, *Musical Creativity*, 33–4; also John Milsom, '"*Imitatio*", "Intertextuality" and Early Music', in *Citation and Authority in Medieval and Renaissance Musical Culture: Learning from the Learned*, ed. Suzannah Clark and Elizabeth Eva Leach (Woodbridge: Boydell, 2006), 141–51 (145).

[9] Julian Grimshaw, 'Sixteenth-Century English Fuga: Sequential and Peak-Note Subjects', *MT* 148 (2007), 61–78.

[10] Dowland's 'tear' motif was widely imitated in the seventeenth century; see Peter Holman, *Dowland, Lachrimae (1604)*, Cambridge Music Handbooks (Cambridge University Press, 1999), 75–80.

different facets of an approach similar to the kind of 'transformative imitation' proposed as the motivation behind Handel's borrowings by John T. Winemiller.[11] Together with the existence in all of these cases of identifiable pre-existing materials, this principle offers an analytical opportunity similar to that identified by Peter Schubert and Marcelle Lessoil-Daelman in their study of Renaissance 'musical modeling':

> ... imitation music is fundamentally like composition from scratch, but when there is a model, we know which musical ideas came first. The composer of the sixteenth-century imitation piece appropriates material from a model – ranging from a single line to a complete block of polyphony – as if it were his own first sketch. Then he modifies, develops, refines and improves the musical ideas, often admixing his own freshly composed material. The simplest type of modification comes from adapting the old music to the declamatory demands of the new text; the most complex comes from changing contrapuntal relationships.[12]

With this in mind, then, the following section considers a detailed case study of the appropriation and transformative reworking of materials in Purcell's fantazias; the final section of the chapter proceeds to assess how the same principle extended into his later music.

TRANSFORMATIVE REWORKING IN THREE FANTAZIAS

The cases of explicit similarity of fugal materials between fantazias described so far in this chapter can easily be understood to indicate that Purcell was selecting contrapuntal subjects simply on the basis of their known suitability for imitative treatment, as a shortcut to successful counterpoint. However, closer examination of the details of Purcell's workings of identical subjects is more suggestive of a process of stretching *fugeing* to its limits, to the extent that his desire to test the potential of his materials to exhaustion required more music than could be accommodated in any one work. Nowhere is this more obvious, or more thoroughly worked out, than in the link between Fantazia VI (bb. 62–82), Fantazia XI (bb. 1–24) and In nomine II (bb. 10–22), excerpts from which are given in Ex. 6.5. Each of these three sections is based on the same simple subject, worked *per arsin et thesin* as in the section from Fantazia VIII analysed in detail in Chapter 2. The use of related materials across these three works is particularly interesting, furthermore, because of the uncertainty regarding their sequence of composition: while the two fantazias are dated, respectively, 14 June and 16 August 1680 in Purcell's autograph scorebook (*Lbl* Add. MS 30930), in the absence of a dated inscription for the

[11] John T. Winemiller, 'Recontextualizing Handel's Borrowing', *Journal of Musicology*, 15/4 (1997), 444–70.

[12] Peter Schubert and Marcelle Lessoil-Daelman, 'What Modular Analysis Can Tell Us About Musical Modeling in the Renaissance', *Music Theory Online*, 19/1 (2013), http://mtosmt.org/issues/mto.13.19.1/mto.13.19.1.schubert_lessoil-daelman.html (consulted 7 August 2016).

Ex. 6.5   The 'cumulative fourth' subject in three consort works

(a)   Fantazia VI, bb. 62–67

(b)   Fantazia XI, bb. 1–6

(c)   In nomine II, bb. 10–15

In nomine it has usually been assumed that this work, with its self-consciously archaic genre, was somewhat earlier. In the following analysis I show how Purcell probes the possibilities of the subject much deeper in

Ex. 6.6   Earlier 'cumulative fourth' subjects in music that Purcell knew

(a)   William Byrd, 'O Lord, make thy servant': subject at 'give him his heart's desire'

give   him   his   heart's   de - sire,

(b)   Orlando Gibbons, 'Hosanna to the son of David': opening subject

Ho - san - na   to the Son   of   Da - vid,

the later of the two fantazias, exploring interlocks that would have been rejected in the more circumspect Fantazia VI section, before going on to consider whether the contrapuntal treatment in the In nomine can tell us anything about its likely place in the sequence of composition.

The subject itself is once again a commonplace contrapuntal fragment, a point labelled the 'cumulative fourth' subject by Grimshaw (one of a group of what he identifies as 'peak-note subjects').[13] In its simple form Purcell might have encountered it in Byrd's anthem 'O Lord, make thy servant [Charles] our [King]', at the words 'give [him his] heart's desire' (see Ex. 6.6a), though the similarity here covers only the overall contour (and not the rhythm, an essential feature of the point's imitative versatility). This was one of a number of earlier vocal works that Purcell copied into his scorebook *Cfm* MS 88, probably only months before he dated the copies of the Fantazias in *Lbl* Add. MS 30930.[14] Indeed, another of the pieces he copied, Orlando Gibbons's 'Hosanna to the son of David', opens with a version of this subject that is even closer to that used by Purcell in these Fantazias (Ex. 6.6b): disregarding Gibbons's opening leap, his point both has the same rhythm as Purcell's version, and adds the same passing note.

To these possible precedents may be added at least two more. The first is the opening of William Young's sixth sonata from the set published in Innsbruck in 1659 (Ex. 6.7a). These were apparently also known in England as fantazias, under which title Stephen Bing copied them into *Lgc* MSS 469–71, and may have been known at court if Shay and Thompson are correct that John Reading Sr – who copied four of them (under the title 'Sonnata') into his scorebook, *Lbl* MS R.M. 20.h.9 – encountered them in the hands of London musicians visiting Winchester

---

[13] Grimshaw, 'Sixteenth-Century English *Fuga*', 73–4.
[14] On Purcell's copying in *Cfm* MS 88 see Shay and Thompson, *Purcell Manuscripts*, 33–47 (especially p. 44 for dates of copying).

Ex 6.7   Two 'cumulative fourth' subjects from the mid seventeeth century

(a)   William Young, Sonata/Fantazia *a* 3 (VdGS M97): opening subject

(b)   Locke, canon 'Domine Jesu Christe': opening subject

in 1682–4.[15] The second is the 'Canon Six in Three' on the words 'Domine Jesu Christe, miserere mei' by Matthew Locke (Ex. 6.7b), published in his *Observations upon a Late Book* (1672). This work ostensibly forms part of his rebuttal of Thomas Salmon's notorious proposal to reform the system of clefs in *An Essay to the Advancement of Musick* of the same year; though – as Locke says – the canon is intended as much to demonstrate the excellence of canon itself (and by extension, one infers, its composer's superior musical learning).[16] From Ex. 6.7 one might assume that the instrumental piece by Young was a clear forerunner of the Purcell examples: after all, it is from a closely related genre and contains the melodic subject in exactly the same form in which it appears in Purcell's Fantazia VI (compare Ex. 6.5a).

In imitative terms, however, Young's three-part piece is far less ambitious than any of Purcell's consort works: Young rarely interlocks the subject with itself, preferring a series of singleton entries with occasional hints of recurring countersubject material (hence the brief modules identified in Ex. 6.8). By contrast, in the opening eleven bars of Locke's canon, each of the seven entries of this subject creates an interlock with at least one other. Moreover, and intriguingly in the present context, six of these imitative entries form a large-scale complex that is closely paralleled in the opening of Purcell's Fantazia VI (Ex. 6.9). Purcell places the entries in different registers, but is no less systematic than Locke: in entries ①–④ Locke's zigzagging entries are replaced by Purcell's straightforward top-to-bottom disposition, and where Locke places entry ⑤ in the bass, Purcell – still opting for an outer voice – selects the treble.

Such beguiling correspondences aside, the point here is not to demonstrate that Purcell modelled these three sections of fantazias on one or another of these works, or even that he must have taken elements from

[15] On Young's 1659 Sonatas see Stephen Morris, 'William Young's Fantazias *a* 3, by Another Name, Still Sound as Sweet . . . ', *Journal of the Viola da Gamba Society of America*, 41 (2004), 5–35; on Bing see Pamela Willetts, 'Stephen Bing: A Forgotten Violist', *Chelys*, 18 (1989), 3–17; for Reading, see Shay and Thompson, *Purcell Manuscripts*, 295–8.

[16] See Benjamin Wardhaugh, ed., *Thomas Salmon: Writings on Music*, 2 vols (Farnham: Ashgate, 2013), I, 127–31.

Ex. 6.8   Young, Sonata/Fantazia *a* 3 (VdGS M97), bb. 1–13

multiple models, but to establish the likely *prius factus* elements of his work on these materials as a background against which to understand his own music. Purcell could have derived his melodic diminution of the subject from Young (perhaps also with Gibbons in mind) and his densely inter-locking imitative texture from Locke (though equally possibly from Gibbons again); at a stretch he could even have reworked Locke's canon itself to produce the first six entries of the Fantazia VI section in their entirety. Yet it is clear that his interrogation of the imitative possibilities of this material went much further than any of these specific instances, to the extent that his approach is truly 'transformative'. In the first place, none of the four works identified here as possible precedents for Purcell's music attempts to invert the subject, whereas in all three Purcell examples inver-sion is ubiquitous; in Fantazia VI it is introduced immediately after the six *arsin* entries which follow the pattern established in the Locke canon. Furthermore, and only partly as a direct result of this observation, the number of different interlocks Purcell used in these three passages (when viewed together) is far greater than that even in the first section of Fantazia VIII. The almost exclusive reliance on imitation at the unison or octave, fourth or fifth in that work, and in each of the pieces identified in Ex. 6.6 and 6.7, contrasts strongly with the much less circumscribed range of intervals Purcell explored in these sections of Fantazias VI and XI, and In nomine II: close imitation occurs literally at every numerical interval. Accounting for the inversion of either the first or second entry, this produces 56 potential two-voice interlocks at the distances of one or two beats alone; many more are possible at greater intervals of time.

Ex 6.9   Fantazia VI compared with Locke's canon: (a) Locke, 'Domine Jesu Christe',
bb. 1–11;   (b) Purcell, Fantazia VI, bb. 62–6

In order to aid in the representation of such an unwieldy body of
information, the imitative possibilities of the subject can be conveniently
notated as a series of alternative canonic entries, adapting the contemporary method for notating vocal canons and rounds on a single stave by
indicating subsequent entries with the symbol ⌖ as in Ex. 6.10. Aligned
with each ⌖ in Ex. 6.10b is a series of numbers indicating the interval above
the written subject of the possible entries, grouped with the letters A (*arsin*)
and T (*thesin*) to indicate the form of the subject implied. Interlocks are
assumed to be inversionally equivalent at the octave, such that the figure 4
indicates an entry either a fourth above or a fifth below the written subject.
The interlocks listed are considered 'intrinsically viable' in that they make
good two-part counterpoint by themselves (the only exception is when the
higher part makes a fourth with the lower part, in which case a conceptual
bass part beneath the interlock is assumed). Each ⌖ in the chart represents
an alternative, rather than a successive place of entry for a further voice;
while it may be possible to construct larger, multi-voice complexes using
entries at more than one such place, no larger complexes are indicated by
the notation unless specifically noted as such.

   The intrinsically viable two-part interlocks that can be formed from the
materials in these three fantazia sections are shown in Ex. 6.11.[17] Since

---

[17] This and all subsequent similar figures are notated with the crotchet as the base unit of time, in order
to facilitate comparison; similarly, all of the interlocks are notated with an assumed key-note of C,
the 'natural' key that Purcell recommends as simplest for beginners. Bar-lines are not notated, since

Ex. 6.10   The 'cumulative fourth' subject: notation of available interlocks

(a)   Three viable interlocks

(b)   Notation on a single staff

many aspects of Purcell's approach to *fugeing* in the three works under discussion here are already familiar from the foregoing analyses, I focus in the following discussions on the ways in which Purcell brought new concerns to bear on the materials in each passage. It is the recognition of unexplored possibilities in Fantazia VI that gives impetus to the resumption of interest in the material in Fantazia XI; my contention is that we can then use these observations to consider how the use of similar materials in the In nomine fits into this sequence of events.

(a) Fantazia VI, Bars 62–82

The information in Ex. 6.12 provides a basis on which to assess Purcell's use of the possibilities inherent in his subject material in this first example. The interlocks heard in Fantazia VI are represented in bold typeface, with the remainder of intrinsically viable (yet unused) interlocks shown in smaller type. The use of brackets for one entry (T:A$^{+3,\,\text{♩}}$) indicates that

the metrical placing of the entries in all of the works in question is variable, and in some cases different interlocks require specific metrical placing in order to make them viable (for example, in order to prepare, strike and resolve a suspension correctly). The differing lengths of the *arsin* and *thesin* forms of the subject given in Ex. 6.11 reflect their use in the fantazias: these are the parts of the subject in each form that remain intact throughout the works, both rhythmically and in terms of pitch.

Ex. 6.11   Intrinsically viable two-part interlocks in Fantazias VI (bb. 62–82) and XI (bb.1–24), and In nomine II (bb. 10–22)

this interlock arises from the shadowing of another part at the third, rather than from an independent imitative entry in its own right.

Two notable characteristics of Purcell's *fugeing* in this section of Fantazia VI are immediately apparent from Ex. 6.12: his marked preference for imitation at the fourth, fifth or octave (nine of the twelve interlocks in total), and at the distance of two crotchet beats (just over half of the interlocks used). This can be seen more clearly when the interlocks are laid out as they appear in the fantazia, demonstrating the imitative frame-work on which the section is built, as in Ex. 6.13. This example retains the continuation of each entry (the portion beyond the fourth note in this simplified form), since it is so prominent melodically in this passage. In imitative terms, however, the notes after those given in Ex. 6.11 and 6.12 are redundant: all instances of imitation at a distance greater than one bar are incidental to other interlocks involving closer imitation, and this portion of the material is freely altered throughout in order to accommo-date otherwise unviable entries.

Just as in other works he confined himself to imitation at the conven-tional intervals of fourth, fifth and octave, so Purcell made these intervals the most important in this first passage in which he explored the potential of this subject. Of the few interlocks involving imitation at other intervals, the one at the third has already been observed as the by-product of a

Ex. 6.12   Fantazia VI, bb. 62–82: interlocks used

Ex. 6.13   Fantazia VI, bb. 62–80: outline score, showing disposition of interlocks in Ex. 6.12

doubling, while the imitation of the subject *arsin* at the lower seventh, three beats later (bb. 65–7) results from the combination of two other interlocks involving imitation at the fourth. This leaves only the two instances of the same imitation at the lower second (bb. 71–2 and 73–4) as evidence of any exploration in this passage of viable interlocks beyond the simplest intervallic relationships.

Purcell's concentration on imitation at the distance of two beats served a particular contrapuntal purpose, preserving the syntactic function of the fourth note of the subject *arsin* (again, in the simplified version shown in Ex. 6.13) as the preparation and striking of a suspension – which depended on the metrical placing of the point. This is why each of the first four entries of the point begins on a strong beat, and each new entry creates a suspension in one of the other parts (bb. 63_1, 63_3 and 64_1). With the point in inversion, though, the situation is quite different: while the melodic element remains intact, the equivalent note can no longer form a preparation and suspension (which would require resolution by a melodic step down, something incompatible with the continuation of the point). As a result, Purcell was less concerned to maintain the metrical placing of *thesin* entries; not being tied to a metre-specific syntactic function, these tend to occur on the weaker beats. Indeed, where they are placed on strong beats the result is a fourth note tied over the bar-line followed by a stepwise ascent, which necessitates unusual voice-leading, such as the 9–10 suspension in bar 76, in an effort to avoid over-static harmony.

The importance of these metrical properties of the subject can be seen in Purcell's approach to interlocks involving the combination of an entry *arsin* with one *thesin*, which appear five times in the course of the whole section. Where this happens at the distance of two crotchet beats, one of two things must happen: either the *arsin* entry is displaced by a beat, thus destroying the syntactic function of its fourth note, as in bars 65–7; or the *thesin* entry is displaced, with the result that its fourth note is tied over the bar-line as it is at the start of bar 76 and bar 79, necessitating some extremely deft handling of irregular dissonances in each case.

Purcell's solutions to this problem can be seen in the two complexes that involve imitation at the crotchet. In bars 78–9, he begins the complex $A{:}T^{+8,\,\downarrow}$ on a strong beat, with the result that the suspension of the *arsin* entry is left intact, and indeed enhanced by the fourth note of the *thesin* entry, which falls on the strong third beat of bar 79 and provides the necessary dissonance; at the same time, Purcell shortens the fourth note of the *thesin* entry by a crotchet. In the case of bars 71–4, however, the potential solution is undermined by the placement of the beginning of the complex $A{:}T^{-2,\,\downarrow}$ not on a strong beat, but a weak one (bb. 71_2 and 73_2). The result is a moment of rhythmic ambiguity reminiscent of Byrd, which relies on exactly the association of melodic and syntactic elements, tied to metrical placing, that had been set up from the beginning of the section.

The sense of rhythmic unrest, enhanced by the unusual imitation at the lower second and the momentary reduction in texture at this point, suggests that Purcell was deliberately upsetting the otherwise stable metrical structure of the section in this passage. At the same time, though, these two sequential statements of the same interlock have a clear relationship to the underlying harmonic purpose of this passage: the movement around the circle of fifths from G (b. 71) to C (73) and F (75) relies on the arrival at each point of rest on a strong beat, a function that this interlock performs perfectly without any need to alter the continuation of the subject.

In this first exploration of these familiar materials, then, Purcell makes good use of the most obvious interlocks of the subject with itself at the conventional intervals of imitation, while introducing the idea of inversion – which, incidentally, also has a clear role in the structuring of the section, with its concentration first upon interlocks involving entries *arsin* (bb. 62–5), then those with entries *thesin* (bb. 66–70), and finally those incorporating combinations of the two, in order of increasing complexity (bb. 71–81). Against the background of this familiar cumulation of artifice, which resembles that observed in Fantazia VIII (see Chapter 2), he makes limited use of interlocks at more unusual intervals, chosen for their specific voice-leading implications and rhythmic qualities. But he also leaves many intrinsically viable combinations as yet untapped (as can be seen in Ex. 6.12). The fact that he was later to return to these materials suggests that he was well aware of their potential for further exploitation.

(b) Fantazia XI, Bars 1–24

It is not known whether the dates at the head of each of Purcell's four-part fantazias in *Lbl* Add. MS 30930 are dates of composition or copying, but if they represent the former, then the date Purcell wrote at the top of Fantazia XI is most revealing. Fantazias IV (the first four-part fantazia) to X are all given dates at roughly equal intervals between 10 and 30 June 1680, but after Fantazia X Purcell seems to have laid aside his 'fantazia project' for some time:[18] Fantazia XI was first dated 16 August, some seven weeks after its predecessor, and completed over two or three days;[19] the last complete four-part work, Fantazia XII, followed a couple of weeks later on 31 August.[20]

---

[18] Bruce Wood suggests that this may have been in order to work on the welcome song *Welcome, Viceregent of the Mighty King* (Wood, *Purcell*, 58).

[19] Purcell first wrote '16', later changing the 6 to a 9. At some stage, seemingly after this, he also tried to alter the same character to an 8 (not a 7 as some authors state); thus it is possible that the work was completed on 18 August – though the possibility that he had mistaken the date in either direction makes it difficult to be certain.

[20] For more on the dates inscribed above the four-part fantazias, and the codicology of their source, *Lbl* Add. MS 30930, see Shay and Thompson, *Purcell Manuscripts*, 85–100.

It seems highly likely that Purcell's return to writing fantazias on 16 August began with – perhaps it had even been motivated by – a browse through some old notes and sketches that he found among his work on the previous fantazias. The opening of Fantazia XI (Ex. 6.5b) deliberately avoids the interlocks that were so prominent in Fantazia VI, instead exploring no fewer than three new two-voice interlocks (A:T$^{+4, \, \text{♩}}$, A:A$^{+5, \, \text{♩}}$, and A:T$^{+7, \, \text{♩}}$) within the space of just three bars.

Despite Purcell's desire to differentiate between his treatment of the material in the two fantazias so early in the piece, the descent of this section of Fantazia XI from the earlier passage is quite clear from his treatment of the continuation of the subject. In Fantazia VI, this material (after the fourth note) was consistently present throughout the section – though, as we have seen, its exact intervallic and rhythmic content was considerably more varied than that of the subject itself. In Fantazia XI, however, Purcell's treatment of this material is much more fluid: the point *arsin* regularly ends with the resolution of the suspension (e.g. bb. 3, 5, 6, 11) or even before it (bb. 13, 16, 17, 19, 23); meanwhile the point *thesin* rarely proceeds beyond this point (the notable exception being the treble 2 entry at bar 6$_4$, in which the entire continuation of the subject *thesin* as it appears in Fantazia VI is retained).

Nevertheless, the impact of these discarded fragments of melody can still be detected in Fantazia XI. This can be seen by reconstructing the beginning of the work as if Purcell had retained the continuation of the subject, as in Ex. 6.14. As in previous 'outline scores', notes that Purcell amended are shown as crossed noteheads, in this case not as part of the subject itself but its continuation. Purcell made two kinds of change to the material in this reconstructed opening. First there were the three voice-leading transgressions marked in Ex. 6.14, each of which he easily rectified either by altering individual notes or by dropping the continuation of the subject altogether (compare Ex. 6.5b). The second kind of change, meanwhile, was a response to more creative concerns. By progressing *upwards* by step

Ex. 6.14   Fantazia XI, opening: reconstructed with continuation of point from Fantazia VI after the resolution of the suspension in the subject *arsin* (tr. 1, bb. 3 and 4–5; bass, bb. 5–6), Purcell was able to make this version of the point imply a melodic cadence, with the resolution of the suspension functioning as a leading note. Remarkably, considering that it is such a simple change and that suspensions in general are such frequent cadential precursors, this was a change that did not occur once in Fantazia VI. Having made the alteration, Purcell proceeded to play with the cadential implication, inserting a series of interrupted cadences that make a notable contribution to the rather unsettling tension between clear harmonic direction and refusal to find resolution that is a feature of this section of the fantazia.

The strong sense of cadential function provided by this alteration to the subject and its continuation also allowed Purcell a much greater freedom of harmonic range in this work than in Fantazia VI. This is particularly obvious later in the section, where a series of entries *arsin* in quick succession on *e'*, *b'* and *f*♯*'* effect a speedy modulation sharpwards from A minor to B minor (bb. 18–20). Without the alteration of the subject, Purcell would have required passages of 'free' counterpoint in order to incorporate the necessary cadential progressions; by modifying the subject to include strongly marked cadential lines, however, he could entrust much of this harmonic work to his imitative materials and thus maintain a higher degree

Ex. 6.15   Fantazias VI and XI: contrasting modulations

(a)   Fantazia VI, bb. 67–71

(b)   Fantazia XI, bb. 18–21

of contrapuntal artifice. Indeed, a direct comparison between Fantazias VI and XI shows this to great effect. Whereas in Fantazia VI (Ex. 6.15a) the modulation from F to G necessitates strongly goal-directed material that is unrelated to the subject, the similar modulation in Fantazia XI (Ex. 6.15b) is achieved almost exclusively using entries of the point; only the bass resorts to harmonic function without thematic reference.

Purcell's exploration of new interlocks in this section of Fantazia XI continued beyond the first platform into the whole passage of *fugeing*. Of those that remained unused from Fantazia VI, he made use of all of the two-voice interlocks involving imitation of the subject *arsin* at the distance of one or two beats, and a further eight of those involving imitation of the subject *thesin* at the same distances. (All of these are shown in larger type and bold in Ex. 6.16; interlocks previously used in Fantazia VI but not present in Fantazia XI remain bold, but are printed in smaller type). Then in three more cases he incorporated imitation that is not intrinsically viable (denoted by an exclamation mark), by removing the problematic part of the initial entry.

When it came to imitation at greater distances, Purcell seems to have chosen interlocks for their specific contrapuntal properties rather than attempting to include as many different complexes as possible as an end in itself. The strong syntactic element of the subject made many of the entries at the distances of three or four beats undesirable, since they obscured the suspension and corresponding cadence associated with the end of the subject *arsin* in this fantazia. In this context, it is revealing that Purcell truncated both entries of the point that are imitated after three beats in Fantazia XI, removing the suspension altogether (ten. and bass, bb. 17–18; tr. 2 and ten., bb. 18–20). Conversely, the interlocks involving imitation after four beats (see, for example, ten. and tr. 1 in the opening platform, Ex. 6.5b) are all chosen for their use of intervals of imitation that intensify the dissonance of the suspension. Purcell's desire to use the most artificial combinations seems to have won out over any attempt to exhaust the possible combinations at these greater intervals of time.

Ex. 6.16   Fantazia XI, bb. 1–24: interlocks used

(c)   *In nomine II, Bars 10–22*

Although this passage occurs latest of the three works examined here in *Lbl* Add. MS 30930, it is, as noted above, unclear exactly when Purcell composed it in relation to the four-part Fantazias. As a result, the findings of any contrapuntal analysis potentially have a bearing on our understanding of its relative dating.

At first glance, this section seems very much in keeping with an assumption that the In nomines were composed in the order in which they appear in the scorebook; that is, after the Fantazias (contrary to the usual opinion). The In nomine passage is apparently consistent with Purcell's gradual exploration of the imitative potential of this simple subject in Fantazia VI and Fantazia XI: he explores still more fugal combinations, again concentrating on the most artificial by aiming for the closest possible imitation (Ex. 6.17). In all, no fewer than eleven additional interlocks appear in this section (those used only in the In nomine are underlined). Given the exhaustive use of imitation after one and two beats in the two Fantazia sections, this often meant making alterations to the substance of the subject itself (as shown by the number of exclamation marks, indicating interlocks that were not intrinsically viable) – something that was comparatively rare in the two fantazias.

One might think that the staggering range of intrinsically viable interlocks of this material makes it unlikely that Purcell would have resorted to some of the difficult imitations incorporated into In nomine II if this was the first time he had used it; the lengths to which he goes to incorporate them seem to make sense only against the background of existing passages on the same subject. Even more than Fantazia XI, for example, In nomine II relies on the shortest forms of the subject material. The continuation of the subject found in Fantazia VI is rare, and very often the point consists only of the stepwise melodic movement through a fourth in both *arsin* and *thesin* forms of the material. There are two prominent exceptions to this, occurring in the treble 1 and tenor 1 parts in bars 11–12 and 12–13, respectively. Both instances involve the interpretation of

Ex. 6.17   In nomine II, bb. 10–22: interlocks used

the fifth note of the subject *arsin* as a suspended fourth degree, resolving to the minor third of a chord on the key-note (see Ex. 6.5c, bb. 11–13). This is important as it is the only instance of such a context for this important syntactic–harmonic event: in Fantazias VI and XI the same suspension is commonly heard as a key-note falling to a leading note, or a fourth resolving to a major third. Since In nomine II is the only one of the three works in the minor mode, Purcell was able to give this suspension a different harmonic context here. The new cadential version of the point *arsin* from Fantazia XI, in which the resolution of this same suspension was followed by a step upwards to the local key-note, is not found at all in In nomine II.

Some of the methods by which Purcell increased the range of available complexes are shown in Ex. 6.18, which shows the imitative parts of the beginning of this section of In nomine II. Several entries proceed only as far as the melodic fourth, and the shortening of the beginning of the point (bb. 10, 11, 12, 13 and 15) is a feature even where Purcell was not forced into it to facilitate otherwise impossible imitation. By introducing this version of the subject from the beginning (bb. 10 and 11), and returning to it periodically throughout the section (bb. 13 and 15), he was able to use it when necessary (as in b. 12) to incorporate more difficult complexes without significantly damaging the melodic identity of the fugal materials. Furthermore, Purcell's incorporation of multiple interlocks through the shadowing of individual entries at the third or sixth enabled him to

Ex. 6.18   In nomine II, bb. 10$_4$–16: disposition of two-voice interlocks build denser textures simply by overlapping straightforward two-voice combinations.

There is, however, an alternative way of understanding these differences of contrapuntal technique that does not rely on the later composition of In nomine II. The much greater tendency in the In nomine to alter the length of the first note of the subject, and shorten it at the end, might be viewed as a less rigorous application of Purcell's 'artificial' techniques, and the greater range of intervals of imitation as indicative of a lack of control of the harmonic context of entries. According to this interpretation, the In nomine might equally be the work of a less experienced composer, and therefore antedate the two Fantazia sections.

Furthermore, even the apparent variety of intervals of imitation found in In nomine II is arguably less audacious than it first seems. A careful reading of this section reveals that all of the interlocks involving imitation at intervals other than the fourth, fifth or octave are created either by the overlapping of interlocks themselves at perfect intervals, or by the kind of shadowing of 'perfect' interlocks already noted. This is a relatively simple strategy for the increase of imitative density, especially given a restrictive *cantus firmus*. In bars 15–16, for example, interlocks involving imitation at the third, second and seventh arise incidentally among three successive interlocks at the fourth or fifth (each shown on its own stave in Ex. 6.18); the unconventional intervals result because Purcell linked these together by having the leading part of each new interlock shadow the following part of the previous one at the third (shown with vertical brackets). All of the unusual combinations in this passage of the In nomine can in fact be explained according to similar reasoning. By contrast, in both Fantazia VI and Fantazia XI Purcell seems deliberately to select more adventurous interlocks in order to exploit their interesting harmonic or expressive potential. This could be a sign of greater confidence of technique in the Fantazias, or simply a function of the restrictive nature of the *cantus firmus* in the In nomine; it seems, nevertheless, that in this case analysis of the contrapuntal methods of these works cannot resolve their problematic sequence of composition.

More generally, the extremely thorough probing of the imitative possibilities of this subject in these three sections clearly shows how Purcell's creative processes could stretch beyond the boundaries of individual works. The lengths to which he pursues increasingly artificial combinations, even incorporating many of the more improbable interlocks through careful manipulation of melodic properties and harmonic context, both reinforce and enhance the image built up in earlier chapters of a composer peculiarly fascinated with the pursuit of contrapuntal artifice as an end in itself. It is clear that whether he took materials from his own earlier works or from the music of other composers, he was more than capable of transforming them through such techniques into something far beyond the ambitions of their original manifestation.

A further glimpse of this process can be seen in one final outing for these same materials in Purcell's instrumental music, the canzona of Sonata II (1697). This movement, probably composed some time in the mid 1680s, has a subject derived from an unviable interlock, $T:A^{+5,\;\downarrow}$, that was not attempted in the earlier works, and its countersubject is clearly related to the complete subject *arsin* from Fantazia VI, complete with continuation (Ex. 6.19). The treatment of this material is very different from that in the earlier consort music, however, as if – having subjected them to the full range of possibilities available in the consort fantazia – Purcell was inspired afresh by the further options available in this different stylistic context.

Firstly, having derived his materials as shown in Ex. 6.19, Purcell used them – together with a third invertible part derived mainly by doubling one or the other of the existing lines at the third or sixth – to create a permutational first platform, just as he did in so many of the sonata canzonas examined in Chapter 3 and 4 above. After a seventeen-bar exposition, he then subjected the main subject to stretto entries a crotchet apart (b. 37, flexing the first melodic step to a third in order to make it work in stretto *fuga*), also introducing an inversion of the subject (b. 42) which is combined with the prime form at varying intervals of pitch and time (bb. 42–7, 53–6, 57–9). Such *fugeing* is closely akin to the fantazias again, but what is not is the way in which these imitative entries are juxtaposed with a more formulaic set of sequential materials based on a 7–6 progression, first introduced in bar 40. In yet another new form of experimentation with his subject materials, Purcell strives to combine the subject and the voice-leading progression throughout bars 51–9, coming closest in bars 51–3, in which what would be three bars of semiquaver divisions on an unfolded-third pattern in the bass viol are interrupted only in bar 52 in order to avoid consecutive fifths with the subject entries above, before being resumed in bar 53. Only after this passage do the semiquavers take over completely, and the subject is not heard again before the end of

Ex. 6.19 Sonata II (1697), second movement (opening): derivation of materials

the canzona. (It does reappear, via an ornamented metrical transformation, as the subject of the concluding triple-time fugue – again using a permutational exposition – of the same sonata; another instance of the *da capo*-like reworking of materials cited in Sonatas V and VIII (1683) at the start of this chapter.)

'AS IT WAS IN THE BEGINNING'

Purcell's final period of engagement with the subject he had already explored so thoroughly in Fantazias VI and XI, In nomine II and Sonata II (1697), returns our focus to the late vocal music, and indeed to the very same Gloria of the D major Jubilate with which this chapter opened. We have already seen that the passage at 'World without end' derives closely from materials and techniques taken from the end of Fantazia XII, and both of these passages will be analysed in more detail in Chapter 7. Looking at the sections on either side of this music, however (Ex. 6.20), it should by now be obvious that both 'As it was in the beginning' and the 'Amen' make use of exactly the same subject that has been the subject of most of this chapter.

Of the two sections, 'As it was' is by far the simpler (Ex. 6.20a; compare Ex. 6.5a): just as in Fantazia VI, the four parts enter in order from top to bottom on pitches alternating between the fifth and first scale-degrees, at corresponding intervals of time (minims in the Fantazia, semibreves in the Gloria owing to the doubling of note-values). Throughout bars 182–7 of the Gloria (the first five bars of Ex. 6.20a), indeed, there are really only two fundamental changes from the basic structure heard in the earlier Fantazia: the fact that the entries fall on the weak beats instead of strong, which is clearly designed to reflect the stress-pattern of the words (that is, on 'was' and '-gin-' rather than 'As' and 'the'); and the flexing of the entries in countertenor and bass such that the version on the first scale-degree provides a tonal answer (D–A to the subject's A–D) rather than the subdominant version (the equivalent of D–G) in the Fantazia. Thereafter, Purcell introduces a *thesin* version of this flexed entry (alto and Tpt 2, b. 187), before using it to create paired entries in thirds and sixths in bars 189–91 in a manner reminiscent of its treatment during In nomine II.

The flexed entry on D again dominates the more extended working-out of the same materials in the 'Amen' in bars 213–26, where this time it leads off rather than entering as an answer (Ex. 6.20b). This version of the subject strips away the rhythmic and melodic diminutions heard in all the passages examined thus far, seemingly returning to the unadorned form heard in Locke's canon 'Domine Jesu Christe' (Ex. 6.7b). In imitative terms, however, it most closely resembles another of the precedents identified earlier, the opening of Gibbons's 'Hosanna to the son of

Ex. 6.20   Jubilate Deo in D, Gloria: use of the 'cumulative fourth' subject

(a)   'As it was in the beginning'

David'. Ex. 6.21 lays out the imitative content of the two sections in parallel, showing shared entries in black, numbered to demonstrate the correspondence. Although Purcell redistributes the subject entries, and exploits his larger ensemble to increase the overall density of imitation, both workings similarly generate an impressive texture by alternating regular entries on the first and fifth scale-degrees, restricting the combinations in play to the two resulting interlocks at the same repeated pitches. Both also use the flexed version of the subject on the first scale-degree freely, after earlier entries that were not flexed.

There is even a remarkable correspondence between the two works that perhaps hints at a more conscious transformation of Gibbons's piece on

Ex. 6.20(b) 'Amen'

Purcell's part: while, as stated, Gibbons freely flexes the answer in his working, he restricts the subject to its strict intervallic content throughout until bar 10, immediately before the cadence of this section, when the second treble part reaches up through a flexed subject entry to a climactic high *g″* (or *e″* at the pitch shown in Ex. 6.21). In his 'Amen' Purcell adopts exactly the same strategy, with the triadic shape of the flexed entry on A appearing in the soprano and first violin at bar 223 and leading – via a registrally climactic high *e″* treated, like Gibbons's *g″*, as a suspension over the pedal fifth degree below – into a cadential progression, now stretched over an additional bar in order to accommodate further entries in countertenor/second violin and tenor/trumpet 2. As in the Gibbons, this is the only time the answer is treated in this way, though Purcell does anticipate the move by flexing the answer differently in the soprano and first violin at bar 219, thereby forcing the only break in his regular minim-alternation of entries on first and fifth scale-degrees (since the expected entry on D at b. 220 is delayed to the second half of the bar, trumpet 2). It may not be too fanciful to suggest that this feint at the pre-cadential climax was inserted specifically to adjust the metrical placing of the final cadence of the section so that it would fall at the start of a bar.[21]

I suggested at the start of this chapter that we might understand the whole of this doxology as a kind of choral reimagination of Purcell's earlier fantazias – as if in Purcell's works of the 1690s the centre of gravity of the English contrapuntal style finally comes full circle, returning to its sixteenth-century origins in sacred music after a lengthy sojourn in the consort repertoire. There are certainly signs that Purcell planned the chorus carefully, with new

---

[21] A consideration with which Gibbons is unlikely to have been so concerned, especially since his working was not the end of a piece.

Ex. 6.21   Parallel score showing Gibbons, 'Hosanna to the Son of David' (a), and the Amen from Purcell's Jubilate in D (b)

materials for each section, contrasting passages of near-homophony at intervals (bars 180–82, 191–6) and varied cadence points (D at b. 182, b at 196, A
(D imperfect) at 212) – all features that can be observed in the fantazias of the
early 1680s. In this context, the use of the same contrapuntal idea for 'As it
was in the beginning' and the 'Amen' takes on a similar role to the *da capo*-like
reworking of materials discussed above in conjunction with Sonatas V and
VIII (1683), and Sonata II (1697), though it must be acknowledged that the
very strong motivic links between all four sections of this chorus if anything
undermine the extent to which this particular relationship comes across in
performance. (See, for example, the correspondence between the arpeggiated
opening of the subject at 'Glory be', b. 170, and the flexed version of the
'Amen' subject on the first scale-degree, b. 213; also the way in which the
soprano at 'As it was in the beginning', b. 182, rises through a fourth before
descending by step to begin another rising fourth, thereby anticipating the
augmented version of the 'World without end' subject (but in *arsin* form)
heard in b. 199.)

The severe restriction of tonal compass and pitch content necessary to
allow the participation of the trumpets arguably further diminishes the
significance of any such apparent connections. Harmonic restraint and
melodic suavity are often cited as key features of the Italianate, high-
Baroque character of Purcell's later music. However, the remarkable closeness of Purcell's 'Amen' to the similar working in Gibbons's 'Hosanna to
the son of David' serves as a reminder that relevant stylistic models could
also be found much closer to home: in a sense these choruses could be
thought of as a Purcellian equivalent of the *stile antico* choral fugue that was
to become so ubiquitous in the music of Bach and Handel, though I
suspect that Purcell maintained a direct connection with this earlier
manner to an extent that was not the case for later composers.

This can be seen in particular in the way that he actively sought materials
and techniques for his late choral music from his fantazias and other
earlier works, and to an extent in the works of other composers as well.
As Table 6.1 shows, nearly every choral passage in the D major Te Deum
and Jubilate derives closely from a model in Purcell's earlier music.
Occasionally, as in the case of 'Thou art the King' (Te Deum, b. 140)
the model is more recent – all of the interlocks of the two subjects used in
this section will be found among the combinations used in the canzona
from *Come ye Sons of Arts* analysed in Chapter 8, for example – but
otherwise only the canon for 'O go your way' in the Jubilate seems to be
completely new, presumably because it had to be freshly conceived according to a technique like that described by Christopher Simpson.[22]

---

[22] Simpson, *Compendium*, Part 5 ('The Contrivance of Canon'). Although Simpson does not discuss
canon 'Four Parts in One' specifically, the techniques he describes for 'Two Parts in One' (148–51)
and 'Three Parts in One' (152–4) hold equally good for four-part canons.

Table 6.1 Creative origins of choral passages in the Te Deum and Jubilate

Bar	Text	Origin
Te Deum		
29	'The Father everlasting'	In nomine II, bb. 1–10 (subject and some interlocks)
59	'Holy Lord God … Majesty of Thy glory'	In nomine II, bb. 49–end; also Fantazia V, bb. 22–5, Fantazia XI, bb. 22–3 (parts paired by shadowing in thirds and sixths; contrary motion)
140	'Thou art the King'	(*Cf Come ye Sons of Arts*, Canzona)
231	'Day by day … worship thy Name'	(*Cf The Fairy Queen*, Act IV, 'Sonata while the Sun Rises'; discussed below)
242	'Ever world without end'	In nomine II, bb. 29–33 (subject, several interlocks and *cantus firmus* treatment)
308	'Let me never be confounded'	(Some similarities with 'Ever world without end' above)
Jubilate		
106	'O go your way'	(Brand new canonic working)
170	'Glory be'	Locke, *Consort of Four Parts*: Fantazia I in F, bb.16–49 (subject, some interlocks, and working *per arsin et thesin*)
182	'As it was in the beginning'	Fantazia VI, bb. 62–82; Fantazia XI, bb. 1–24; In nomine II, bb. 10–22 (subject and interlocks, working *per arsin et thesin*; discussed above)
196	'World without end'	Fantazia XII, bb. 58–end (subject and interlocks, working *per arsin et thesin* and *per augmentation*)
213	'Amen'	O. Gibbons, 'Hosanna to the Son of David', bb. 1–11 (subject and several details of working, discussed above; also Fantazia VI, bb. 62–82; Fantazia XI, bb. 1–24; In nomine II, bb. 10–22)

Earlier on, I pointed out that Purcell's creative reworking of materials in this way drew on principles of imitation and emulation derived from approaches to creativity theorized at the time in relation to rhetorical practices. In effect, what I wish to suggest here is that in this creative re-working of materials from so many earlier works, Purcell is treating his earlier music as a kind of commonplace book.[23] The frequency with which In nomine II appears in Table 6.1 would suggest that he found this work especially useful in this context, though clearly some other works within *Lbl* Add. MS 30930 were also important. Indeed, it is perhaps worthy of note that nearly all of the music of the early 1680s and before on which he drew in the Te Deum and Jubilate came from what are believed to have been his own personal file copies: *Lbl* Add. MS 30930 for the Fantazias and other consort music, of course, but also (admitting examples from other composers) *Cfm* MS 88 for his score of Gibbons's 'Hosanna to the son of

---

[23] On the evidence for more conventional collecting practices relating to this tradition in Restoration music see Herissone, *Musical Creativity*, 5, 7, 16–25.

David', and *Lbl* Add. MS 17801 – which Purcell is thought to have owned after Locke's death – for Locke's *Consort of Four Parts*.[24]

In some of these later reworkings, as with the 'As it was' and 'Amen' from the Gloria in the Jubilate, Purcell seems to have lifted only the melodic subject and a limited range of imitative or contrapuntal fragments from the model, rather than subjecting them to the sort of rigorous re-examination we saw in the successive workings of the subject shared by Fantazias VI and XI and In nomine II. Much as with the example of the re-use of these materials in Sonata II (1697), it was enough that the same contrapuntal materials and techniques were reinterpreted in the new stylistic context. One final example in this chapter, however, demonstrates that far from simply selecting and re-using passages that already suited his needs, even in 1694 Purcell remained adept at identifying and exploiting unrealized potential in the materials of his earlier music.

The longest choral movement in the Te Deum is the passage from 'Day by day' to 'Ever world without end', a chorus in two main sections, the first of

Ex. 6.22   Te Deum in D, chorus 'Day by day' compared with part of the 'Sonata while the Sun Rises' from Act IV of *The Fairy Queen*

(a)   'Sonata', fourth section, opening (i); Te Deum, bb. 231–6 (ii)

[24] See Herissone, *Musical Creativity*, 104 (*Lbl* Add. MS 17801), 94–5, 216–17 (*Cfm* MS 88); also Shay and Thompson, *Purcell Manuscripts*, 43 (*Cfm* MS 88).

Ex. 6.22(b)   'Sonata', fourth section, bb. 34–6 (i); Te Deum bb. 236–9 (ii)

Ex. 6.22(c)   'Sonata', fifth section, opening (i); Te Deum, bb. 239–42 (ii)

which draws its techniques firmly from the 1690s: its close imitation of an arpeggio-derived subject, followed by antiphonal exchanges between trumpets and chorus/strings and then a homophonic convergence on the dominant via a brief chromatic digression (bb. 240–41), all closely parallel equivalents from the fourth and fifth sections of the 'Sonata while the Sun Rises' in Act IV of *The Fairy Queen* (see Ex. 6.22).[25] The next eighteen bars, however, are a most

---

[25] Incidentally, this setting of 'Day by day we magnify thee' is the previously unidentified source of the 'Alleluia' attributed to Purcell in several eighteenth-century printed volumes of anthems and psalmody, listed in Zimmerman's catalogue as N110. Who made the adaptation as an alleluia is

Ex. 6.23   Te Deum in D, chorus 'Ever world without end' compared with part of In nomine II

(a)   In nomine II, bb. 29–34

resourceful adaptation of materials taken from Purcell's favourite port of call in this work, In nomine II – and magisterially transformed from a simple passage, in a minor key, of *fugeing* against a *cantus firmus*, into a fine major-key working in four parts *per arsin et thesin* and *per augmentation*.

'Ever world without end' begins with a straightforward incorporation of the four entries of the subject heard in bars 29–31₃ of the In nomine (Ex. 6.23), the only substantive change being to the distribution of these entries ⓐ–ⓓ among the parts of the ensemble. The first sign of an increased level of artifice is the introduction of the inversion of this point in the bass in bar 246, as part of an interlock at the octave with the tenor (also inverted) a bar later. What happens over the ensuing double-augmented subject entry in the bass (which thus proceeds in semibreves) is as ingenious as it is exhilarating in performance: rather than inventing new counterpoint or seeking fortuitous imitative entries of the subject, Purcell looked for fragments of counterpoint in the In nomine which would serve just as well over this new '*cantus firmus*' (that is, the augmented entry).

Since the original *cantus firmus* fell from *a′* to *g′* in breves in bars 31–2 of the In nomine, the second treble line in bar 31 (when diminished by half) made an ideal counterpoint to the similar bass semibreve in bar 249 of the Te Deum (☒); Purcell's response to the additional stepwise descent in the

unknown, but it does not look sufficiently skilful to have been Purcell. Neither is the piece a canon in any strict sense, making Zimmerman's classification of it as a canon puzzling – especially given that the sources do not name it as such.

Ex. 6.23(b)   Te Deum, bb. 242–55

'*cantus firmus*' of the Te Deum was simply to repeat this bar in sequence in the countertenor part (x–2). The soprano and tenor parts in these bars follow the imported countertenor line from the In nomine in stretto *fuga*, made possible by its 'down 4/up 3' contour at the minim level, while the inverted entry of the subject at bar 250_3 seems to grow almost accidentally out of the repetition of this pattern in the countertenor part. (Whatever its origins, though, Purcell meant it to be noticed – hence its prominent doubling an octave higher in the second trumpet.) Finally, the two entries of the original version of the subject in soprano and countertenor in bars 252–4 may repeat the original interlock of this section, but they too follow voice-leading from the In nomine (y) in their relationship with the underlying double-augmented entry. This section of the Te Deum ends with a further four entries combining *arsin* and *thesin* forms of the subject over a fifth-degree pedal, before the instruments recall the arpeggiated subject of 'Day by day' over the final D major chord.

Such an extremely creative approach to the reworking of materials shows Purcell in full command of his technique, and reveals much about how he sought out and made use of suitable music from his earlier works. This passage is particularly interesting for the way in which he made use of music originally conceived against a *cantus firmus* in order to construct a passage of *fugeing* incorporating one of his favourite devices of the 1690s, a greatly augmented subject entry elaborating the arrival at an important structural dominant. And as so often, this augmentation has a specific textual prompt, the illustration of the words 'Ever world without end': an almost identical conceit to the example with which this chapter began, and one which leads directly into the further consideration of augmentation in Chapter 7.

CHAPTER 7

Augmentation as Artifice, Artifice as Augmentation

Some of the most conspicuous moments of artifice in Purcell's vocal music of the 1690s arise from the deployment of contrapuntal augmentation, or 'fugeing *per augmentation*' as Purcell calls it in 'The Art of Descant'. This chapter examines this phenomenon largely by delving again into the case of transformative self-borrowing identified at the start of Chapter 6: the relationship between the setting of 'World without end' in the orchestral Jubilate of 1694 and its antecedent – in terms of materials and contrapuntal treatment – in the last section of Fantazia XI. The technical resources necessary to devise such sustained passages of imitation *per augmentation* are worthy of consideration in their own right, and provide a fresh avenue for inquiry into Purcell's compositional choices. Moreover, the incorporation of such techniques into vocal music constitutes a rhetorical augmentation not just of the music on its own terms, but also of its ability to enhance the setting of text – much as I have observed elsewhere that Purcell used ground bass for similar ends.

Purcell's use of augmentation to increase the level of artifice in his later vocal works arguably appears to buck the widely recognized trend of increasingly Italianate stylistic influence in Purcell's mature style, instead harking back to his youthful preoccupation with arcane contrapuntal experiments. Martin Adams, in particular, is at pains to understand the best such examples as the fruits of Purcell's reconciliation of competing stylistic preoccupations. Perhaps the most famous case is the double fugue to the words 'Who whilst among the choir above/Thou dost thy former skill improve' in the second section of the closing chorus of *Hail, bright Cecilia*, as discussed in Chapter 5; a prime example of what Adams calls Purcell's 'consolidat[ion of] modern methods with that thoroughgoing polyphony which was so important to him'.[1] No less pervasive is the idea that such passages somehow redeem music otherwise weakened by the new tonal simplicity and apparent reliance on jingoistic bombast. Westrup, indeed, applied this argument to the very same passage from *Hail, bright Cecilia*,[2] and it persists in Adams's discussion

---

[1] Adams, *Henry Purcell*, 81.
[2] 'The finale . . . is weakened by the conventional jubilation of the orchestral fanfares. But there is a splendid moment when the subject of the fugato . . . is heard simultaneously in the bass in ponderous augmentation . . .': Westrup, *Purcell*, 191.

of the 1694 *Te Deum*: having generally concurred with Westrup's scathing criticism of the work's 'reliance on largely superficial effects' and 'disconnected structure', he concludes nevertheless that the work's 'forceful deployment of figuration and display of peerless technical skill deserve our acclaim'.[3]

It is perhaps worth considering whether this much later critical viewpoint might in fact preserve something of Purcell's own motivation for continuing to pursue such highly artificial techniques, as a way of compensating for the harmonic and tonal simplicity demanded by the new Italianate style and also, arguably, by the much more public nature of this later repertoire. This would certainly accord with the impression given by the preface to his 1683 *Sonnata's of III Parts*, and would also ring true with Arthur Bedford's later enthusiasm for what he identified as '*Intention of Mind*' (see Chapter 4). In another sense, however, it will emerge in the course of this chapter that the technical demands of augmentation themselves had a profound effect upon the aural impression of Purcell's music. Paradoxically, it was Purcell's very attempts to increase the rhetorical and contrapuntal artifice of his music – far beyond that to be found in any Italian model – that caused it to sound in the end so uncompromisingly 'Italian'.

THE TECHNICAL DEMANDS OF FUGEING PER AUGMENTATION

Fugal writing is so common in Purcell's choruses after the late 1680s that it is easily forgotten that such techniques, especially handled with such refinement and including multiple subjects and melodic inversion almost as a matter of course, were relatively unusual in the music of his close English contemporaries. Given this situation, the comparatively small number of these works that feature augmentation makes a convenient subset of passages 'marked' as more complex, while also offering a useful analytical window into the techniques required to compose such music. An examination of the technical resources behind the deployment of contrapuntal augmentation in the Fantazias and Sonatas will prepare the way for an examination of the same techniques in later choral works.

While not as common in the early instrumental music as the near-ubiquitous *fugeing per arsin et thesin* (by inversion), *fugeing per augmentation* [*sic*] is nevertheless frequently found both in Purcell's fantazias and in his two sets of trio sonatas (see Table 7.1). When it comes to understanding how such passages were composed, three principal techniques seem instructive: firstly, the incorporation of augmented entries derived through a process of contrapuntal research and experimentation, much as I have shown for simple *fugeing* in earlier chapters; secondly, the simultaneous

---

[3] Adams, *Henry Purcell*, 191.

Table 7.1 *Fugeing per augmentation* in the Fantazias and Sonatas

Work (key)	Movement	Bars	Remarks
Four-part Fantazias			
Fantazia IV (g)		9–18_3	
Fantazia VIII (d)		12_3–15_3	
Fantazia XI (G)		4_3–18_2	Rhythmically free
		32–50	Rhythmically free
Fantazia XII (d)		58–99	Whole of last section
1683 Sonatas			
Sonata II (Bb)	1	17_3–20_1	
Sonata VI (C)	1	1–47	Whole movement
Sonata VII (e)	1	1–26	Whole movement
Sonata X (A)	4	124_2–6_1	Augmented entry truncated
1697 Sonatas			
Sonata III (a)	1	1–7_1	
	3	61–7	Prefigured in bb. 54_3–56_2
Sonata IV (d)	2	57_4–9_3	
Sonata IX (F)	1	1–26	Whole movement; see discussion below

derivation of multiple imitative parts at different levels of augmentation, following a modified version of contemporary procedures for devising strict canons; and, thirdly, treatment of greatly augmented subject entries as *cantus firmus* lines with conventional *fugeing* devised against them. This first section of the chapter will take each of these techniques in turn, explaining them through specific examples from Purcell's early instrumental music.

(a) Contrapuntal Research with Pre-Existing Subjects

A simple instance of the incorporation of a near-exact augmented entry has already been discussed briefly in Chapter 2: twelve bars into the first section of Fantazia VIII, Purcell accompanied a statement of interlock G (see p. 69), T:T ♩, in the inner parts, with an entry of the same form of the subject a fourth higher, augmented to double the note-values (Ex. 2.12, b. 13). As noted before, the feature that marks this out as an instance of augmentation researched from pre-existing subjects is the fact that Purcell was forced to shorten the length of the first note of the augmented entry (shown shaded in Ex. 7.1) in order to avoid an unresolved dissonance in the treble with the ab' in the second tenor; to compensate, Purcell cleverly preceded the treble augmented entry with a long note on the same pitch. As

Ex. 7.1   Fantazia VIII, bb. 12–16: rhythmic modification of augmented entry necessitated by existing interlock

we shall see in the coming pages, in the construction of *fugeing per augmentation* by design Purcell found it no problem to devise subjects that could imitate by augmentation – that is, overlap with statements of the original subject – in exact form. That he did not in this instance suggests that it was instead the result of experimentation with a subject whose pitch content and rhythmic profile were already determined – perhaps even that it was arrived at serendipitously in the course of the creative process.

Such an element of opportunism also seems to be in evidence in the treatment of augmentation at the beginning of Fantazia XI: as well as the extremely dense *fugeing* on the main subject *per arsin et thesin* examined already in Chapter 6, the first 17 bars incorporate ten loosely augmented entries of the subject, in which the initial dotted-minim–crotchet figure remains unchanged but the ensuing stepwise motion through a fourth proceeds at a slower pace (these are shown in black in Ex. 7.2).[4] The idea to treat this subject in augmentation perhaps arose first from an attempted simultaneous interlock $A:T^{-8}$, in which the parts would collide on an unprepared second on the fifth note. By augmenting the *thesin* entry, however, Purcell could create a useful cadential fragment, which he then treats as a module, $\boxed{M}$; this is stated three times, as shown in the shading in Ex. 7.2. Nearly all of the elements of $\boxed{M}$ are in fact also present (in inversion) between treble 1 and bass as early as bars 2–3.

Whatever the origins of these augmentations, however, it is clear that their melodic identity as subject entries is crucial to Purcell's conception of the piece. In the first place, this is evident from the role they play in the harmonic planning of the opening section. From bar 5 to bar 13, this

[4] The augmentation to quadruple note-values marked in the tenor at bar 9 is an exception to this remark about the beginning of the subject: here, the initial dotted-note figure is apparently absent, though it can be heard in double note-values beginning with the bass d at bar 8 and moving to the tenor d at bar 8_4, when both parts suddenly exchange registers.

Ex. 7.2   Fantazia XI, bb. 1–18: incorporation of loosely augmented entries alongside
main subject

unfolds as a progression flatwards around the circle of fifths, initiated by
$\boxed{M}$ in bars 4–5 and continued as far as F major in the restatement of $\boxed{M}$
a tone lower, in the same parts in bars 11–12. Between these statements of
$\boxed{M}$ is a long ascending scale in the bass initiated by the double-augmented
entry in bar 6, and passing into the tenor during bar 8. The circle-of-fifths
pattern is arrested by a turn to the relative minor of F, which becomes D
major and heralds a third statement of $\boxed{M}$, in bars 15–16, now placed
more prominently in treble 1 and bass. The very brief return to G major
that results in bar 16 then serves as the starting-point for a second,
unrelated harmonic process, which balances the previous flatwards motion

Ex. 7.3   Fantazia XI: recurrence of subject from first section in last section
(a)   bb. 31–9

by proceeding in the opposite direction (from A minor via E minor to B minor; see Ex. 6.15b).

Secondly, and perhaps even more persuasively, it is the augmented version of the subject of this first section that reappears as one of three subjects in the final section of this same fantazia, a unique instance in the fantazias of the kind of thematic link between sections also explored in trio sonatas such as Sonatas V and VIII (1683), and Sonata II (1697).[5] This link could be made through these augmented forms alone (see the black notes in Ex. 7.3a), but Purcell pushes the point home by including further versions of the same subject as the final section progresses (Ex. 7.3b): the original form *thesin* in the bass (b. 40$_2$) and tenor (b. 41$_4$), several augmented entries of varying rhythmic precision (*thesin,* tr. 1 b. 41$_2$; *arsin,* bass b. 41$_3$; *thesin,* bass b. 45; *thesin,* ten. b. 46$_2$), and even a fleeting diminished statement *thesin* on the second crotchet of bar 49 (tr. 2). Though most of these combine with one or both of the other quaver-based subjects of this section, Purcell approaches the final cadence with a closing imitative flourish in the form of a tenor and

---

[5] Peter Holman finds further thematic links between sections in Fantazias V and IX (*Henry Purcell,* 82–3), though in each case these constitute less systematic melodic resemblances rather than the kind of careful contrapuntal reworking and recontextualization I observe in Fantazia XI.

Ex. 7.3(b)   bb. 40–43, 45–50

bass duet in bar 48 that reimagines the original module M of the first section by augmenting the bass *arsin* entry instead of the tenor *thesin* statement (Ex. 7.3b).

What these passages in Fantazias VIII and XI show is that the augmentation of melodic subjects whose rhythm and contour are fixed in advance almost inevitably involves a degree of compromise, for all that Purcell goes to some lengths to ensure that the subject *per augmentation* remains recognizable. Yet despite its less exacting requirements in terms of melodic identity, this method of incorporating augmentation into a passage of *fugeing* – by research and experimentation – remains fundamental to all of Purcell's imitative writing involving augmentation, inasmuch as it allowed him to explore further potential combinations even when dealing with materials derived through the conceit of augmentation from the start. It is to this conceit that we now turn, in order to see how Purcell was able to derive much stricter augmentations: by designing them into the materials from the start of the creative process.

(b) Canonic Invention

Perhaps the most extreme example of artifice through *fugeing per augmentation* is the celebrated opening of Sonata VI (1683) in C major, a strict canon three in one combining the subject with simultaneous entries in twofold and fourfold augmentation (Ex. 7.4). Successive commentators have cited this passage as the quintessence of Purcell's continued obsession with formal counterpoint in the sonatas – and evidence of his mastery of the craft – yet few seem to have considered it from a compositional perspective. Indeed, as we shall see, it is arguably not the opening that would have cost the most compositional effort, but rather the ensuing 38 bars, in which these same materials were exhaustively probed using the methods of research and experimentation described above.

The aura of near-mystical contrapuntal facility that attaches to this opening is perhaps unsurprising given the conventional emphasis on the compositional priority of imitative subjects: theorists from Morley's time up to and including both Simpson and Purcell consistently stated that the first stage in writing a passage of *fugeing* was to select a point consisting of several notes, to serve as the subject. Yet it does not take much consideration to realize that the arbitrary or fortuitous selection of a point of imitation is almost vanishingly unlikely to yield material susceptible to simultaneous presentation in prime, twofold- and fourfold-augmented forms. Rather than simply marvel at Purcell's unerring ability to select a fully-formed subject suited to his purpose, then, we can seek an explanation elsewhere in contemporary theory; specifically, in the extremely helpful description given by Christopher Simpson of the method for deriving canons by working concurrently in multiple parts:

Ex. 7.4   Sonata VI (1683), first movement: opening platform

... first set down the Beginning Notes of each Part ... That being done, the first business is, to fill up the second Bar of the Leading Part, with some Note or Notes which may agree with that Part which came in next after it; and add the said Note or Notes to [the end of] each of the other Parts ... Then fil [*sic*] up the third Bar of the Leading Part ... still adding the said Note or Notes to [the end of] the other Parts. And thus you are to do from Bar to Bar.

... But if you perceive that your following Parts begin to run counter one upon another by these additional Notes; you must then try some other way; either by putting in a Rest, or by altering the course or Notes of the Leading Part ...[6]

The difficulties of composing the opening of the C major sonata become far less daunting under these conditions, since the material with which to create the canon can be developed step by step, working perhaps one or two notes at a time and in all voices concurrently, in order that the contrapuntal implications of each decision can be grasped immediately. Indeed, it is quite possible to reconstruct the process by which Purcell might have arrived at this passage by following Simpson's method almost exactly. In Ex. 7.5 the canon is built up by stages beginning from the initial selection of pitches and levels of augmentation, in such a way that an addition or alteration to one part is replicated at the end of each of the two remaining parts (indicated in square brackets). As Simpson predicted, Purcell's successive additions to the subject would have demanded alterations to the existing material (as in Ex. 7.5e) or precluded particular continuations that would have been otherwise desirable (Ex. 7.5d). Furthermore, the additional complication of the two levels of augmentation – not discussed anywhere by Simpson – meant that some notes had to serve equally well in different functional contexts (Ex. 7.5e).

Understood in this way, the opening of Sonata VI is a valuable demonstration of the derivation of contrapuntal materials from the very process of contriving counterpoint. As Simpson implies, although the technique he describes is directed towards the construction of extended canons, it is no less useful in the design of shorter subjects for fugal treatment:

I am the more inclined to offer unto you this little Essay upon [the making of a Canon], because the exercise thereof will much enable you in all other kinds of Composition; especially where any thing of Fuge is concerned, of which, it is the principal.[7]

Having devised his materials through the construction of this opening canon, though, Purcell still had the rest of the movement to compose. It was at this point that his creative process reverted to something more like the procedure of research and experimentation traced earlier in this chapter and, indeed, throughout his extended fugal writing. The remainder of the piece consists of a series of secondary imitative inventions apparently designed to probe the ability of the (now fixed) subject to combine with its two augmentations in different configurations. As Table 7.2 shows,

[6] Simpson, *Compendium*, 152–3.   [7] Ibid., 147.

Ex. 7.5   Sonata VI (1683), first movement:
hypothetical reconstruction of composition of opening platform

(a)   Opening pitches and relative note-values

(b)   Bass, b. 1 'filled up', and other parts continued accordingly

(c)   Continuation of bass in sixths with violin 1

(d)   Continuation of rising scale prohibited in violin 2 by violin 1; interpolation of falling third

(e)   Resolution of implied suspension in violin 2, b. 3

Resolution of suspension (i.e. consonant)

Accented passing note (i.e. dissonant)

(f)   Addition of passing notes (final form of canon)

these inventions encompass what appear to be a number of specific imitative aims, the results of which are carefully disposed within the movement. Perhaps Purcell's first priority was to consider alternative combinations of the subject with its simultaneous twofold and fourfold augmentations; like the augmentations explored above in Fantazias VIII and XI the resulting inventions both required compromise, but their importance is nevertheless evident from the way that Purcell used them to articulate a simple harmonic structure, with invention **E** appearing in the dominant and invention **G** marking the return to C major. A second process of research appears to have involved the attempted combination of the original subject, in two parts creating *stretto fuga*, with a third part carrying the subject in augmentation; this process, described in Ex. 7.6, produced the compromised but usable inventions **B** and **C**, before arriving at the successful invention **D** – which Purcell again highlighted by placing it at the start of a new section beginning in G major (b. 18). The remaining inventions shown in Table 7.2 all incorporate two-voice elements extracted from other inventions, supplemented with a third part either shadowing one or other of the structural voices (**F, J, K**) or exploring a new imitative relationship (**H**).[8]

The use of canonic technique to invent fugal materials suitable for augmentation in this way is not unique to this sonata: indeed, the very next sonata of the 1683 set, Sonata VII in E minor, has an opening movement that combines a similar approach to augmentation (this time at only two levels) with entries *per arsin et thesin*. This movement incorporates many combinations that must be the product of research carried out after the invention of the opening augmentation canon on the subject *thesin*, a canon that must have been deliberately – and ingeniously – contrived from the start to permit its wholesale intervallic and melodic inversion (b. 5, transposed to the dominant). Then there are the isolated instances in which a fugal invention *per augmentation* is stated at the outset without being developed further: at the words 'He hath shewed strength with his arm', in the Magnificat from the Service in B♭ major, for example, or at the start of Sonata III (1697) in A minor, in which a brief invention involving the augmentation of the first violin line two octaves lower in the bass is used as the start of a harmonic proposition phrase, and consequently repeated a fourth lower four bars later.

A more unusual example is provided by the 'Golden' Sonata, no. IX (1697), in which the opening derives from what appears to be an attempt at *fugeing per augmentation* on a subject closely related to that of the last section of Fantazia XII. As Ex. 7.7a shows, the violin parts at the start outline a much-modified, augmented version of the sequential pattern in the bass; the melody in the violins might seem to be fatally compromised

---

[8] Though in fact, since the first violin and bass entries in **H** never overlap, it might be better to think of **H** as a two-voice interlock joined to the following three-voice invention **J** by the entry of 2S+5 in the second violin, which continues intact from bar 39_3 to bar 43_1.

Table 7.2 Imitative inventions in the first movement of Sonata VI (1683)

Invention	Key	Bar	Configuration	Comments
A	C	1 $\quad$ 1_3 $\quad$ 1	4S $\quad$ 2S+5 $\quad$ S	Original canonic invention combining S, 2S and 4S
B	C	11_2 $\quad$ 11_3 $\quad$ 12	S+5 (altered; see below) $\quad$ S (altered; see below) $\quad$ 2S	Attempt to combine S in *stretto fuga* with 2S
C	C	14_3 $\quad$ 14_2 $\quad$ 12	S+4 $\quad$ S (much alt.; see below) $\quad$ 2S	*Cf* **B**: second attempt to combine S in *stretto fuga* with 2S
D	G	19 $\quad$ 18_2 $\quad$ 18_3	2S+5 $\quad$ S+5 $\quad$ S	*Cf* **B** and **C**: successful attempt to combine S in *stretto fuga* with 2S
E	G	19 $\quad$ 21 $\quad$ 21	2S+5 $\quad$ S (note 6 stretched) $\quad$ 4S (note 1 compressed)	*Cf* **A**: attempted second canon combining S, 2S and 4S
F	(V of) G	27_3 $\quad$ 28 $\quad$ 28	2S+5 (notes 1–3 compr.) $\quad$ (2S+3) (note 1 delayed) $\quad$ 2S (notes 1–6 only)	Based on 2S in *stretto fuga* (Vn1+BC); Vn2 shadows BC at tenth (attempted 3-voice interlock using 2S?)
G	C	30_3 $\quad$ 31 $\quad$ 31	2S (nn.1–2 compr., 3 str.) $\quad$ 4S+5 $\quad$ S (note 8 stretched)	*Cf* **E**: more successful canon combining S, 2S and 4S; additional S+5 (becoming 2S+5 (alt.)) in bass at 33
H	C	39_2 $\quad$ 39_3 $\quad$ 41_3	S $\quad$ 2S+5 $\quad$ S	Violins *cf* **G** (note-values halved)
J	C	42 $\quad$ 42 $\quad$ 41_3	2S+5 $\quad$ (2S+7) $\quad$ S	S and 2S+5 (BC+Vn1) from **A** (Vn2 shadows Vn1 at third)
K	C	42 $\quad$ 42 $\quad$ 42_3	2S+5 $\quad$ (2S+7) (notes 1–2 compr.) $\quad$ 2S (starts at note 3, b. 43_3)	*Cf* **F**: 2S in *stretto fuga* (Vn1+BC) again, but now Vn2 shadows Vn1 at third

S=subject, 2S=augmented subject, 4S=double-augmented subject; 'Configuration' column lists contents of parts in the order Vn1/Vn2/BC

were it not that Purcell makes clear the relationship in the second half of bar 3, when the breaking of the bass pattern allowed the augmented version to proceed unaltered for the first time (the same happens in the bass in the bar following the end of the example). The roles are then reversed from bar 4 onwards. The segmented lines in the example pick out the notes of the subject shared with Fantazia XII, here disguised by a sequentially repeating, upward-fourth anacrusis and the filling in of the falling fourths; the presence of the basic pattern from Fantazia XII is nevertheless clear, and made more so by its diminution to unadorned quavers at the end of bar 6. The rest of this first movement proceeds to research alternative

Ex. 7.6   Sonata VI (1683), first movement

(a)   Properties of material

(b)   Unsuccessful combination with augmented entry (bass), demanding alterations to both parts of stretto *fuga* (Vn1/2)

(c)   Further unsuccessful combination; one part of stretto *fuga* (Vn1) left intact

(d)   Successful combination of stretto *fuga* (Vn2/bass) and augmented entry (Vn1)

combinations of these three related elements, in prime and inverted forms. The identification of the role of this subject in the conception of this movement is also key to the recognition of another, hitherto unremarked case of Purcell's reworking of the same materials in multiple movements of the same sonata: two successive statements of the same four-note motif *thesin* provide the bass over which eight bars of the second-movement

Ex. 7.7   'Golden' Sonata, no. IX (1697): augmentation as a creative impetus

(a)   First movement, opening (bb.1–7)

(b)   Second movement, bb. 37–44

(c)   Last movement, opening (bb. 124–35)

Adagio are composed (Ex. 7.7b), after a briefer appearance *arsin* in the violins in bars 3–5 of this movement; it then makes occasional appearances in the canzona, before providing the first subject of a triple-invertible complex for the final fugue (Ex. 7.7c).

One final instance of augmentation probably conceived canonically concerns the opening of Fantazia IV, in which the canonically invented augmentation appears not at the head of the movement, as in all of these instances from the Sonatas, but fourteen bars into the music, where it provides an artificial climax much like that provided by the *stretto fuga* invention beginning at bar 16 of Fantazia VIII (see Chapter 2, pp. 57–8). The passage concerned (Ex. 7.8) places a fourfold augmentation in the second tenor, against which the prime subject appears five more times in the surrounding imitation (three *thesin*, then two *arsin*). Purcell even prepares for this extreme augmentation by placing twofold-augmented entries in the treble (b. 9, *thesin*) and bass (b. 11, *arsin/thesin* hybrid) in the preceding bars. Tellingly, however, neither overlaps substantially with any other entries: these augmentations are not imitatively conceived, suggesting that the canonic invention at bar 14 had compositional priority.

The passage in Ex. 7.8 might easily have been invented using the canonic process described above for Sonata VI (1683), but there is at least one crucial detail in the Fantazia that suggests a useful shortcut to

Ex. 7.8   Fantazia IV, bb.14–19: canonically conceived fourfold augmentation (ten.)

similar results: unlike that in the Sonata, the first note of the subject is comparatively long, to the extent that its fourfold augmentation produces a single note of greater duration than the entire subject in prime form. This single feature could have enabled Purcell to plan the melodic content of the subject from the start in order to permit the climactic treatment heard from bar 14, without actually having to write it out note by note. All that was required was to select the structural pitches of the subject solely from those consonant with its own first note: if we disregard the passing notes, the subject proceeds, as predicted by this observation, to the third and then the fifth below (in its *thesin* form), before returning via the third to the unison (and when stated *arsin*, to the third and fifth above and back). In effect the degree of augmentation combined with the choice of a long first note has transformed the canonic conceit here into one in which Purcell's main task was the composition of *fugeing* against an internal pedal – or rather, a series of pedals on the pitches of the subject. This is a *cantus firmus* in all but name, which leads to the third and final method by which *fugeing per augmentation* could be devised.

(c) *Augmentation and* cantus firmus *Technique*

This is the kind of contrapuntal invention most relevant to the artificial climax of the last section of Fantazia XII: the augmentation to eightfold note-values causes the subject to function as a *cantus firmus* (highlighted in Ex. 7.9) against which Purcell incorporates *fugeing* on the original subject (in crotchets).[9] Much of the structural and harmonic planning of these final bars is thus determined at a very early stage, since the music is constrained by the successive statements of the augmented subject *arsin* starting on the key-note (D, b. 79, ten 2) and then *thesin* starting on the fourth scale-degree (G, b. 88, ten 1). An additional, unusual property of this subject is that its inversion is intervallically equivalent with its retro-grade, thus creating a large-scale palindromic design in the *cantus firmus* that is interrupted only by the transposition at the moment of its migration from the first to the second tenor. The degree of influence that this has on the harmony is evident even in the range of keys implied, from E♭ major at bar 87 as far as E minor in bars 94–5. The latter is caused by the arrival on *b*♮ in the first tenor in bar 94; a bass entry beginning an octave lower in bar 95 (now augmented only to fourfold note-values) ends on a low *D*, enabling Purcell to create the effect of a large-scale *tierce de Picardie*.

Purcell's harmonic treatment of this passage will be the subject of further comment much later on in relation to his later handling of such grossly

---

[9] Martin Adams too describes this section as 'more or less in cantus firmus style' (*Henry Purcell*, 99); what follows in in large part an attempt to flesh out this passing insight into a more sustained analytical investigation of the usefulness of *cantus firmus* techniques in understanding Purcell's approach to augmentation.

Ex. 7.9   Fantazia XII, bb. 78–99: eightfold and fourfold augmentation

augmented subject entries – such as in the 'World without end' passage from the Gloria of the Jubilate in D. Of greater interest in the present context are the technical resources that permitted him to devise successful *fugeing* against these *cantus firmus*-like augmentations of subjects composed, or selected, expressly for the purpose. In order to understand this better, we can begin by looking at a similar example in which we nevertheless know that the pitch content of the subjects was to some degree fixed from the start of the compositional process: Purcell's six-part In nomine I.

As Holman and Adams both note, the six-part In nomine adopts a particularly arcane form of *cantus firmus* technique in which each of the three imitative subjects is derived closely from the chant that serves as the foundation of the piece.[10] The different intervallic properties of the three subjects in fact had a profound effect on the approach to *fugeing* that Purcell was able to take in each section, the reasons for which will help to illuminate the selection of his subjects in other cases (like Fantazia XII) where the potential for augmentation is designed in from the start.

In the first section of the In nomine (bb. 1–14) Purcell based his subject on the first five pitches of the *cantus firmus* (shaded in Ex. 7.10), four of which are repeated later on in the chant, up a fifth; this conveniently built-in feature was no doubt a factor in his selection of this fragment for imitation, though as the opening of the chant it is the obvious place to start. Each of the other parts has a single entry of the subject based on these pitches (shown with black noteheads). Purcell seems to have designed the subject primarily around the two-voice interlock heard at the start of the third treble and second tenor parts, using a canzona-like rhythm to establish the metre and extending the fifth note of the leading part to create a suspension, which when stated in the following part overlaps with a new entry in the second treble.

Only after this opening does the *cantus firmus* begin, and against it Purcell brings in the remaining two parts with singleton entries (b. 6_3, bass; b. 11, tr. 1). This is despite the fact that, remarkably, at least one segment of the chant would combine with *fugeing* in two voices simultaneously: an additional entry on G in the second half of bar 10 is perfectly possible, and indeed in bars 11_4 to 12_4 the second tenor even accompanies the first treble entry with a fragment of counterpoint from the opening interlock, completing a module first heard in the third treble and second tenor in bars 2_2–3_2 (as shown in Ex. 7.10). Purcell may have been aware of the imitative possibility, given that he incorporated the module – indeed, given the pattern proposed elsewhere in his consort music we might even propose that the invention of the opening interlock against this portion of the chant represents the creative origin of the subject materials. If so, the absence of a complete statement of the interlock at this point in the *cantus firmus* is curious. Perhaps in the end he decided to prioritise the harmonic shift towards D minor, which the interlock would have precluded, as a counterbalance to the C minor of bars 6–8; or perhaps he was concerned with the strict presentation of just one subject entry in each part, in contrast with the denser imitation of the succeeding sections. Alternatively, it may be that he designed the opening interlock independently and the particular combination I have described simply never occurred to him. In which case, it might be argued, the omission of this viable combination here only

[10] Holman, *Henry Purcell*, 85; Adams, *Henry Purcell*, 11, 95. On the origins and characteristics of the In nomine see Gustave Reese, 'The Origin of the English "In Nomine"', *JAMS*, 2/1 (1949), 7–22; Robert Donington and Thurston Dart, 'The Origin of the In Nomine', *ML*, 30/2 (1949), 101–6; and, at greater length, Robert Weidner, 'The Early *In Nomine*: A Genesis of Chamber Music' (unpublished PhD thesis, University of Rochester, 1960).

Ex. 7.10   In nomine I, complete: *fugeing* based on *cantus firmus* in all three sections

Ex. 7.10 (cont.)

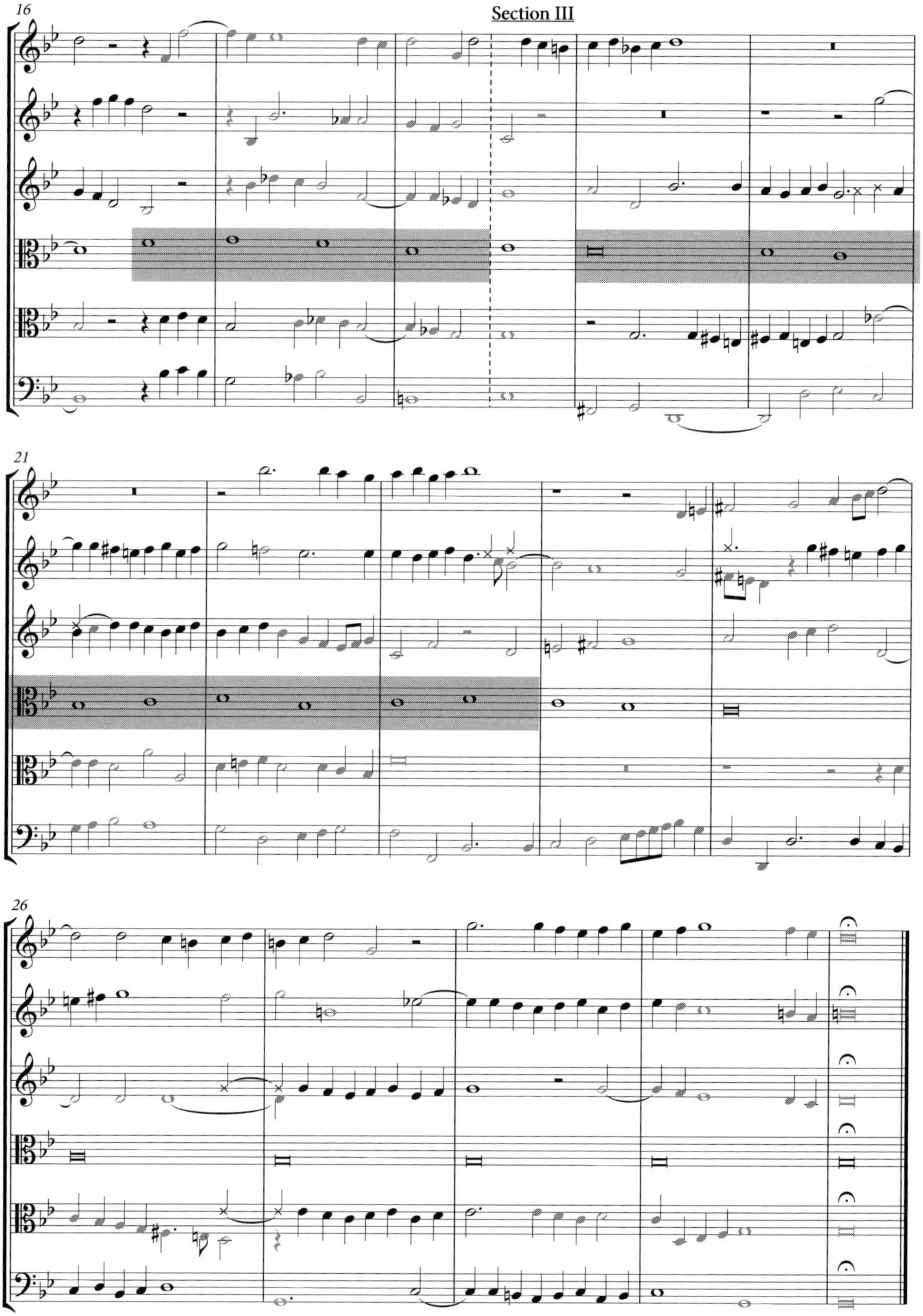

strengthens the proposition that when they do occur, the most artificial interlocks and subject complexes are there by design: they do not arise fortuitously.

Leaving aside Section II for a moment, and regardless of the situation in Section I, Purcell seems to have been considerably more ambitious in contrapuntal terms in Section III of this In nomine. The subject chosen is considerably longer, spanning eight notes of the plainsong, and Purcell combines it into several different two-part interlocks – even one in three parts – against the *cantus firmus* (see Ex. 7.10, bb. 18₃–30). Part of the reason why this works well, and one that will be highly relevant when it comes to the original derivation of materials in Fantazia XII and elsewhere, is that the level of augmentation (or rather diminution in this case) is much greater than in Section I: a semibreve in the plainsong becomes a crotchet in the imitative subject, for the most part, so that the prevailing note-values are much shorter than the harmonic rhythm implied by the *cantus firmus*.

This feature makes it particularly straightforward to construct *fugeing* against an extended pedal note, as in bars 25–6 (two breves on *a* in the *cantus firmus*) and 27–30 (four successive breves on *g*). Indeed, the paradigm here is probably the closing three bars, in which the main two-part interlock, $S^{+5,\,\downarrow}$, appears in the bass and first treble parts, the bass shadowed up a tenth in the second treble, and the first treble shadowed down a tenth in the second tenor. This same interlock accounts for the pairs of entries in bars 20–21 (tr. 2/3), 22–3 (tr. 1/2) and 25–6 (tr. 2/bass), while that in bars 19–20 (ten. 2/tr. 3) uses the version $S^{+3,\,\downarrow}$, equivalent to the bass and second tenor in bars 27–9.

A closer look at the *cantus firmus* itself in this piece, however, reveals the level of compromise involved here in the treatment of the chant; comparable, indeed, to the other augmentations composed by experimentation and research examined earlier on. The version of the In nomine plainsong used in this piece by Purcell is isolated in Ex. 7.11. Since we do not know what Purcell's source was for the chant, it is difficult to be certain about the form in which he found it, but the much greater similarity of the version Purcell used in his other In nomine (of seven parts) to the original found in Taverner's Mass permits a number of striking observations about Purcell's manipulation of the chant in his six-part work, particularly in relation to the derivation of usable materials for *fugeing* and its maintenance against the plainsong in the final work.

One of the notable features of the *cantus firmus* in the six-part In nomine is its comparatively short note-values (semibreves rather than breves), and the opportunity this presents for audible rhythmic effects (most often achieved by Purcell through the grouping together of repeated pitches into sustained notes, but also notably through the doubling of the length of the first note of the chant, thereby making the start of the *cantus firmus* closer to an exact rhythmic augmentation of the opening point of

Ex. 7.11   The In nomine *cantus firmus* in three versions: (a) John Taverner, Mass 'Gloria tibi Trinitas', Benedictus (beginning at the words 'In nomine Domini'); (b) As in In nomine II; (c) As in In nomine I

imitation). Furthermore, the long pedals at the end of the piece that facilitated such dense imitative entries are to some extent imposed upon the original chant: both of Purcell's In nomines omit note 52 of the original plainsong and extend the final pitch repetitions, so that whereas Taverner's *cantus firmus* closes with three breves of D, Purcell's seven-part work concludes with six breves, and his six-part work with eight semibreves' worth of final G (after a chant presented mainly in semibreves). In addition, the six-part work also quadruples the comparative length of note 50. It seems logical to attribute these characteristics of Purcell's six-part work directly to the intensity of imitative work he was attempting in these closing bars. Meanwhile, the omission of notes 45–9 of the plainsong in the In nomine of six parts (despite their presence in the seven-part work) probably had a harmonic and structural rationale, since the deployment of the main interlock $S^{+5, \, \downarrow}$ against this portion of the chant would have extended the B♭ major reached in bar 23 by another 5 bars, incorporating a strong local inflection further flatwards towards E♭ major and additionally demanding a repetition of the already prominent subject entry on *bb''* (tr. 1, b. 22).

One more change is even more important, though, in terms of imitative invention: the omission of notes 34 and 35 of the chant (again these are present in the seven-part work). This omission is directly related to the success of the *fugeing* in bars 20–23, when the *cantus firmus* is more mobile, since neither the interlocks beginning at bar 20_4 (tr. 2/3) nor bar 22_2 (tr. 1/2) would combine acceptably with the relevant notes of the plainsong if their component subject entries included these additional pitches as

Ex. 7.12   In nomine I, Section III: subject interlock with implied voice-leading (below)

crotchets. Their omission allowed Purcell to create a subject inter-lock elaborating simple two-part motion in semibreves (Ex. 7.12), ideally suited to combination with a *cantus firmus* that itself moves stepwise up and down within the compass of a third (Ex. 7.10, bb. 19–23). Here as elsewhere, then, Purcell compromised pre-existing materials – in this case, through the omission of the two corresponding notes from the chant – in order to maintain the artificial relationship between the *cantus firmus* and the subject in the final work.

If the first and last sections of In nomine I both involved a process of contrapuntal experimentation and, correspondingly, compromise of mat-erials, it was in the shorter Section II that Purcell hit upon a section of the chant that could be treated strictly with very little pre-compositional research required (see Ex. 7.10, bb. 14_3–18_2). The *fugeing* here is based on a four-note fragment encompassing notes 25–8 of the plainsong. Already conspicuous by their status as the registral peak of the chant, these notes are also ideal for the construction of close imitations, forming a series of entries at the unison and octave a minim apart. This works against the plainsong because of the level of diminution in the subject, making it short enough to be repeated several times against the *d'* in the *cantus firmus* in bars 15–16, and because all four notes are consonant both with this note and with (and indeed, in the case of the Gs, because of) the bass *B♭'* that supports it. When the plainsong again becomes more mobile, in its own statement of this sequence of pitches in bars 16_3–18_2, the density of subject entries against it drops considerably, with only the bass entry at the fifth below (b. 16_3) and its shadow at the third in the second tenor.

It is the principle established in bars 15–16, though, which brings us closest to the method by which Purcell conceived of the *cantus firmus*-like *fugeing per augmentation* at the end of Fantazia XII: both passages employ principles derived from the composition of canons in unison (and octaves) against a plainsong. The advantage of this method was that, unlike any of the techniques explored so far in this chapter, it offered a set of melodic characteristics that would allow Purcell to compose a subject in advance that would be susceptible to close *fugeing* against a plainsong derived from a grossly augmented version of itself. Once again, it is Christopher

Simpson who gives the most insight into the demands of this kind of composition.

The relevant passage of Simpson's *Compendium of Practical Musick* is his discussion 'Of Canon in Unison', which begins with the observation that such canons can be composed in the same way as I explored above in connection with the opening of Sonata VI (1683): 'that is to say, The Leading Part must be accommodated to the following Part, when it comes in; and to both Parts when they sound together'.[11] Simpson goes on to observe that because in canons at the unison all three parts begin on the same note ('Tone'),

> ... it necessarily follows, that the foregoing Parts must move into the Concords of the said Tone; either ascending or descending; and by this means the Sound of the same Tone will be continued so long as the Parts move in the Concords of that Key.[12]

Here, then, is a shortcut to the composition of a successful canon, since as long as one restricts oneself to intervals consonant with the first note of the leading part (illustrated with the example shown in Fig. 7.1a), one can be sure of producing successful canon. In reality the situation is not quite so simple. Simpson's verbal instructions hold good for leading parts constructed solely of pitches taken from a root-position triad on the first note of the subject, but Fig. 7.1a is not so restrictive, admitting the sixth as well as the fifth scale-degrees. Close examination of Fig. 7.1b, Simpson's worked example of the principle – actually composed out closely from Fig. 7.1a – reveals the additional condition that must be met in order for this collection of pitches to yield successful canon: if adjacent pitches in the scale are to be used without need for fully notated trials, the leading part must confine the even- and odd-numbered pitches (by interval from the first note) of the pair of notes concerned, respectively, to the same part of the *tactus* throughout. Thus in the first four bars of Fig. 7.1b, in which the 'root' is *g*, all *d*'s (a fifth higher) occur on the first or third beats of bars, while *eb*'s (a sixth higher) occupy the second or fourth; in bars 5–8$_2$ the 'root' is *d'*, and all *f♯*s and *a*s (respectively sixths and fourths below) are on strong beats, while *g*s and *bb*s (fifths and thirds below) are on weak beats. As we shall see, exactly the same principle holds for the *Fugeing* in the last section of Purcell's Fantazia XII.

The next section of Simpson's *Compendium* discusses what he calls 'Syncopated or Driving Canon', a refinement of the same technique that, as Simpson points out, 'may be applied to any Ground or Plain-song'.[13] This is treated at length, including discussion of how the leading part should behave in order to accommodate both stepwise movement and motion by leap of various kinds, in the plainsong (or ground, since

---

[11] Simpson, *Compendium*, 154.   [12] Ibid.   [13] Ibid., 156.

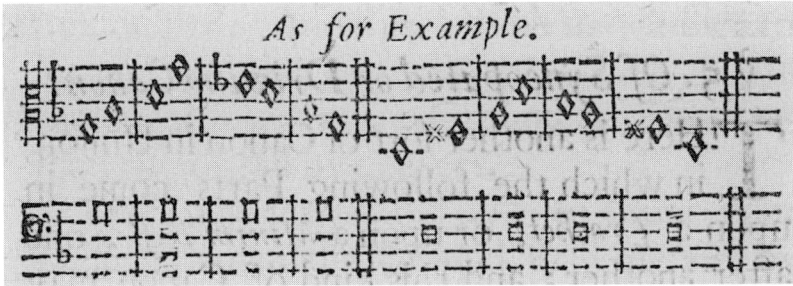

(a)   Permitted intervals, measured from the first note of the subject (p. 155, top)

(b)   A worked example (p. 155, bottom)

Fig. 7.1 Christopher Simpson, *A Compendium of Practical Musick* (1667): examples illustrating canon at the unison (courtesy of the Bayerische Staatsbibliothek, Munich)

Simpson notates it throughout as a bass part). Despite the potential relevance of this technique to the last section of Fantazia XII, however, Purcell does not seem to have followed similar rules in this case; perhaps this was in part because he found them over-restrictive, limiting the structural notes to consonant pitches (decorated with fleeting passing notes) and yielding no suspensions at all. In any case, Simpson's instructions are necessary only when the canon is sustained at length over a moving plainsong, which is not the case in Purcell's Fantazia; rather the *fugeing* there only continues exactly for durations shorter than the length of each note of the 'plainsong' (though as we shall see, more extended imitation probably played a part in the compositional process). Though he does not make it explicit, Simpson's instructions for simple canon at the unison are sufficient for such cases, since the key-note of the subject provides a notional *cantus firmus* (so in Fig. 7.1b above an inner pedal G could sound throughout the first four bars, and a D during the remainder of the example).

There is nevertheless one more aspect of Simpson's discussion of canon at the unison that links it closely to Purcell's Fantazia XII: Simpson's crowning example of 'Canon in Unison to a Ground' (Fig. 7.2), in which his ground exactly matches the contour of Purcell's subject as it appears both in Fantazia XII and in the Gloria of the Jubilate in D (where it also appears exclusively as a bass part). Perhaps Purcell's interest in the potential of this subject for this sort of treatment might even have begun with a desire to go one better than Simpson's example by

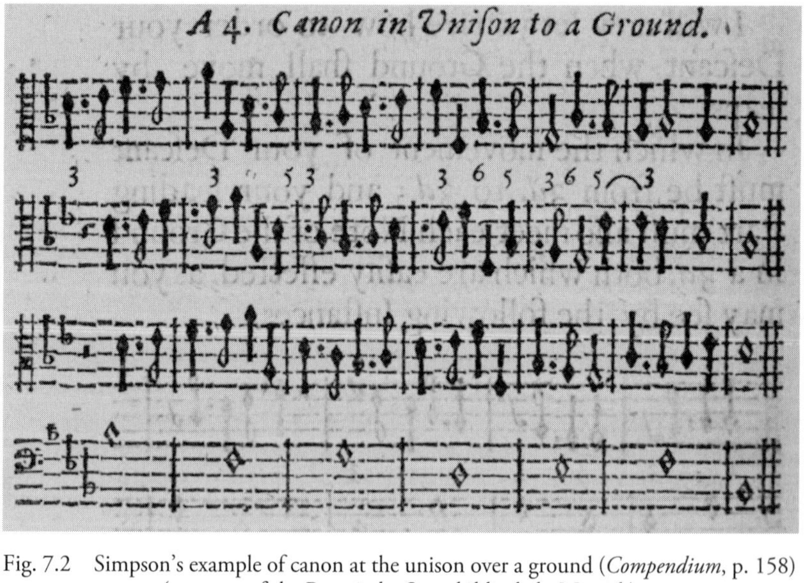

Fig. 7.2   Simpson's example of canon at the unison over a ground (*Compendium*, p. 158) (courtesy of the Bayerische Staatsbibliothek, Munich)

constructing the canons over the plainsong from the same material. At
the same time, like the examples of pre-existing subjects analysed in
Chapter 6, Purcell's familiarity with this particular subject doubtless
stemmed from multiple sources. He is very likely to have encountered
it in the Magnificat from Thomas Tomkins's Fifth Service, for example,
in which the verse 'He hath put down' (see Ex. 7.13a) uses it in both
thesin and *arsin* forms, in minims, against a series of sustained notes in the
organ (thereby demonstrating its suitability for Purcell's similar later
treatment in Fantazia XII and the Jubilate); meanwhile, the prominent
use in Fantazia XII of a version of the subject in which one of the fourths
is diminished (see bb. 65–7, 71–2, 79–84, 88–93) can be heard as early as

Ex. 7.13   Earlier instances of the subject from Purcell's Fantazia XII, last section

(a)   Thomas Tomkins, Fifth service, Magnificat (bb. 54–63)

Ex. 7.13(b)   John Dowland, 'In darkness let me dwell'

John Dowland's song 'In darkness let me dwell' (Ex. 7.13b) – and indeed more generally in the near-ubiquitous 'lachrimae' motif, to which it is more distantly related.

Whatever the pre-history of the motif, Purcell's adoption of it as the subject for the concluding section of Fantazia XII, with its grossly augmented subject entries, can be quickly understood in conjunction with Simpson's advice for unison canons. The advantages of this motif for such treatment are obvious: its first four notes (the main part of the subject treated consistently throughout) all form consonant intervals with a notional root, as shown in Ex. 7.14a (compare Fig. 7.1a, from Simpson's *Compendium*); furthermore, they combine well in canon at the unison or octave, against this same root, at the distance of two metrical units – as in Simpson's worked example (Fig. 7.1b), the adjacent fifth and sixth degrees above the root are confined to consistent metrical placement in order to facilitate this feature (the sixth on a strong, the fifth a weak beat for *arsin*, vice versa for *thesin*; see Ex. 7.14b).

Although, as observed already, the strict imitation of the subject at this distance never continues longer than the duration of each note of the 'plainsong', the *fugeing* surrounding both entries at eightfold duration of the subject (bb. 79–86 and 88–95, respectively) does appear to derive from experiments in more sustained canonic working. Ex. 7.15 shows the apparent origins of bars 79–86, against a plainsong-like subject-statement in the second tenor (in fact the lowest sounding part in these bars). During the first two notes of the 'plainsong' the upper parts proceed in a

Ex. 7.14   Fantazia XII, closing section: derivation of subject

(a)   Possible consonant notes above a one-note *cantus firmus* in the bass

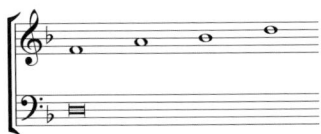

(b)   Subject *arsin* and *thesin* above bass pedal (*cf.* bb. 79–80)

canon at the lower octave based on the subject interlocks $\boxed{\text{A}}$ (A:A$^{-8,\,\downarrow}$) and $\boxed{\text{T}}$ (T:T$^{-8,\,\downarrow}$). Purcell then repeated this invention, labelled 'X' in Ex. 7.15a, up a minor third, for the third and fourth notes of the 'plainsong' – reflecting the sequential relationship between notes 1–2 and 3–4 of the motif. The shading in Ex. 7.15a highlights the one place where this canonic relationship fails to yield good counterpoint with the bass; as Ex. 7.15b shows, Purcell corrected this detail with the minimum possible alteration to the following part (shown in black noteheads in the third and seventh bars; notes unchanged from part (a) of the example are shown in grey). At the same time he made a small adjustment to the leading part in order to start the second interlock an octave lower in the seventh bar.

Having constructed the two statements of 'X' in this way, Purcell then would have set about joining them together, beginning by continuing the canon in the fourth bar by Simpson's method (adding to the end of the leading part to agree with the following part; see Ex. 7.15b, bb. 82–3). On reaching the stepwise descent into note three of the 'plainsong', however, he chose to suspend the treble *eb″* over the bar-line rather than sustain the canonic motion between treble and tenor 1, additionally implying a continuation that would overlap with the beginning of 'X+3' in the treble (shaded in Ex. 7.15b). This made strong counterpoint with the second tenor, and provided a viable harmonization of the problematic root movement down a tone. In order to accommodate this treble line in the final text of this passage, the first tenor's imitation of the treble shifts down a fourth at the start of bar 83 of Ex. 7.15c (the final form of this passage), setting up a cadence on Bb and linking directly into its following role in 'X+3'.

In the treble, meanwhile, Purcell resolved the suspended *eb″* before, having missed the lead entry for 'X+3', beginning a statement of the subject *arsin* a third lower and one minim later than in the original invention (see the black notes in Ex. 7.15c). This decision caused a reduction in

Ex. 7.15   Fantazia XII, bb. 79–86: likely compositional process

(a)   Two-part canon at the octave (X) repeated in sequence up a third

(b)   Attempted canonic continuation joining X with X+3

(c)   Final version

compositional artifice – in effect, the treble here now simply shadowed the first tenor entry at the upper sixth – for which Purcell originally attempted to compensate by beginning a new interlock A in the first tenor, starting at bar 83_2 (see the crossed noteheads in Ex. 7.15c). In what is a highly unusual piece of evidence showing genuine compositional activity in the *Lbl* Add. MS 30930 fantazia scores, this intermediate reading is actually preserved in the manuscript: in bar 83 the first tenor originally had crotchets $a - f - bb - a$, as can clearly be seen in the manuscript excerpt reproduced in Fig. 1.1 (top system, third bar from end; and in colour on the jacket of this volume). Only after notating this passage did he decide to bring forward the tenor bb in order to create a properly prepared suspension, thereby compromising the rhythm of the subject.

Although the original conceit is somewhat masked in the final version by these necessary changes, then, these eight bars are clearly derived from an

underlying canon over a 'plainsong' that greatly augments the same subject. A similar observation could be made of bars 88–95, in which the
'plainsong' has migrated to the first tenor and the outer parts carry a
different canon (this time beginning afresh at b. 90$_2$ and thereafter spanning notes two and three of the 'plainsong'). Indeed, the fundamental
nature of this canonic invention can also be observed elsewhere in the final
section of Fantazia XII, not least in the near ubiquity of the basic $\boxed{\text{A}}$ and $\boxed{\text{T}}$
interlocks even in the passages in which imitation is confined to original
note-values – to the exclusion, indeed, of several other viable combinations
that, from Purcell's habits in similar sections of other fantazias, one might
expect to have been explored. This may partly result from the brevity of the
subject, and Purcell's well-judged decision to confine entries of the subject
in crotchets to the weak beats of the bar (since much of its rhythmic
identity, and the cadential drive of the section, derive from this anacrustic
placing). However, even these strictures leave available imitation of the
subject *arsin* at the upper fifth or sixth, or *thesin* at the upper fourth, none
of which Purcell incorporates into the section (though one of these, A:A$^{+6,\,\downarrow}$
does arise in bars 71–3 as a result of the shadowing of the second tenor
entry at the third). Similarly, several combinations of the subject mixing
entries *arsin* and *thesin* are possible but not used.

As in the case of the simpler canonically conceived augmentations
already encountered, the plainsong-like approach to augmentation in
this movement also sits alongside other passages in which *fugeing per
augmentation* has seemingly been researched beyond the process of initial
invention, and in which the fugal materials show corresponding signs of
melodic compromise. Indeed, in the last section of Fantazia XII the one
passage of dense four-part fugeing (bb. 74–6) betrays the considerable
problems Purcell must have had with its creation. This passage apparently
preserves the remnants of an attempt to combine prime and augmented
fugal entries, along the lines reconstructed in Ex. 7.16. Since there are no
intrinsically viable combinations of the subject *arsin* in augmentation (2A)
with the prime form as a following part, Purcell began by attempting to
combine three of the least problematic attempts into one larger four-part
complex, then making the necessary adjustments to the resulting texture –
the temporal displacement in several parts producing an unsettling rhythmic effect. In fact had he simply reversed the order of entries, he would
have found that an A:2A$^{+8,\,\downarrow}$ interlock is perfectly viable, though similarly
problematic from a rhythmic perspective.

Purcell's difficulty in contriving this passage only seems at odds with the
techniques observed in other fantazias when viewed in isolation; from the
point of view of his creative process, it simply indicates a difference in
compositional priorities in this section right from the moment of the initial
invention. In Fantazia VIII, for example, Purcell's intention to create a
climactic four-voice interlock in stretto *fuga* affected the very creation of

Ex. 7.16   Fantazia XII: possible derivation of bb. 75–6

(a) Attempted two-voice combinations

(b) All three
     combined

(c) Treble corrected by
     doubling length of
     second note

(d) Last note of bass brought
     forward to eliminate fourth
     on second beat of second bar

(e) Alto entry stretched, trans-
     forming appoggiatura into
     properly prepared suspension

(f) Final form of
     passage

the fugal materials, and all of the most artificial passages of *fugeing* could be seen to belong to the beginning of his compositional activity; by contrast, in Fantazia XII the qualities of the subject and the similarity with *cantus firmus* techniques suggest that it was the inclusion of grossly augmented subject entries that guided Purcell's earliest phase of composition, and not the construction of dense passages of *fugeing* in four parts.

MUSIC AS RHETORICAL AUGMENTATION

The basic contrapuntal technique examined in detail so far in this chapter remained constant throughout Purcell's deployment of augmentation in his later vocal music, though – like his more general approach to artifice during the 1690s – it entailed considerable stylistic transformation. Before examining this in detail, however, we need first to consider his motivation for maintaining this intellectualized manner in spite of the 'extraordinary surface changes in style'[14] observed more generally in this later repertoire. No doubt in part, at least, this can be attributed to his more general musical personality, his love for artifice *per se*. But as I have argued before, Purcell's use of compositional artifice in vocal music throughout his career went far beyond the mere exercise of contrapuntal virtuosity. By bringing it to bear on the very semantic content of the texts he set, Purcell was able to transform this aspect of his technique into a vehicle for rhetorical intensification.[15] For Dryden in his preface to *The Prophetess*, 'As poetry is a rise above prose and oratory, so is Musick the exaltation of poetry'; it seems Purcell took him at his word.[16]

One illustration of the importance Purcell attached to the rhetorical deployment of artifice in vocal music is that he seems to have resorted to augmentation as a device in a very limited range of textual contexts (see Table 7.3).[17] Indeed, the relative infrequency of contrapuntal augmentation in Purcell's vocal music paradoxically throws into relief its rhetorical importance: its impact upon the listener is all the greater for its singularity. It is for this reason – together with the notable prominence of the device among some of Purcell's best-known works of the 1690s – that inquiry into the technical resources he deployed in this context can contribute to

---

[14] Adams, *Henry Purcell*, ix.

[15] See Howard, 'Composition as an Act of Performance: Artifice and Expression in Purcell's Sacred Part Song *Since God so Tender a Regard*', *JRMA*, 132/1 (2007), 32–59 (esp. 51–7). This article is reprinted in Peter Holman, ed., *Purcell*, The Baroque Composers (Farnham: Ashgate, 2011), 353–80.

[16] Quoted in Burden, *Purcell Remembered*, 89.

[17] Purcell never made extensive use of augmentation in his later instrumental music; an exception is the opening symphony of *Now Does the Glorious Day Appear* (for Queen Mary's birthday in 1689), in which the bass at bar 15_3 carries an augmented entry of the trumpet-like subject that simultaneously reaffirms the key-note and prepares for the half-cadence on the fifth degree that concludes this first, repeated section. (I thank Bruce Wood for reminding me of this instance.)

Table 7.3 *Fugeing per augmentation* in Purcell's vocal music

	Year	Work	Bars	Text set
(1)	*c.* 1680	Service in B♭ (Magnificat)	$31–4_1$	'He hath shewed strength with his arm'
(2)	1685	*I was Glad* (coronation anthem)	$105_3–8_2$	'World without end, Amen'
(3)	1690	*The Yorkshire Feast Song*	$570_3–74$	'Let Music join in a chorus divine / the praise of all that celebrate this festival'
(4)	1691	*Welcome, Welcome Glorious Morn*	$573_3–82_2$, $595_3–600_2$	'Sound, all ye Spheres, confirm the omen, Heav'n/ And long preserve the blessings thou hast giv'n'
(5)	1692	*Hail, bright Cecilia*	2. $38_3–41_1$	'Fill ev'ry heart with love of thee and thy celestial Art'
(6)			13. $38–42_2$	'Who whilst among the choir above / Thou dost thy former skill improve'
(7)	1694	Te Deum in D	249–55	'Ever world without end'
(8)	1694	Jubilate in D	201–8	'World without end'

the emerging picture of his compositional character even in spite of the fact that most works do not inspire such treatment.

Several of these examples are linked conceptually through a general association with the notion of technical accomplishment: 'celestial Art' (no. 5 in Table 7.3) and 'skill' (6) in a textually explicit sense, and 'Let music join in a chorus divine' (3) inasmuch as compositional artifice might be conceived of as a key tool in the accomplishment of this invocation. Perhaps unsurprisingly, though, the most common context for contra-puntal augmentation in these instances is its use to set passages of text explicitly dealing with the idea of longevity (four out of the eight cases identified). In Anglican service music the doxology was a traditional site of technical display, Purcell's own B♭ major service incorporating six canonic settings of the words 'Glory be to the father' (together with four more passages labelled as canons), drawing on the precedent established in works by Blow, Child and others.[18] The association of this text in general with compositional artifice together with the presence of the words 'world without end', then, would have made the use of augmentation an attractive option.

The increasing use of longer note-values towards the end of an otherwise rhythmically active concerted choral texture is relatively common in late seventeenth-century Italian music, for example in the oratorios of Alessandro Stradella or Legrenzi; Michael Talbot even quotes an example from Benedetto Vinaccesi's eight-part Compline setting in which the

---

[18] On the tradition of canonic display in such pieces see Rebecca Herissone's comments on Daniel Henstridge's collection of canons in *Lbl* Add. MS 30933: *Musical Creativity*, 17–24.

words 'longitudine dierum replebo eum' (With long life will I satisfy him) prompt the introduction of a hexachord-like melodic idea in the sopranos moving in semibreves, against crotchets and quavers in the remaining parts.[19] While Purcell's adoption of this strategy was eminently in keeping with contemporary Italian developments, then, he might equally have looked to earlier English precedents in which, unlike the Italian examples, the slower-moving parts are fully integrated into the fugal texture. Almost a century earlier, in fact, Thomas Weelkes had used the same device to conclude several six-voice madrigals from his 1600 *Madrigals of 5 and 6 Parts*. Both 'As Vesta was from Latmos hill descending' and 'Like two proud armies' feature bass augmentation to eight times original note-values towards the end, like Purcell in response to the text: 'Long live fair Oriana' in the former, and 'dazzl'd reason yields as quite undone' the latter.

While in one sense the use of long note-values for texts invoking concepts of longevity resembles simple madrigalian word-painting, it is arguably different in its relationship both to the creative process and to the musical texture as a whole. Inasmuch as music in performance unfolds in time, changes in harmonic rhythm directly alter the listener's perception of the passage of time in a way that more pictorial devices – such as the depiction even of simple concepts such as 'high', 'low' or 'round', which rely on linguistic metaphor for their melodic equivalence – could rarely be argued to operate.

The aural effect of one part singing longer note-values than the surrounding voices is to foreground a slower harmonic rhythm than is immediately audible on the surface, as can be heard in the last section of *I was Glad* (Ex. 7.17). In the initial entries, the harmony progresses in crotchets despite the quaver-based subject; this is made more audible when the subject enters for the first time in augmented form (S, b. 102_2). Later, a thrilling bass entry in fourfold augmentation (b. 105_3) actually dictates a further slowing of the harmonic rhythm, now to minims. This has a direct effect on the harmonic syntax, and through this on Purcell's very ability to create the senses of tension and release that were central to the tonal language of Italianate Baroque music. It is as if, rather than the music acting as a vehicle for the eloquent delivery of the text, the idea in the text at this point has hijacked the internal logic of the music to its own ends: with the arrival at a dominant pedal in bar 108 comes a further slowing of harmonic rhythm, and ultimately, the realization that the entire double-augmented bass entry has functioned to withhold a cadence on G that has been inevitable for some time – it could indeed have occurred as early as bars 106–7 with minimal adjustment to the existing counterpoint.

[19] Michael Talbot, *Benedetto Vinaccesi: A Musician in Brescia and Venice in the Age of Corelli* (Oxford: Clarendon, 1994), 254.

Ex. 7.17   *I was Glad* (1685), conclusion

This association of augmented bass entries in particular with the harmonic function of the dominant (in modern terms) is common in Purcell's music, as will become clear in examining the other instances listed in Table 7.3. The more pressing point, though, is that while many forms of word-painting operate essentially on the ornamental surface of the music, *fugeing per augmentation*, like other forms of contrapuntal artifice, operates at a deeper structural level, with the result that the very fabric of the musical texture interacts with the verbal meaning of the text.

In this sense the rhetorical power of contrapuntal augmentation in Purcell's vocal music is strongly reminiscent of his similar approach to the use of ground bass. As in the case of contrapuntal augmentation, and notwithstanding Rosamond McGuinness' observation, in relation to Purcell's odes, that there is no common thread linking the texts that he chose to set to ground basses,[20] there are in fact a number of textual references which can be seen as likely indicators for a ground-bass setting when the full range of his grounds is taken into account. References to music, for example, frequently inspired ground-bass settings – think 'Music for a while' (*Oedipus*), 'Hark each tree' (*Hail, bright Cecilia*), or twice in *Come ye Sons of Arts*, with 'Sound the trumpet' and 'Strike the viol'. Here the prompt would seem to be the exercise of particular compositional skill in such textual contexts, much as in the case of the chorus from the *Yorkshire Feast Song* shown in Table 7.3. Another common feature of the texts set to ground basses is association with the erotic, a tradition derived from Venetian opera and one that extends in Purcell (as in Italian music) both into the realms of the lament ('When I am laid in earth' or 'The Plaint' being the obvious examples) and, conversely, to notions of the ecstatic more generally, as in the use of ground-bass 'Alleluia' sections in works such as *Beati omnes qui timent Dominum* of the late 1670s, or the anthem *Awake, Put on thy Strength* of a few years later. Also related to the idea of love are ground-bass texts that explore concepts related to loyalty and fidelity – 'She loves and she confesses too', or in a converse, ironic sense, 'She is unconstant' (from 'Love, thou can'st hear'), both of which form part of a much larger category in which the repetition of the ground appears to act as a symbol of constancy in general. This usage can be heard in several examples that celebrate the repetitive cycles of nature ('He appointed the Sun', from *Praise the Lord, O my Soul, O Lord my God*; 'What makes the Spring retire?', from the song 'Young Thirsis' fate'; 'Now the night is chas'd away', from *The Fairy Queen*; 'April who till now', from *Celebrate this Festival*) or the omnipresence of God ('Since God so tender a regard'; 'The Lord is great', from *O Sing unto the Lord*).

---

[20] Rosamond McGuinness, 'The Ground Bass in the English Court Ode', *ML*, 51/3 (1970), 118–40 and 265–78 (118).

As in the use of augmentation, the point about this careful matching of technique and verbal text extends beyond the general compatibility of the two into the detail of the compositional process, such that the music is harnessed, through application of the technique, in order to enhance and deepen the semantic content of the text. I have shown elsewhere how Purcell manipulated the harmonic implications of the unchanging ground in the final stanza of 'Since God so tender a regard' to produce a vivid musical corollary to the paradoxical final couplet, 'The very bonds which thou hast loos'd/Shall tie me faster unto thee': for all that the voices revel in the potential freedom of the ground, with its many possible harmonic inter- pretations, in the end they must conform to its simple tonic cadence.[21]

A slightly simpler, though no less effective example can be heard in one of Purcell's most famous ground-bass songs, his setting of William Fuller's *An Evening Hymn*. Ground bass is an obvious choice for this text, with its references both to divine constancy and the daily rhythms of life. The five- bar ground, with prominent arrival on the fifth scale-degree at the start of bar 4, offers much potential for varying phrase lengths, which Purcell exploits fully from the start. Most effective in this respect is the way in which the certainty of the opening line, 'Now, now that the sun . . . ', coinciding with the beginning of the ground, is contrasted with the questioning 'But where, where shall my soul repose?', set to the same rhythm but starting on the less stable second bar of the ground (b. 22, plus anacrusis), the repetition of the adverb in each case reinforcing the parallel (see Ex. 7.18a). It is really only from bar 31, however, that the ground is fully activated as a partner in the effective (and affective) delivery of the concept implied in the text.

Arriving at the line 'And can there be any so sweet security', not only does Purcell choose to transpose the ground up a third – a shocking harmonic twist given the unchanging pitch of the ground up to this point, and uncomplicated G-major key context – but he also ends the phrase with an interrupted cadence exactly coinciding with the word 'security' (Ex. 7.18b). If this first setting of these words harnesses radical harmonic volatility to the ironic representation of the concept of 'security', it also acts as a foil to the proceeding six bars, in which the ground acquires the comparative 'security' of transposition down a fourth from original pitch, and the phrase ends with an emphatic perfect cadence. The ground then remains at this pitch for two statements of the invocation 'Then to thy rest, O my soul' – complete with long held notes on the word 'rest' – which is fulfilled in harmonic terms with the return of the ground to its original pitch in bar 54; only now is the soul free to indulge in the singing of joyful praise, complete with dotted-note figurations prefiguring those in the concluding 'Alleluia'.

Together with examples like this from Purcell's ground-bass songs, the very specific but telling examples of contrapuntal augmentation assembled

---

[21] Howard, 'Composition as an Act of Performance', 57.

Ex. 7.18   *An Evening Hymn*

(a)   bb. 6–25

Now,   now   that the   sun＿＿＿＿   hath   veil'd＿＿ his＿ light,   and   bid   the＿

world＿   good night;   to the   soft＿＿＿＿＿   bed,   to   the   soft,＿   the   soft＿＿

bed＿   my bo-dy I＿＿ dis-pose;   But where,   where shall my   soul＿   re - pose?

(b)   bb. 31–55

arms: And can there be   a - ny so   sweet＿＿＿＿＿＿   se - cu - ri -

- ty?   Can there be   a - ny so   sweet,   so   sweet＿ se - cu - ri -

- ty?   Then   to thy   rest＿＿＿＿＿＿＿＿＿＿＿＿＿＿   O＿ my soul!

Then   to thy rest,＿＿＿＿＿   O＿ my＿ soul! And sing＿＿＿＿＿

in this chapter demonstrate how Purcell, in using compositional artifice in his vocal music, was able to take what in the instrumental music functioned as an inspiration for invention and at times a vehicle for abstract musical expression, and turn it into one of the most powerful tools at his disposal for the heightening of the verbal meanings and expressive contents of the texts he set. In the final part of this chapter I examine how, having made the decision to harness the technique of contrapuntal augmentation in this way, Purcell revisited the approaches to its derivation described above in the new stylistic context of the 1690s.

AUGMENTATION IN THE LATE VOCAL MUSIC

In the context of the examples listed in Table 7.3, the final movement of *Welcome, Welcome Glorious Morn* is something of an exception: like the passage at 'He hath shewed strength' from the earlier Magnificat in B♭ (discussed on p. 197), this is not strictly a fugal movement. 'Sound, all ye Spheres' begins rather as a binary-form tenor solo, its 'A' section exploiting fanfare-like figures punctuated by the real thing from two obbligato trumpets. In the 'B' section Purcell retains the trumpet style, but constructs solo and thoroughbass parts opening with a canon two in one at the fifth by augmentation (Ex. 7.19a). (There is a slight, and contrapuntally unnecessary flex in the tenor melody at bar 574_2: Purcell could have written the $f\sharp'$ implied by the bass *b* at bar 574_3, though this would have been detrimental to the sense of resolution and stability required by the text at this point, and provided by the *e'* he chose instead.) This, then, is the only example from the late vocal music of Purcell's use of canonic invention (as described earlier in this chapter) for the simultaneous composition of prime and augmented forms of a subject. The remainder of the movement is built on the same subject material as the canon; the whole is then repeated by the chorus, the 'B' section preserving the original entries intact and simulating a full imitative texture with opportunistic entries of the head of the subject wherever a few notes can be made to fit (Ex. 7.19b). Just as in the instrumental music, then, materials invented canonically are later treated more variably through contrapuntal research, though in this case the wholesale repetition of the original bass and tenor parts as the basis of the choral movement limits the additional entries to a series of less ambitious 'reports' rather than any more systematic probing of the potential combinations.

　　Beginning with the passage from the *Yorkshire Feast Song* of 1690, in the remaining five examples from Table 7.3 we can observe Purcell attempting to recapture the success of his use of an augmented bass entry towards the end of *I was Glad*, of five years earlier. All five share the relationship of the augmented entry to the dominant identified in relation to *I was Glad*, yet in terms both of contrapuntal artifice and more general musical interest they achieve varying levels of success; Purcell's increasing tendency to

Ex. 7.19   *Welcome, Welcome Glorious Morn*

(a)   bb. 573–9

(b)   Excerpt from final chorus

resort to materials used successfully in his Fantazias suggests a conscious attempt to assimilate this technique into the new stylistic context. Indeed, in some ways it was this very Italianate style that created the opportunity for Purcell to revive his interest in augmentation at this stage in his career: dominant pedal-points[22] are by far the most common context in which Italian composers introduced notes of radically longer rhythmic value towards the ends of sections, and already in the 1683 Sonatas Purcell had mastered the use of these pedal-points to create the expectation of resolution to the key-note, thus building tension towards a final cadence (see for example Sonata III, second movement; Sonata IV, second and fourth movements; Sonata VI, second movement; Sonata IX, second movement). Bearing in mind his penchant for contrapuntal artifice, it

---

[22] In the absence of a consistent contemporary term for the phenomenon, modern tonal language seems the best way to convey adequately the clear 'dominant' function of these pedal notes and the harmonies they support; hence the increasing use of modern terminology in this chapter and even more so in Chapter 8.

would have been an obvious step to attempt to integrate this harmonic function with the melodic materials of a given passage.

This would demand a very different approach, however, from that taken in the final section of Fantazia XII, which arguably plays on exactly this conceit. The two successive statements of the subject augmented to eight times original note-values in the last 21 bars of this piece – *arsin* from bar 79 (ten. 2) and *thesin* from bar 88 (ten. 1) – both underpin a succession of dominant sonorities implying different keys, each ultimately frustrated only for another 'dominant' to be set up in its place. The result is a remarkable tension between expected closure and tonal instability: the music seems to be propelled headlong towards an unknown harmonic goal.

In fact throughout the last section of Fantazia XII Purcell explores the potential of augmented entries to imply potential cadence. Three examples are given in Example 7.20, in which the thoroughbass lines beneath the main system extrapolate the implied cadential voice-leading using crossed-out figures and note-heads to show expectations that are never realized. The same principle applies throughout the section, and equally when the augmented entry appears in an upper voice (bb. 88–95). Purcell uses the very progressions prescribed for cadences by Matthew Locke in *Melothesia* (see Fig. 7.3a); indeed, his treatment of the double- and triple-augmented subject entries in Ex. 7.20b and c is strongly reminiscent of the second of Locke's examples of 'transition' or modulation, in which a long series of breves progresses around a circle of fifths, each harmonized with a variation on the same basic 7/3 – 6/4 – 5/3 pattern (Fig. 7.3b).[23]

Despite the strongly directional voice-leading supplied by this approach, it is the melodic shape of the subject that ultimately determines the harmonic trajectory. Purcell uses the tension between these two aspects of his music to create a sophisticated commentary on the nature of cadence and closure. As shown in Ex. 7.20, the expected cadential direction is continually confounded by the presence of the triple-augmented subject entries. Purcell gradually increases harmonic tension by introducing successively greater augmentation of the subject: twofold in bar 59, fourfold in bar 68 and finally eightfold augmentation in bar 79. Although this outwardly resembles the principle of cumulation of artifice observed in Fantazia VIII (see Chapter 2), its main purpose here is the intensification of cadential implications; since, as noted above, the greatest degrees of augmentation function essentially as notes of a *cantus firmus*, their presence hardly represents any significant increase in the level of fugal artifice. Instead, the strength of the resulting desire for resolution, combined with its denial by the melodic shape of the subject, results in an increasingly

[23] Locke, *Melothesia*, n.p. (second page of 'Examples of the Precepts'). On Locke's treatise see also Chapter 3, pp. 87–90. Note that the plate of examples is bound before p. 9 in the copy from King's College, London reproduced in the illustration; the editorial page numbers in the captions reflect the more usual position of this plate in other copies.

Ex. 7.20   Fantazia XII, last section: harmonic treatment of augmented subject entries

(a)   *Arsin*, twofold note-values (bb. 59–61)

(b)   *Thesin*, fourfold note-values (bb. 61–5)

(c)   *Arsin*, eightfold note-values (bb. 79–87)

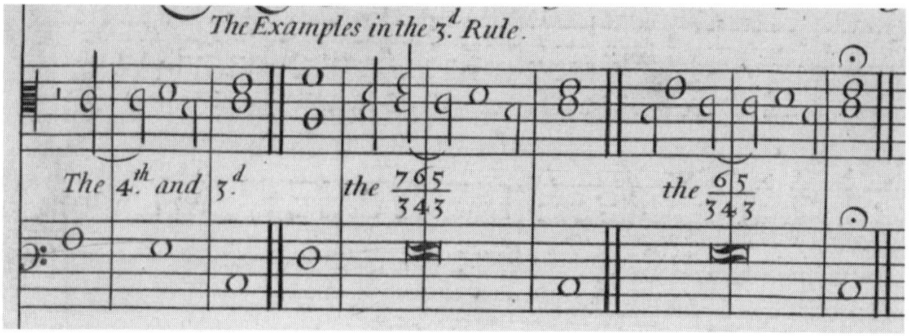

(a) Examples of cadential progressions (p. [10], top)[24]

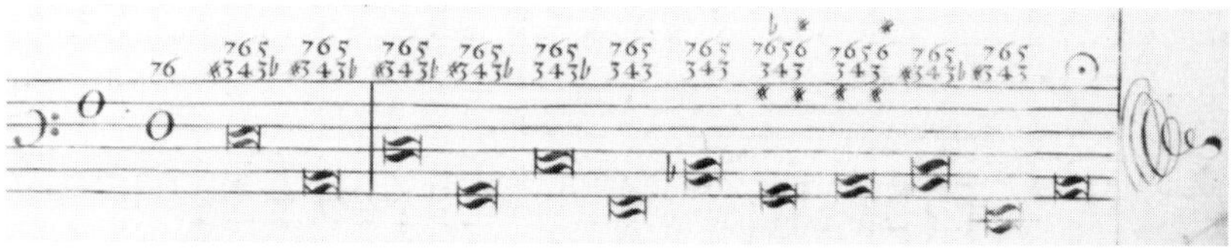

(b) Second example of 'transition' (p. [11], bottom)

Fig. 7.3 Matthew Locke, *Melothesia* (1673) (courtesy of King's College London, Foyle Special Collections Library)

wayward-sounding harmonic structure. In the end the final cadence represents a rhetorical defeat for the kind of strongly directed cadential progressions that had pervaded throughout (see Ex. 7.9): lacking any kind of 'full close' on D in the entire section, the last augmented entry – *thesin* in the bass, at fourfold note-values – even displaces the minor third of the key, creating an expanded *tierce de Picardie*, and the piece ends with a plagal cadence.

This kind of harmonic rabbit-warren would have been entirely out of place in the final chorus of the *Yorkshire Feast Song* of 1690 – due to stylistic change in part, but also for reasons of functional suitability in relation to the public and occasional nature of the work. Nevertheless, Purcell's strategy for avoiding it is entirely in keeping with his earlier experience (Ex. 7.21): by designing a subject based primarily on the extension and repetition of a single note, he could use it in the bass augmented to quadruple note-values to produce a pedal point on the fifth scale-degree. In terms of the techniques described above for the invention of counterpoint involving extreme augmentation, then, this is quite clearly a return to the *cantus firmus* technique. Within this context, the prime entries above the pedal remain strictly limited in their intervallic relationship with the bass, being restricted to entries involving the repetition of the first and fifth

---

[24] The second bar of the second example here contains a misprint: in the highest sounding voice, the first note should have been an F, tied to the previous note (as indicated by Locke's figuring).

Ex. 7.21 *Yorkshire Feast Song*, bb. 568–76

scale-degrees. Apart from the regular flexing of the opening interval, and shadowing of main entries in thirds or sixths (bb. 570–1 and 574, both tenor) the only exception is the countertenor in bar 573 (which still retains the consistent relationship with the bass, even if not with the prevailing key). Yet arguably, as a combination of the principles of artifice through augmentation and harmonic pedal-point, this passage is heavily skewed towards the latter function: the reliance of the subject upon repetition of the fifth scale-degree is so prominent that although the bass line unquestionably carries an entry of the subject, it might just have well have been a plain pedal note. And the restricted pitches of entries in relation to the pedal and the overall key represent a considerable impoverishment of harmonic interest when compared even with the ending of *I was Glad*

(Ex. 7.17), in which the prime subject is heard at seven different pitches (four *arsin*, three *thesin*) in relation to the key, and at varying intervals with the bass note at any given time.

The next three instances of bass augmentation in Table 7.3 each show Purcell attempting to improve upon the characteristics of its deployment in the *Yorkshire Feast Song*. In the first chorus of *Hail, bright Cecilia*, at 'Fill ev'ry heart', the subject used for the augmented entry has much more individuality and variety of pitch, but as a result of this – and of the fact that Purcell only augments to double the note-values – the necessary melodic compromise considerably reduces the artifice of the resulting passage. Neither of the two augmented bass entries is sustained, and this passage gives the impression of an idea researched after the prior selection of materials. It is possible, of course, that Purcell deliberately held back in this passage in order to enhance the effect of the more virtuosic application of the technique in the final chorus, especially given the verbal cues in the text ('Thou dost thy former skill improve', as explored in Chapter 5, pp. 143–7).

From this point onwards all of Purcell's augmented bass entries make use of materials imported from earlier works, perhaps in an attempt to overcome the limitations of the passage at 'Fill ev'ry heart'. Returning to the final chorus of *Hail, bright Cecilia* in the light of the discussion of Purcell's technical approaches to augmentation above, it is possible to see why the material at the start of the second In nomine was particularly suited to his purposes in this chorus. In line with the 'cantus firmus' approach, the first note of the subject is sufficiently extended that a quadruple augmentation produces a pedal note long enough to support an entire prime subject entry; in accordance with Simpson's instructions for canon over a plainsong, meanwhile, the structural notes of the subject are limited to pitches consonant with its first note. The density of contrapuntal elaboration here is strongly contrasted with the passage at 'Ever world without end' in the Te Deum, however, in which Purcell re-uses voice-leading from later in the same In nomine (as described in Chapter 5, pp. 149–50). In this passage the augmented entry itself is mainly of melodic significance, while the *fugeing* above is seemingly opportunistic rather than systematically researched.

Finally, the setting of 'World without end' at the end of the Jubilate is Purcell's last and most successful attempt at this fusion of contrapuntal augmentation and pedal-point harmonic function. The model here – the end of Fantazia XII – is by now very familiar, but the harmonic effect is profoundly different in the later work from the labyrinthine diversions of the Fantazia. As in the other examples from the 1690s, starting with the *Yorkshire Feast Song*, the augmentation in the bass is strongly linked with the establishment of a dominant pedal. The bass entry in bar 201 briefly interrupts a pedal *a* (doubled in BC an octave lower) first established at bar

200, before returning to it in bars 203–4 and again in bar 210; despite the movement away from the fifth degree in bars 201–2 and 205–9, in fact, the whole passage from bar 200 to bar 212 can be understood in modern terms as a dominant prolongation, with the eightfold-augmented entry effectively in parentheses (Ex. 7.22; the full vocal texture is shown in Ex. 6.1a). In the *fugeing* that accompanies this in bars 201–10 Purcell achieves a compromise between the colourful but harmonically volatile working of Fantazia XII and the tonal clarity – verging on sterility of effect – in the *Yorkshire Feast Song*.

As in the fantazia, Purcell builds his texture from structural subject-entries that reiterate the same contrapuntal interlocks over each note of the bass augmentation (see Ex. 7.22). Furthermore, he again divides the augmented subject in half, treating its second falling fourth as a sequential repetition of the first (compare Ex. 7.15). But now, rather than couching the entries in the upper parts within a series of dominant harmonies over each bass note, Purcell uses the third note, *b*, to prolong a simple minor chord; only at the bass *f♯* do we depart any real distance from the key-note. While this is indeed heard locally as a cadential preparation in the relative minor – already anticipated by the sopranos' *thesin* entries in bars 205–6 with their *a♯*'s – the pedal *a* is so firmly established in the surrounding bars that this momentary digression never threatens the pull of D major, and still less produces the sense of disorientation felt in the closing bars of Fantazia XII (compare Ex. 7.22 with the cases in Ex. 7.20). Paradoxically, by framing this whole passage of *fugeing per augmentation* securely within the prolongation of the fifth degree, Purcell is able to free up the 'middle-ground' (again, borrowing modern terminology) to introduce harmonic variety without threatening the overall sense of key.

* * *

The greatly augmented fugal entries favoured by Purcell here and in some of his best known music of the 1690s can be understood – in addition to their textual–rhetorical function – as characteristically brilliant responses to the demands of and possibilities afforded by the Italian style: by harnessing his deployment of grossly augmented fugal entries to the harmonic function of the dominant pedal, Purcell could make clearly audible by thematic means the long-range tonal organization of the music, itself perhaps one of the most important and, in Westrup's words, 'novel and striking' features of the concerted style that was gaining popularity in 1690s England.

The converse of this, however, was a corresponding loss of the kind of harmonic flexibility seen earlier in Fantazia XII. This brings us to the heart of the reason why Purcell's augmented entries paradoxically produced some of his most Italianate-sounding choruses, despite their origins in

Ex. 7.22   Jubilate in D, bb. 200–210: harmonic treatment of augmented subject entries, with analysis of *fugeing* above his much more idiosyncratic love of artificial creative strategies. As we have seen, the context for these passages was most often the desire for simple, diatonic progression towards the dominant; moreover, the techniques Purcell used to guarantee viable augmentations – whether conceived canonically or in line with *cantus firmus* techniques – made repeated or extended pitches and simple triadic melodies ubiquitous. Furthermore, even when not harmonized as a dominant, the slow-moving bass still dictated the pitches of the entries above and, by extension, the surface harmonic progressions, making straightforward triadic harmony almost inevitable.

Purcell's use of compositional artifice in the expressive setting of text in these passages clearly drew profoundly on his experience in the instrumental music he composed around 1680, both in terms of technique and the re-use of actual materials. Nevertheless, it is an oversimplification to consider these instances as aberrations or distractions from the adoption of 'true' Italian style. Such artificial techniques, including (but not limited to) augmentation, were key components of Purcell's musical poetics, as well as invaluable tools for the expressive setting of text; furthermore, within the context of a general move towards more Italianate harmonic traits, this concern for artifice may actually have contributed to rather than detracted from the more Italianate sound of the later music. This specific observation may apply only in very limited contexts, and it remains to be seen whether such complex relationships between styles can be observed more widely; the potential rewards are a deeper and more sophisticated appreciation not only of how Purcell conceived some of his most memorable and popular music, but also of his own understanding of the musical styles current in late Restoration London, and how he was able to turn these to his own expressive ends.

CHAPTER 8

'Italian sonatas in orchestral garb'

It has frequently been observed that the techniques that Purcell employed in his trio sonatas found a new outlet in his orchestral symphonies and overtures of the 1690s.[1] Giovanni Battista Draghi's 1687 Cecilian ode had shown how a large-scale work could begin with an Italianate orchestral sinfonia rather than the more conventional English take on the French overture, and in their odes and theatre music of the 1690s Purcell and Blow embraced this feature with enthusiasm.[2] What is not often acknowledged is that, Draghi's example aside, Purcell was effectively forced to invent this genre for himself, adapting the chamber sonata to the larger orchestral resources available at performances of court odes and in the theatre. The textbook Baroque distinction between the French and Italian overture types only really emerged towards the end of Purcell's life: the Italian fast–slow–fast scheme is usually credited to Alessandro Scarlatti, who first used it in 1687 (the same year as Draghi's ode),[3] but Purcell is unlikely to have known any such examples at first hand. The extensive use of antiphonal exchanges between trumpet and strings in the Trumpet Sonata in D, which has been thought likely to belong to a lost ode, *Light of the World* (though it is not clear whether Purcell ever actually set Matthew Prior's text for New Year 1694[4]), supports Don Smithers's suggestion that Purcell was familiar with Bolognese trumpet sonatas like those in Cazzati's Op. 35 (1665) and Andrea Grossi's Op. 3 (1682), but these works are much less sophisticated than Purcell's great trumpet overtures of the 1690s, such as those in *The Fairy Queen, Hail, bright Cecilia* and *The Indian Queen*.[5]

---

[1] Westrup, *Purcell*, 232; Bukofzer, *Music in the Baroque Era*, 214; Tilmouth, 'The Technique and Forms', 109; Adams, *Henry Purcell*, 32, 76–7.

[2] Holman, *Purcell*, 4, 20; Draghi's ode has recently been printed for the first time in Giovanni Battista Draghi, *From Harmony, from Heav'nly Harmony*, ed. Bryan White, Purcell Society Edition Companion Series, III (London: Stainer & Bell, 2010).

[3] Stephen C. Fisher, 'Italian Overture', in *Grove Music Online* (accessed 22 November 2018).

[4] See Bruce Wood, 'Only Purcell e're shall Equal Blow', in *Purcell Studies*, ed. Curtis Price (Cambridge University Press, 1995), 106–44 (139, note 53).

[5] Tilmouth, 'The Technique and Forms', 109 (note 2); Don L. Smithers, *The Music and History of the Baroque Trumpet before 1721* (London: Dent, 1973), 194.

In this chapter I argue that Purcell's individual approach to these movements drew on multiple stylistic resources. In the melodic character of the writing for trumpet and the antiphonal writing suggested by the contrast of timbre between trumpet(s) and strings, the Bolognese repertoire was no doubt influential.[6] But the style of these pieces would have seemed unduly restrictive to a composer so deeply in thrall to the 'great deal of Art mixed with good Air' which he found in the Italian sonata. It is against this background that we should understand the revival, noted by Martin Adams, of Purcell's interest in the duple-time canzona in the overtures and sinfonias of the 1690s.[7] The trumpet overture in particular proved to be an ideal site for the indulgence of his liking for contrapuntal ingenuity: as in the earlier sonatas, the incorporation of a canzona provided a clear focus for artificial techniques; conversely, the very presence of one or more trumpets provided a textural clarity that could sustain much greater levels of artifice than could have been supported by homogeneous ensembles of stringed instruments in the public settings of court and theatre.

As in previous chapters, the principal focus here is not the establishment of precedent or patterns of influence, but the development of more fruitful lines of analytical inquiry. Put simply, it is my contention that all of Purcell's canzonas of the 1690s were composed, so to speak, against the background of examples from the sonata repertoire. Analytical commentary on these works has focused on the improvements brought about by his long-term stylistic development and increasing maturity as a composer – 'Purcell's flawless sense of proportion, now liberated from that comparatively uncritical parading of combinatorial possibilities which affected some sonatas'.[8] Yet as the example of the Trumpet Overture from Act III of *The Indian Queen* shows, the exploration of specific compositional decisions with respect to the re-use of earlier material can be equally revealing in terms of Purcell's later compositional strategies. Moreover, even in the absence of particular models, the permutational approach to fugal exposition can be shown to be alive and well in works such as the Canzona in the overture to *Come ye Sons of Arts* of 1694. The situation is more complicated in canzonas like that in the 'Sonata while the Sun Rises' from Act IV of *The Fairy Queen* (1692): the subtle refinement of Purcell's technical ability with respect to the balance of melodic invention and invertible counterpoint in this work casts new light on his achievements, as well as suggesting a more specific origin for his interest in the trumpet sonata in general than has hitherto been identified.

---

[6] Ibid.   [7] Adams, *Henry Purcell*, 76.   [8] Ibid.

PURCELL'S REVIVAL OF THE CANZONA

Purcell seems to have sensed from the start that the most frequent type of fugue encountered in the canzonas and elsewhere in his sonatas – with multiple subjects wittily passed between members of the ensemble for the delight of the performer – would be unsuitable for the Italianate sinfonia attached to a large-scale work for public performance, which must appeal to a listening audience with members of varying tastes and musical abilities.

In the symphony at the start of his Cecilian ode, Draghi had built an impressive fugue by concentrating primarily on a single, well-defined subject; this is given a series of expositions which progressively introduce increasing levels of fugal complexity (the opening of the fugue is shown in Ex. 8.1).

The absence of a true regular countersubject means that the initial presentation of material is not over-complicated, though a recurring suspension idea against the subject (bb. 13–14, 15–16) serves a clear role later in the movement as the basis for episodes based on chains of suspensions. Length is also increased by the introduction of a further idea consisting of violinistic string-crossing semiquavers (first heard in bb. 17, Vn1, and 18, Vn2); the successive expositions introduce first a recurring subject stretto (bb. 21_4–23, Va2/BC), and then increasingly dense combinations of subject stretti with both the suspension and string-crossing ideas, such that the texture becomes increasingly saturated with motivic material towards the end. Thus although the fugue combines several ideas, its structural handling is such that each is clearly introduced before gradually increasing the textural complexity towards the climactic combinations at the end; a notable difference of approach from Purcell's sonata canzonas, in which the interplay between multiple subjects was a feature from the start, and later contrapuntal artifice relied primarily upon more elaborate treatment (inversion, close stretto and augmentation) of single subjects.

The second section of one of Purcell's earliest Italianate sinfonias, the opening of the 1688 anthem *O Sing unto the Lord*, adopts a very similar subject to Draghi's fugue, though Purcell does not attempt anything as ambitious. Instead, he presents a fugue whose structure and imitative technique resemble closely the single-subject imitative passages of some of his three- and four-part fantazias, yet which derives an Italianate character primarily from the simple voice-leading of the subject and the relatively restricted range of pitches and key contexts in which it appears – together with a preponderance of writing in parallel thirds and sixths. Purcell's more concentrated fugue again uses no regular countersubject, and has no episodes from its beginning in bar 19 until bar 35, where the subject is dropped in favour of new material which pits the violins against the viola and bass in antiphonal exchanges. Up to this point, however, the single

Ex. 8.1   Giovanni Battista Draghi, *From Harmony, from Heav'nly Harmony* (1687): opening of second section of symphony

subject is heard first in a straightforward exposition (Ex. 8.2a), then in inversion, including passages combining the *arsin* and *thesin* forms in alternate orders (Ex. 8.2b). This leads to a climactic three-voice stretto (bb. 30–31; Ex. 8.2c) with entries of the original subject on successive

Ex. 8.2   *O Sing unto the Lord*, second section of symphony

(a)   Exposition (bb. 19–23)

(b)   *Fugeing per arsin et thesin* (bb. 25–8)

(c)   Three-voice stretto, followed by subject fragmentation (bb. 30–35)

crotchets, before the subject becomes fragmented in the lead-up to the new section at bar 35.

Purcell is clearly concerned here with the same kinds of techniques he deployed in his earlier instrumental music, complete with cumulation of artifice. By contrast, in the French-influenced overtures that were still more common in the odes and theatre music of this time, his fugues make frequent use of melodic inversion and even occasionally augmentation, but extensive *fugeing* with complexes of overlapping subject entries is rare; after the exposition the subject is primarily of melodic interest.[9] For all this greater level of artifice, nevertheless, the fugal section of the symphony from *O Sing unto the Lord* illustrates some of the limitations of this approach to canzona composition. When compared with earlier sonata canzonas, the absence of multiple subjects not only makes it less artificial but also makes formal expansion more difficult; techniques from the earlier music that could compensate for this – the permutational repetition of the sonata canzonas, or the progressive exploration of more extreme harmonic regions and more complex imitative combinations found in the fantazias – are unavailable in this style which favours clarity in the relationship between harmony and melody and a relatively restricted pattern of modulation, both of which also suit a more audience-centred approach.

Purcell's last canzona of this kind,[10] written as part of the Act III Trumpet Overture in *The Indian Queen*, shows how some of these limitations could be overcome in an orchestral adaptation of the sonata canzona for a trumpet along with the usual string parts. Furthermore, because it is an actual adaptation of a sonata canzona, or at least an appropriation of its materials for use in the new context, this movement provides the ideal opportunity to see how Purcell responded to the demands of the more public orchestral sinfonia to produce a different working from that found in the original canzona from Sonata VII (1697).[11]

Apart from the notion that Purcell had a particular fondness for this sonata movement,[12] it is surely no coincidence that in looking for materials for a canzona with trumpet solo, Purcell turned to a sonata movement that had made overt use of the trumpet-style writing for violins that was so popular in the Italian repertoire.[13] The situation is further complicated by the fact that Purcell left two versions of the sonata canzona. Both follow the catch-like, permutational exposition, in which the violins take turns in imitating the trumpet in its high register, with episodic material of exaggeratedly violinistic character, with wide string-crossing leaps, as if to negate the preceding implications of trumpet style and so reaffirm the

[9] An example would be the second section of the overture to *The Gordian Knot Untied* of 1691, a fine work but much less demanding in fugal terms than any of the pieces under discussion in this chapter (for an analysis see Adams, *Henry Purcell*, 140–43).

[10] The canzona for four trumpets Purcell wrote for the funeral of Queen Mary is a work of a rather different sort, though the generic label retains its implications of contrapuntal interest even there.

[11] Adams, *Henry Purcell*, 113, 161–3.   [12] Ibid., 113.

[13] Christopher Hogwood uses the convenient term *violino in tromba* in this connection in his discussions of both Italian works and sonatas by Purcell (*The Trio Sonata* (London: BBC, 1979), 29, 87). However, it is unclear whether this terminology would have been familiar to seventeenth-century musicians in that context; Hogwood may have mistakenly applied the term back from its appearance in certain works by Vivaldi which specify *violini in tromba [marina]*, hence in imitation not of trumpet but the esoteric single-stringed 'trumpet marine'. Eleanor Selfridge-Field considers this to have been a style of violin-playing using harmonics in her article 'Vivaldi's Esoteric Instruments', *EM*, 6/3 (1978), 332–8 (335–6); more recently, Michael Talbot has proposed that the designation entailed physical adaptation of the violin; see Michael Talbot, 'Vivaldi and the "Violino in tromba marina"', *The Consort*, 61 (2005), 5–17.

qualities of the violin. It is not entirely clear which version is the later, since it has been argued that the autograph in *Lbl* Add. MS 30930 could be a revision of an earlier manuscript version that later found its way into the 1697 print;[14] certainly the contrast between the extreme flatwards plunges in the print and the more restrained, more consistently sequence-driven counterpoint of the autograph would bear this out.

The *Indian Queen* canzona follows neither version closely, instead triumphantly reclaiming the materials of the sonata for the trumpet, in a movement that more than any other Purcell trumpet canzona makes a feature of the trumpet as a solo instrument. Its densely worked fugue leads into a series of increasingly fanfare-like antiphonal exchanges in the Bolognese manner, neatly dovetailed into the fugue by deriving their materials closely from the main subject. The assurance with which Purcell handles this style in 1695 belies the close links between this canzona and the earlier sonata movements, however: in composing the trumpet work Purcell cannot but have been aware of his earlier treatment of the same materials, with the result that an analysis which begins from the comparison of his strategies in each case can reveal much about his approach to the later work.

Unlike the other two late canzonas discussed below, in which artifice is pursued through the juxtaposition of multiple fugue subjects, the canzona in the *Indian Queen* trumpet overture presents an ingenious working of a single subject in close imitation. At the climax of the first fugal passage, the trumpet enters with the subject (b. 24) initiating a remarkable passage of five bars in which the characteristic triple-anacrusis head motif is heard twice in every bar. While this kind of dense texture is familiar from the fantazias and sonatas, where the close imitation would be immediately apparent to the participants in the ensemble, it is much more risky in a listener-oriented genre such as this. Roger North articulated the problem when he wrote in his *Musical Grammarian* of 1728 that 'Fuges and swift movements doe not agree well together', for 'unless it be at the entrance after a resting, the audience will have no knowledge of any [fugal] point. Perhaps an ear placed in the midst of the performers may distinguish somewhat, but at a decent position, the sume is a musicall din, and no better.'[15] North's view of the style proper to theatre music was rather that it was 'chiefly compounded of melody, and pulsation or time: the consort is not much heeded, and if the melody is ayery ... the ground may be of a common style':

And all the force of these consorts lyes in the upper part, to which all the rest and even the base sometimes is subservient. Therefore it is to litle purpose to crowd in

[14] Purcell, *Ten Sonatas in Four Parts*, ed. Christopher Hogwood, I, iv–vii; see also Shay and Thompson, *Purcell Manuscripts*, 113–17.
[15] Wilson, *Roger North on Music*, 188–9.

accords by inner parts, for (if they could have any melody) care is taken, by doubling the superior, to drowne them.[16]

Although North is thinking here primarily of common 'playhouse tunes', his description applies well to much theatrical instrumental music by Purcell's contemporaries, especially by comparison with Purcell's own. The French overture that opens Eccles's music for the first Musical Entertainment in John Dennis's *Rinaldo and Armida* (1698), for example, fine though it is in melodic terms, would lose almost nothing from the complete omission of the second violin and viola parts – with such parts 'no better than hum-drum drudges', small wonder that 'scarce any but hirelings will be concerned with them', as North observed.[17] Yet North's typically acerbic observations also contain hints as to why Purcell evidently felt able to indulge his penchant for contrapuntal display in the *Indian Queen* canzona, despite such concerns. The clear differentiation of the trumpet in terms of timbre provides a strong aural focus on a top line as 'ayery' as could be wished, without its either being lost 'as in a mist' in the blend of ensemble parts or, conversely, requiring reinforcement to the extent that any detail in the supporting texture is rendered futile. Purcell further draws attention to the status of the trumpet by reserving it until after the initial exposition, setting the stage for its entry with a drawn-out cadential progression over a long bass pedal A:[18] although the trumpet shares thematic material with the strings, then, its presence has clear structural implications not unlike those of later Italian concerto styles. In terms of texture, meanwhile, the clear melodic focus provided by the trumpet liberated Purcell to provide a level of detail in the accompanying parts that would impress his performers and any listening colleagues, and satisfy his own pride in his contrapuntal prowess.

The density of imitative entries is made possible – indeed, the whole outline of the trumpet's first entry in bars 24–9 is determined – by the specific alterations Purcell made to the material he took from Sonata VII (1697). Or, to put that another way, the changes Purcell made to the familiar subject material demonstrate the importance he placed upon its potential for close imitative treatment in its new context. The sonata canzona had begun with a permutational exposition whose three-part subject complex is subjected to five complete iterations; a sixth is interrupted somewhat unexpectedly with an abrupt cadence on the third scale-degree. Two features of this complex (shown in both subject and answer forms in Ex. 8.3) are particularly worthy of note: the use of a real answer in

---

[16] Ibid., 271.

[17] Eccles' music for *Rinaldo and Armida* has been published as part of the ongoing series of the composer's *Works*: John Eccles, *Rinaldo and Armida*, ed. Steven Planck, Recent Researches in the Music of the Baroque Era, 176 (Middleton, WI: A-R Editions, 2011). Quotations from Wilson, *Roger North on Music*, 272.

[18] Adams makes a similar point (*Henry Purcell*, 162).

Ex. 8.3   Sonata VII (1697), canzona: three-part subject complex (bb. 81–5)

circumstances that arguably suggest a tonal answer would be more appropriate, and the fact that the second countersubject is designed to invert with the subject at the twelfth, rather than the octave, when serving as the bass (as indeed it does in bars 85–6 and 91–2).

The canzona from the *Indian Queen* trumpet overture, by contrast, opens with an immediate stretto at the distance of a minim (Ex. 8.4a). It was this stretto that shaped the new form of the subject when compared with the version in the earlier canzona: the original head-motif would have created consecutive octaves from the moment the second part entered, and the stretto would have become even less viable from the end of the second bar (as shown on the small stave above the main system). In the new subject, Purcell took the opportunity to introduce the characteristic triple anacrusis of the canzona; having chosen a repeated fifth scale-degree for this figure, he then also supplied the expected tonal answer. At the end of the subject, he rewrote the leading part to continue in the parallel thirds established earlier in the second bar, with the result that the subject now elaborated a scale in minims from the fifth towards the key-note. Although it is correct (as Martin Adams has noted) that this made the subject readily extensible, in fact Purcell never extended it beyond the length found in this first entry. Rather, in making the subject more regularly sequential, its end was less clearly defined: after the initial four quavers lead into the running semiquavers, the part in question dissolves back into the texture and the ear is free to listen for the next entry – a quality that is essential to the success of the denser passage in bars 24–9.

It is striking how much of the creative work of the first fifteen bars of this canzona followed directly from the establishment of this opening stretto. In the first place, the fact that the new canzona opened with a subject–answer pair of voices called into question the form of the entry in the third bar, which had been an answer in the sonata. In the trumpet canzona Purcell opted to introduce the viola with a subject entry, perhaps prompted by the strong implication of impending cadence at the start of bar 17 and the resulting opportunity to overlap the next subject entry with this cadence. Thus although the exposition so far retains the two-bar phrasing

Ex. 8.4   Trumpet overture (*The Indian Queen*, Act III), canzona, bb. 15–29: subject origins and parallel construction of the sonata canzona, the elision of cadence and subject entry at this point creates a very different effect, going some way towards explaining the avoidance of 'clipped, two-bar phrasing' observed by Adams.[19] As shown in Ex. 8.4a, this entry in the viola is accompanied by a countersubject ('CS') identical in function to the first countersubject in the sonata canzona (compare Ex. 8.3 above).

Having established these four bars, Purcell set about deriving the next eleven bars directly from them – as shown in the remainder of Ex. 8.4, which aligns bars 19–23 and 24–9 with the framework in bars 15–18. (To make the parallels easier to see, material not directly related to the subject or countersubject is shown using grey noteheads, while the interlocks established in bars 15–18 are labelled respectively $\boxed{A}$–$\boxed{C}$). The way in which Purcell first introduced the bass part is particularly subtle. As at the start of bar 17, he timed a subject entry to overlap with the expected cadence. This entry is technically redundant (the second violin already having played the subject in b. 15), though if so it is in name only, since it turns out to lead to a new statement of the opening interlock $\boxed{A}$ – thereby producing the tonal answer heard in the bass.

Whereas in Ex. 8.4a it is the leading voice that controls the harmonic direction, however, in Ex. 8.4b Purcell allows the bass (the following voice in interlock $\boxed{A}$) to take over, leading to a cadence on A and the establishment of the pedal in bar 22. The foundation of interlock $\boxed{B}$ on this following voice of $\boxed{A}$ then produces the violin 1 entry in the second half of bar 21, effectively inserting an extra half-bar – shown in Ex. 8.4 by the dotted lines opening up to the first half of bar 21 – which Purcell covers up with an opportunistic (and defective) entry in the viola. By adopting the tonal answer form of the subject in the first violin entry at bar 21_3, and deriving the accompanying second violin from the countersubject, Purcell established a sequence of suspensions over the bass pedal that seems to push inexorably towards the cadence in bar 24 and the entry of the trumpet, which once again elides with the end of the previous phrase.

From this position we are well placed to understand exactly how Purcell achieved the much greater density of entries in bars 24–9 (Ex. 8.4c). Disregarding for a moment those subject entries which are severely truncated or defective in other ways (shown here in small noteheads to distinguish them from the structural voices), it becomes clear that the three-part framework from Ex. 8.4a is replicated fully intact in these bars, the trumpet and first violin taking the parts originally assigned respectively to violins one and two and the bass taking the original viola part down an octave. Purcell's only significant modification is to stretch out the trumpet part by the addition of an extra semibreve in bar 26, thereby making his audience wait even longer than in the equivalent bars (17 and 22) for the

---

[19] Ibid., 161.

expected cadence. In imitative terms, this is achieved by delaying the entry of the first violin by a bar, so that it makes use of a flexed version of the incidental interlock $\boxed{C}$ first heard between the inner parts in bars 15–18. Even the 'free' first violin part in bars 27_3–8 imports voice-leading wholesale from the second violin in bars 17–18 (*x*), while the trumpet countersubject in bars 27–9 concludes with a transposition of the version in the first violin in bar 21 (*y*).

It would be easy to dismiss the remaining entries in bars 24–7 as opportunistic surface echoes of the subject, but this would be to miss the resourcefulness with which Purcell exploits the opening of interlock $\boxed{A}$ in bars 24, 25 and 26–7 to provide each of the full subject entries with a further close stretto. In each case the semiquavers persist as long as the surrounding structural parts permit, though the second violin entry in bar 24 demands more radical revision to avoid parallel octaves with the bass and to prevent interference with the entry in the first violin at bar 25_3; the even less exact entry in the second violin in bar 26 is explained as the surface ornamentation of a descending scalic line ultimately derived from the suppressed continuation of the subject entry it began at bar 24_3. Only in the paired second violin and viola parts of bars 27_3–8 does Purcell resort to mere surface ornamentation, these parts deriving from obvious sequential fillers rather than from the imitative processes at the core of his invention in this passage.

As in most of his later canzonas, Purcell does not tax the attention of his audience much beyond this concentrated opening, which accounts for less than half of the canzona in raw length. The remaining passages, though no less attractive, were technically much less demanding for the composer: most make use of simple melodic exchanges between trumpet and strings, whether based on contrasting material (bb. 30–33 and 44–48) or treating the fugal head-motif antiphonally (bb. 38_3–42 and 49–53). The exception to this is the brief return to fugal procedure in bars 34–8 in order to articulate the main area of harmonic contrast, B minor (Ex. 8.5). In these bars Purcell never states the subject in the full form heard at the start of the movement. Yet rather than a relaxation of technique, this appears to result from the desire to permit the trumpet to carry the subject in this key. Thus its entry in bar 34 breaks off only where a further sequential repetition (shown in Ex. 8.5 with crossed noteheads) would lead the instrument into unplayable notes. At this point he turns instead to a Phrygian cadence that demands an answer cadencing on the local key-note, B – a function he duly fulfilled with a liberally flexed first violin and bass stretto beginning in bar 36. The entries in the inner parts here are more opportunistic, and correspondingly less exact, though the viola does appear to preserve fleeting remnants of experimental entries on the off-beat (bb. 34 and 35–6, shaded) and in inversion (b. 36, also shaded; an interesting echo of the fuller inverted entries in the original sonata canzona).

Ex. 8.5   Trumpet overture (*The Indian Queen*, Act III), canzona, bb. 32–9: later treatment of subject

The connection between this canzona from the *Indian Queen* trumpet overture and the earlier canzona from Sonata VII (1697) unquestionably provides a valuable starting-point from which to understand Purcell's compositional decisions. For all the justified praise of Purcell's last contribution to this genre, however, this canzona is not typical of his practice in the 1690s: we know he considered 'double and treble fuges' superior to single-subject workings, and this is borne out in the fact that most of his late canzonas present multiple subjects. The remainder of this chapter is concerned with two such examples, both of which demonstrate that Purcell's techniques had changed remarkably little, for all that he made telling changes to their execution and keenly exploited the potential of the larger ensemble.

'SKILFUL NUMBERS': THE CANZONA IN COME YE SONS OF ARTS

One of Purcell's best known instrumental works is the symphony today associated with Purcell's last ode for Queen Mary's Birthday, *Come ye Sons of Arts*, which also appears (a tone lower, in C major, and with an additional closing fast movement in compound time) in Act II of *The Indian Queen*.[20] Adams considers its canzona to '[outdo] even that from *Hail, bright Cecilia* in being based on three simultaneously presented subjects',[21] which impressive feat was no doubt Purcell's motivation, though it is a matter of opinion whether or not the result is ultimately more successful than the two-subject canzona in *Hail, bright Cecilia* (discussed in Chapter 5), or for that matter the very similar canzona in the 'Sonata while the Sun Rises' from Act IV of *The Fairy Queen*, which is the subject of the final part of this chapter. The *Come ye Sons* canzona is nevertheless a fine work, and one that perhaps more than any other late instrumental work lays bare its technical resources, making it an ideal case study in the present context.

At first hearing this canzona presents a bewildering display of contrapuntal skill. The first half of the movement works out possible combinations of its three subjects in exhaustive fashion: armed with a score one can easily find more than thirty different two-voice interlocks formed from its three subjects in the space of a mere 15 bars, and over half of these are also repeated. Such an outwardly complex texture would appear to be closely akin to the technique of Purcell's fantazias, but appearances in this case are certainly deceptive: in fact, the central idea of the canzona marks a wholesale return to the 'catch-like' permutational style of exposition found in the majority of trio sonata canzonas. Thus although no specific earlier model exists for this work, the idea of comparing it with Purcell's earlier techniques proves if anything even more revealing in this case.

Like those of his earlier sonatas, the opening of this canzona is built from a basic group of three subjects that form a self-contained musical phrase. The character of the material, however, is now much more harmonically oriented: rather than outlining a repetitive sequential progression, the three-part subject complex in the *Come ye Sons* canzona outlines a simple structural descent from scale-degree 5 over strongly cadential harmony (Ex. 8.6). The character of the three subjects is carefully judged, too, with clearly differentiated voice-leading (scales in contrary motion in the outer parts, and successive leaps in the inner) and rhythmic character (crotchets on the beat in the bass, triplet quavers off the beat in the treble, and repeated duplet quavers in the inner part). In terms of the key issue of

[20] I do not intend to dwell here on whether or not, as Rebecca Herissone has recently questioned, the symphony in fact belongs to *Come ye Sons of Arts* at all; see Herissone, 'Robert Pindar, Thomas Busby, and the Mysterious Scoring of Henry Purcell's "Come Ye Sons of Art"', *ML*, 88/1 (2007), 1–48 (22–3). Herissone's full reconstruction of the work is also published as Henry Purcell, *Come ye Sons of Arts*, reconstructed by Rebecca Herissone (London: Stainer & Bell, 2010); the passage under discussion here is as given in the Purcell Society edition of the ode. My reference to 'Skilful numbers' comes from the second half of the third movement of the ode (the famous countertenor duet 'Sound the trumpet'): 'All the instruments of joy/That skilful numbers can employ'.

[21] Adams, *Henry Purcell*, 268.

Ex. 8.6   *Come ye Sons of Arts*, canzona: tonal content of subject material

audience comprehension, then, these features achieve two aims in particular: the subjects are immediately recognizable, yet so closely derived from
the underlying progression that the listener is relieved of the task of relating
the melodic surface to the underlying harmonic process. The appearance of
one or more of the themes implies the model, and vice versa, so that it is not
necessary to discern every entry in order to grasp the desired effect. Indeed,
the close and consistent relationship between the three subjects and the
underlying cadential progression helps explain why Purcell presented all
three subjects simultaneously from the start, rather than successively (as
was his habit in the sonatas): the basic idea here is not a melodically
conceived subject or even three subjects of equal status, but the whole
three-part texture shown in the model in Ex. 8.6.

Purcell's use of this three-voice complex is nevertheless virtually identical to his procedure in the earlier sonata canzonas, as shown in Ex. 8.7.
The main staves represent the actual structural voices of the canzona as a
continuous three-voice texture constructed from eight iterations of the
original three-subject complex, in different permutations (small notes
represent essential material that is present in Purcell's score, but not
derived strictly from the subject complexes). When these parts are played
on their own, there is very little indeed to distinguish this procedure from
that employed in earlier examples such as the C major canzona from
Sonata VII (1697) discussed above, from the basic alternation of tonic
and dominant in regular two-bar phrases to the frequent inversion of the
third subject at the twelfth to open up permutations that would not be
viable using inversion at the octave alone (bb. 14–15, 16–17, 18–19, 20–
21). The quasi-canonic structure of most catch-like expositions (see
Chapter 3), in which the subjects follow one another in the same order
in each part, is no longer relevant here given the distribution of the three

Ex. 8.7 *Come ye Sons of Arts*, bb. 11–25: permutations of basic three-part complex, with additional entries on uppermost stave

structural voices across a larger, six-part texture. Remarkably, though, Purcell has replaced this aspect of systematization with another, according to which the six available permutations of the three subjects are exhaustively exploited: the fugal treatment comes to an end immediately after the introduction of the sixth different permutation at bar 23_3. Only twice is a given permutation repeated, and in each of these cases Purcell uses other strategies to maintain variety: while bars 14_3–16 repeat the S1/S2/S3 subject-order of bars 11–12, the later statement is over a dominant pedal in the bass and Purcell transposes most of the second subject down a fifth; in bars 22–3 he repeats the S2/S1/S3 configuration of bars 12_3–14_2, but transposes the whole to conclude with a cadence on the key-note rather than the fifth.[22]

What differences there are between the texture shown in Ex. 8.7 and the simple canzona expositions of the sonatas can all be explained with reference to the larger ensemble or as improvements to the basic model of cyclic repetition. One way Purcell expanded the number of parts, for example, was to shadow the first subject at the third or sixth (as shown using small notes in bb. 13–18, 24–5); the extra voices also allowed him to introduce five subject entries that overlapped with the two-bar phrases of the complete three-voice complexes (shown on the additional stave at the top), thereby disguising the regularity of the design. Both of these changes are largely cosmetic, however, leaving the underlying cyclical recurrence of the three-part complex intact. By contrast, in iterations **ii**, **iv** and **viii** Purcell brought forward the beginning of the three-voice complex by a minim such that it overlapped with the cadence at the end of the preceding statement, thereby causing genuine disruptions to the two-bar cycle (shown in Ex. 8.7 using brackets beneath the bass part). The strategic positioning of the start of a new imitative complex to overlap with a cadence had of course been common in the fantazias, and was a key feature of the canzonas of the 1690s (as indeed we saw in the canzona from the *Indian Queen* trumpet overture analysed above).

In an extraordinarily subtle move, Purcell further concealed the cyclical pattern in these same three statements of the three-part complex by offsetting the first subject by a minim in each case, such that (unlike the other two subjects) it begins only after the completion of the preceding cadence. Bars 11–14 are paradigmatic, and the technical means by which Purcell delayed the entry are in fact relatively straightforward: since the first subject simply elaborated a falling scale in minims it could easily start on the second note of this scale, its new beginning strongly defined by its highly characteristic rhythm. Having in effect removed the first off-beat group of triplets from the start of the subject (see the crossed noteheads in Ex. 8.7,

---

[22] Note that the configuration of the subjects in bars 18–19 is S3/S2/S1, since the viola part represented on the highest main stave in Ex. 8.7 sounds an octave lower than written there.

bb. 12_4 (Vn2), 16_2 (Ob2) and 23_4 (BC)), Purcell could then easily add an additional group at the end in place of the original minim (bb.14_2 (Vn2), 17_4 (Ob2), 25_2 (BC)).

This simple change may originally have been prompted by nothing more complicated than the need to complete the melodic cadence in the second violin in bars 12–13, but proves significant in remarkable ways – not least the fact that it allowed Purcell to supply something resembling a tonal answer to the initial entry of the first subject. Furthermore, given the disrupted internal alignment of the subjects in statement **ii**, the entry of the second subject in the same part at bar 13_3 appears to overlap with the end of the first subject (and this despite the fact that iteration **iii** as a whole begins only after the completion of the cadence). Finally, it was the delay of the first subject in iteration **ii** to the start of bar 13 that permitted Purcell to insert the additional overlapping statement of the second subject in the first violin at bar 13_3, which would otherwise have formed consecutive unisons with the second violin moving into bar 14 (as shown in Ex. 8.7). Such effortless control, the way different aspects of the technical treatment seem to fall into place inevitably as the result of apparently unrelated decisions, is surely a key contributing factor to the suave assurance of Purcell's style in these late instrumental works.

Perhaps most impressive of all, however, is the way in which Purcell is able to subsume the two-bar oscillation between tonic and dominant iterations of the subject complex within a longer-term harmonic process which overrides any vestiges of the periodicity that was a feature of the sonata canzona (and which again was unlikely to attract a listening audience). The clear cadential implications of the three-voice complex conversely offered great potential for building longer passages of music by evading and denying the expected resolution, a potential that Purcell exploited in order to build tension across greater periods of time. Thus although the first five subject complexes alternate conventionally between tonic and dominant, their aural effect is somewhat different: iteration **i** is never allowed to confirm the tonic, since the elision with iteration **ii** results in an interrupted cadence at bar 13; after a cadence in the dominant, iteration **iii** then follows in the tonic, but Purcell introduces it over a dominant pedal (which in turn demands the transposition of most of its second subject down a fourth). The harmonic tension built up by this pedal is further prolonged by iteration **iv** in the dominant. It is only resolved with the arrival of a strong tonic chord at the start of iteration **vi**, accompanied by peals of overlapping first-subject entries in the first violin, trumpet/first oboe and second oboe parts.

At this moment, Purcell pushes the point home with a further statement of the complete fugal complex in D major (iteration **vii**). The resulting three consecutive tonic statements go some way towards balancing the previous emphasis on the dominant and establishing tonic

harmony firmly, but the bass part does not descend to the low *A* of its
pedal again until bar 21 (as part of the second subject) and we do not hear
it rise to *d* in a clearly cadential progression until the end of the fugal
section in bar 26. Purcell further compensates for the arresting of harmonic tension in these bars with his favourite earlier device of building
tension through increasing levels of artifice, culminating in bars 23–4
where, through the combination of elision of statement **viii** with the
preceding cadence, additional entries in trumpet/first oboe and second
violin, and the delaying of the first subject in the bass (as in bb. 12–13),
he builds a five-voice imitative complex incorporating new entries on
three consecutive minims.

As in the opening bars of the canzona, the seeming inevitability of the
cadence in bar 26 belies Purcell's highly calculated manipulation of
materials, not to mention the skill with which he deployed the resulting
combinations. Thus the introduction of iteration **viii** in the dominant,
on the heels of the three previous tonic subject-statements, clearly signals
a fresh increase in harmonic tension; Purcell's selection of the S2/S3/S1
configuration here places the scalic descent in the first subject towards the
low *A* in the bass part, connecting this cadence with the register of the
dominant pedal of bars 14–15. The approach to the cadence is remarkable for the way in which Purcell integrates the harmonic and imitative
aspects of his technique: the entry of the third subject in the second violin
at bar 24, though notionally not one of the three structural voices of the
texture, assumes great importance by precluding the *g*♯″ in the second
subject (Ex. 8.8), and thus the resulting dominant cadence that would
otherwise conclude iteration **viii**. Purcell makes it fit by altering the
end of the second subject in the second oboe (b. 25), resolving the
suspended *a*″ to a *g*″ *natural* which initiates a stepwise descent to the
tonic (see the shading in Ex. 8.7, which shows Purcell's solution to
the solecism also shaded in Ex. 8.8). Just as in many earlier works,
then, harmonic events are made to arise directly from imitative processes.
Purcell could have incorporated this combination at any point in the
fugue, but chose to reserve it for the end of the strictly fugal section where
it could be put to work at the climax of a highly sophisticated tonal game.
The tension introduced by the transposition of the subject complex to the
dominant in bars 12_3–13_2 is not resolved simply by the return to the
tonic; instead, the tonic is only truly affirmed when the transposed

Ex. 8.8   *Come ye Sons of Arts*, bb. 23_3–25: incompatible subject entries

subject complex has itself been neutralized by subjugation into tonic harmony, as a direct result of the surrounding imitative activity.

After the concentration of these opening sixteen bars, the remainder of the canzona – as in the *Indian Queen* trumpet overture, more than half the length of the canzona as a whole – seems almost bereft of contrapuntal interest by comparison. Purcell all but abandons his subjects, presenting no further complete statements of the three-part complex; the only obvious reference to the previous material is a seemingly half-hearted statement of the first and third subjects in bars 38–40, hidden away in the viola and bass. It would be easy to settle for the conclusion that, having exhausted both the contrapuntal potential of his materials and the probable attention span of his audience, Purcell simply resorted to empty orchestral gestures in the remainder of the movement.

Yet this is decidedly not the impression gained by the listener. The rapid succession of cadences that follows the tonic resolution in bar 26 – B minor (b. 27), F♯ Phrygian (b. 28), F♯ minor (b. 30), E minor (b. 32) – provides a most effective contrast with the stability of the foregoing tonic harmony and the restriction of the opening sixteen bars to tonic and dominant cadences. From bar 32, Purcell then turned to the antiphonal style discussed in relation to the *Indian Queen* canzona above, using its lively exchanges to resolve this new harmonic tension through a return to the tonic and then a series of melodic fifths which propel the harmony towards the establishment of a final descent from the fifth scale-degree in bars 38–40$_1$ (the additional bars 40–44 adopt a new, fanfare-like figure to reiterate this cadence, strengthening the sense of finality with a long descending scale in the bass). The return in bars 33–40$_1$ to diatonic D major harmonies, with clear articulation of cadential goals, then, creates a strong aural link with the earlier fugal section; indeed, the melodic fifths in particular are strongly redolent of the original second subject. This raises the possibility that there is something more strategic going on beneath the bombastic surface.

In one sense this is a feature of Purcell's derivation of the fugal materials here from such basic harmonic commonplaces: it suggests perhaps that Purcell's technique has moved closer to the manipulation of 'tonal models' that Christopher Wintle observed in Corelli (see Chapter 4), with at least this passage of the canzona being fundamentally 'about' the underlying progressions rather than the surface forms of the subjects.[23] The use of similar progressions in sections otherwise unrelated is an obvious way of establishing coherence in a thematically and texturally diverse movement such as Purcell's canzona. Thus at one level the scalic descent to the tonic in bars 38–40 could be understood as a new manifestation of that from the first subject of the fugal section, now articulated through antiphonal semiquavers rather than off-beat triplet quavers. Supporting this reading is the additional presence of the third

---

[23] Wintle, 'Corelli's Tonal Models', 49.

subject in the bass at this point. But why, if the upper line was a version of the first subject, would Purcell have placed the same subject in the viola part a fifth lower? Apart from anything else, this doubling produces blatant consecutive fifths (which, indeed, remain barely concealed in the final texture irrespective of one's understanding of the origins of this material).

The presence of the first and third subjects in bars 38–9 does, however, provide a clue to a more attractive analysis of bars 33–40_1, according to which this passage has an even more artificial basis. Given that throughout the sixteen bars of strict fugue that began the canzona all three subjects were stated together, where is the second subject in bar 38? In fact, the whole of the treble line in bars 32_3–9 can be understood as an expanded and ornamented version of the second subject up a fifth, leading to a tonic cadence – as heard in the second oboe in bars 23_3–6 and discussed above (see Ex. 8.9). The harmonic rhythm is exactly matched with that of the subject in double augmentation in bars 32_3–8_2, before an acceleration to original note-values for the final scalic descent to the tonic in bars 38_3–40_1. The possibility that this happened fortuitously cannot be entirely ruled out, especially given the commonplace character of the subject in the first place and the metrical regularity that results from the antiphonal exchanges, but the known importance of augmentation to Purcell's fugal technique (see Chapter 7), together with the exactness of the rhythmic profile – the tonic chord could easily have arrived a minim earlier in bar 34, for example – and the missing second subject in bar 38, strongly suggest

Ex. 8.9   *Come ye Sons of Arts*, bb. 36–9: derivation from augmented version of earlier second subject

that the passage should be taken seriously as an orchestral division on the second subject. Furthermore, Purcell would have had good reason to base this passage on the close of the fugal section, where as we have seen the manipulation of the dominant form of the second subject to end in the tonic formed a significant structural cadence.

Whether one attributes these links between the fugal section of this canzona and the antiphonal material towards the end to such compositional ingenuity or to a more general concentration on increasingly stereotyped 'tonal models' and their varied surface ornamentation – or, indeed, one conceives of both explanations operating concurrently, as a function of Purcell's fluent synthesis of his artificial manner with the Italian style – it is clear that despite the real changes in his musical language, works such as the canzona from *Come ye Sons* show Purcell every bit as concerned with the promotion of musical artifice as he was in his earlier instrumental music. The tonal character of the materials in this canzona inevitably invites comparison with Corelli's sonatas (and indeed even more so in the final analysis of this chapter) though, as we have seen throughout, Purcell continued to cultivate a technique of *fugeing* that was never matched by Corelli. He also persisted in his reliance upon the compositional processes that allowed him to sustain this technique, while at the same time modifying the repetitive structures of his permutational approach to fugal invention: overlapping complexes with cadences, designing subjects that could overlap with the main cyclical repeats, and working hard to conceal the regular harmonic oscillations.

Just how successful Purcell's canzona is in this regard can be heard by comparing it with the canzona from Daniel Purcell's 1698 Cecilian ode, *Begin the Noble Song*, which – as Bryan White points out – is closely modelled on Henry's canzona.[24] Daniel's apparent admiration for this canzona, which was no doubt familiar from its place in Act II of *The Indian Queen* (whose Act V masque was added by Daniel after the death of Henry), is evident in many details of his own work, from the scoring and key down to the materials themselves – which echo Henry's almost to the point of parody. But Daniel's piece falls flat in exactly the areas of techique where Henry's was most successful: in the course of seven iterations of his three-subject complex, not once does Daniel introduce additional subject entries to overlap with the periodic repetitions; the first five iterations remain firmly in the tonic key, and only after a half-hearted attempt at invertible counterpoint at the twelfth in the fifth iteration does Daniel transpose the subject complex wholesale to the dominant. Iteration seven then returns immediately to the tonic, and after a brief flirtation with the relative minor the piece breaks down into antiphonal semiquaver figurations without any hint of the underlying motivic significance heard in

---

[24] See White, *Music for St Cecilia's Day*, 149–51, including a full transcription of Daniel's canzona.

Henry's work. The later work provides compelling evidence that at least one contemporary understood the technical basis of Henry's *Come ye Sons* canzona, then, even as its own shortcomings accentuate the success with which the older composer had escaped the potential for monotony by judicious use of supplementary *fugeing*, increased subtlety of phrasing and an ability to harness both in the projection of longer-range tonal processes. If the *Come ye Sons* canzona is impressive in this regard, however, the technique had already reached its apogee in Purcell's hands two years previously, in one of the few Italianate instrumental symphonies that the composer wrote expressly for the theatre.

'IN ITS FULL LUSTRE'

Purcell's most virtuosic deployment of the permutational exposition is the canzona from the 'Sonata while the Sun Rises' at the beginning of Act IV of *The Fairy Queen*. In this work, Purcell rings the changes on a set of largely commonplace materials no doubt known to countless Baroque composers – not least J. S. Bach, who was to use a very similar subject in the 'Gratias' and 'Dona nobis' of the B minor Mass – and used in almost identical form by at least Stradella and Corelli before him. The bewildering array of combinations Purcell presents of his two simple subjects far outstrips the ambitions of either Italian composer, and indeed any other canzona by Purcell (and here I would include that in *Hail, bright Cecilia*, despite its outward similarity). Indeed, this canzona seems wilfully to disregard the concerns over intelligibility touched on above, to the extent that one can only suppose Purcell to have been intent upon inspiring a sense of dumb-founded wonder in his audience – much the same response, perhaps, as might result from contemplating the splendours of a fine dawn.[25]

Notwithstanding Adams's observation that the two subjects of this canzona are closely related to the material of the first section of the symphony, it is hard to escape the conclusion that Purcell based his fugue on either or both of the similar movements from Stradella's *Il barcheggio* and Corelli's Sonata *a* 4, WoO4 (Ex. 8.10).[26] Both Stradella and Corelli use a subject identical in all but very superficial details to

---

[25] I thank Bruce Wood for suggesting the title to this section, which comes from the stage directions describing the rising sun at the start of Act IV of *The Fairy Queen*.

[26] Stradella also made use of a similar subject in the canzona from his *Sonata a otto Viole con una Tromba*, which Peter Holman dates to before 1675; here the subject arrives at the suspension a minim earlier, with the initial entries at the fifth only after the cadence (*Italian Baroque Trumpet Music*, Steven Keavy and Crispian Steele-Perkins (trumpets), The Parley of Instruments, directed by Peter Holman; Hyperion CDH66255, 1988, re-released on CDH55192, 2005). In what follows I assume, as no doubt did Purcell's English contemporaries, that WoO4 is indeed by Corelli. Recent accounts of Corelli's works give credence to this claim, while acknowledging that documentary proof is lacking; see Peter Allsop, *Arcangelo Corelli: 'New Orpheus of our Times'* (Oxford University Press, 1999), 8–9; Michael Talbot, 'Corelli, Arcangelo', in *Grove Music Online* (accessed 22 November 2018).

Ex. 8.10   Shared materials in three trumpet canzonas: (a) Alessandro Stradella, *Il barch-eggio* (1681): Sinfonia I, canzona (opening); (b) Arcangelo Corelli, Sonata *a*4, WoO4, second movement (opening); (c) Purcell, 'Sonata while the Sun Rises' (from Act IV of *The Fairy Queen*), bb. 43–7; (d) 'Sonata while the Sun Rises': three-part complex with additional, overlapping subject entry

Purcell's first subject **A**, introduced after the same recurring interval of one and a half bars (Ex. 8.10a–c; the same is true of Purcell's exposition in bb. 16–18). Even more telling, though, is the way in which Purcell turns the descending-scale bass line also used by both Italian composers into a second fugue subject. Characteristically, he reserved the fullest expression of this principle for the climax of his fugue, following bar 43 (Ex. 8.10c): the groups of quavers in the bass in bar 43 (**B**) elaborate Corelli's descending minims, and are answered in the second trumpet a bar and a half later. Even Corelli's uncharacteristically bland root-position tonic–dominant oscillation in bars 3–5, a serious weakness so early in the piece, is transformed by Purcell into an exciting plummet towards the structural cadence in bar 48, further intensified by extra rhythmic activity and octave transpositions in the bass.

Though it is not essential to my purposes to prove that Purcell must have known either Italian work, it is well within the bounds of possibility that he could have encountered one or both of them first-hand. Stylistically these works are far more like Purcell's trumpet sonatas than either the Bolognese examples or the operatic Italian overture as it was to develop in the hands of Scarlatti and his contemporaries, making the idea that Purcell knew either work an attractive one. Furthermore, the Stradella and Corelli works together offer a stock repertoire of trumpet figures that could be traced in numerous different works by Purcell in this style (though these are of course related to the wider Italian repertoire, not to mention being restricted by the capabilities of the Baroque trumpet). Of the two, the Corelli work is certainly the more likely to have been familiar to Purcell, given its survival in several English sources of the period.[27] Don Smithers suggested that it may have arrived in England by way of Mary of Modena, James II's Queen Consort, who was the sister of Francesco II d'Este, Duke of Modena.[28] The notion that Corelli visited Modena is now discredited, but he did contribute instrumental music to Giovanni Lorenzo Lulier's oratorio *Santa Beatrice d'Este* in honour of the investiture of Mary's uncle Rinaldo d'Este as cardinal in 1689, and also in the same year to Bernardo Pasquini's oratorio *Il colosso della costanza* celebrating James II's escape from England.[29] The latter work even included a *Sinfonia da guerra con tromba* which could conceivably be the trumpet sonata in question, though of course the Jacobite court had by this stage moved into exile in France and thus any source that reached Mary at Saint Germain en Laye would not necessarily have reached England thereby.[30] A slightly earlier date for Corelli's work would open up another plausible route to England via James's *maestro di capella* Innocenzo Fede, who was recruited in Rome probably in 1686: two of Fede's uncles continued to serve as castrati in the Papal Chapel, including the Giuseppe Fede who in 1687 took the

---

[27] Arcangelo Corelli, *Werke ohne Opuszahl*, ed. Hans Joachim Marx, Arcangelo Corelli: Historische-kritische Gesamtausgabe der musikalischen Werke, v (Cologne: Arno Volk Verlag Hans Gerig KG, 1976), 112–13.

[28] Smithers, *Music and History of the Baroque Trumpet*, 107.   [29] Allsop, *Corelli*, 41–2.

[30] On the Stuart court in exile see Edward T. Corp, 'The Exiled Court of James II and James III: A Centre of Italian Music in France, 1689–1712', *JRMA*, 120/2 (1995), 216–31.

allegorical part of London in Queen Cristina of Sweden's entertainment in honour of the then English ambassador to Rome, Lord Castlemaine (another work featuring instrumental music by Corelli).[31]

Another prominent musical visitor to London in 1687 may have been the Milanese violinist Carlo Ambrogio Lonati who, according to John Hawkins, accompanied the castrato Siface (Giovanni Francesco Grossi) to London when Francesco d'Este sent him to entertain his sister there.[32] Lonati had been a direct predecessor of Corelli in the musical establishment of Queen Cristina (where he acquired the well-known sobriquet 'il Gobbo della Regina'), but his main significance in this context is his close friendship with Alessandro Stradella: the two musicians left Rome in 1677 and by the following year were together again in Genoa. There they remained until Stradella's murder in 1682, less than a year after the performance of the serenata *Il barcheggio* as part of the marriage celebrations between Carlo Spinola and Paula Brignole.[33] Carolyn Gianturco has pointed out that one of the extant sources of *Il barcheggio* is partly in a hand thought to be Lonati's, and further suggested that the other extant manuscript was produced to be sent to Francisco d'Este as a demonstration of Stradella's latest work.[34] If so, it is easy to imagine Stradella's trumpet canzona making its way to London either with Lonati or indirectly through the same Estense family links noted in connection with the Corelli work.[35] Another anecdote repeated by Hawkins concerns Purcell's reaction to the news of Stradella's death, and has Purcell specifically praising the Italian composer's contrapuntal skill;[36] if accurate, it shows at least that Purcell knew some of Stradella's music. It is even possible that Purcell learned of Stradella's death from Lonati himself, though there is no direct evidence to confirm that the two ever met.[37]

In spite of all these opportunities to have encountered Stradella's and Corelli's fugues first-hand, it remains perfectly possible that Purcell arrived at the texture in Ex. 8.10c independently: the first subject is commonplace, and the intervals of entry and accompanying lines would have been obvious solutions for any competent seventeenth-century composer. Yet

---

[31] Ibid., 218–19; Allsop, *Corelli*, 43–4; see also Jean Lionnet, 'Fede, Innocenzo', in *Grove Music Online* (accessed 22 November 2018).

[32] John Hawkins, *A General History of the Science and Practice of Music* (London: T. Payne, 1776), ed. Charles Cudworth, 2 vols (New York: Dover, 1963), ii, 808; see also Norbert Dubowy, 'Lonati, Carlo Ambrogio', in *Grove Music Online* (accessed 22 November 2018).

[33] Ibid.; Carolyn Gianturco, 'Music for a Genoese Wedding of 1681', *ML*, 63/1 (1982), 31–43; see also Gianturco, 'Stradella, Alessandro', in *Grove Music Online* (accessed 22 November 2018).

[34] Gianturco, 'Music for a Genoese Wedding', 33, 42–3.

[35] The likelihood that Lonati returned to Rome in 1682–3 (Dubowy, 'Lonati'), incidentally, also provides a route by which the work could have come to Corelli's attention; it is notable that, like Stradella's sinfonia, Corelli's sonata is scored for trumpet, two violins and continuo, apparently the only instance of three-treble-and-bass scoring in the whole of Corelli's output.

[36] Hawkins, *General History*, ii, 653–4.

[37] Purcell's famous keyboard piece 'Siface's Farewell' may seem suggestive, but need not necessarily imply any direct contact with the Italian visitors.

whether or not the direct connection is real, the fact is that all three composers began with the same essential structure; what the comparison reveals is the vast scope of Purcell's additional interrogation of these same materials, which sets his canzona quite apart from either antecedent work.

One of the characteristics that make this canzona so much less predictable than the *Come ye Sons* work is that the basic imitative materials he employed allowed Purcell to combine his *two* subjects in such a way as to form a *three*-part invertible complex (Ex. 8.10d) – one that is not only irregular in length, at one and a half bars, but is also itself shorter than the perceived length of the first subject. Thus any repetition of the basic materials necessarily produced irregular phrases and overlapping subject entries, without the need to add them to the basic permutational structure as Purcell would later do in *Come ye Sons*. On top of this Purcell also added a new subject entry (labelled x in Ex. 8.10d) further cutting across the repeating cycle, which together with the material shared with the Stradella and Corelli fugues makes a serviceable basis for an analysis of the *Fairy Queen* canzona as a series of repeated blocks of material with incidental entries introduced opportunistically, as in both of the canzonas analysed already in this chapter. This, however, would be to underestimate considerably the extent to which Purcell pushed his exploration of these materials.

In fact, every subject entry he employed in this canzona derives from a single, and remarkable underlying conception: a canon 9 parts in 1 alternately at the fifth and octave, from which he carefully selected and deployed individual strands in order to create his six-part texture. The canon itself arises logically from the process of experimentation already evident in Example 8.10d: Purcell's addition of x already suggested its replication in answer form, for example, but the real leap of imagination came in recognizing the possibility of overlapping the entire three-part structure with itself at intervals of one bar, founded on the entries of the head motif at that distance represented by x and the answer form of S3. The resulting nine-part canon is shown in Example 8.11a–b, firstly as a single line, and then in the form of a repeating nine-part complex, the latter as would arise at the entry of the bass assuming all nine parts entered in order beginning with the first treble, and continued to play without rests thereafter.

Every bar of the two fugal sections of Purcell's canzona presents a selection of between one and six parts of this single bar of music, combined with rests and (only very rarely, in fact) free material. Yet because of the huge number of permutations available, Purcell did not need even to come close to repeating the same selection and permutation. When compared with the six available permutations of the three-part cell he later used in *Come ye Sons* the possibilities in the *Fairy Queen* canzona are staggering: there are in fact more than 60,000 different ways to select six voices from a

Ex. 8.11 'Sonata while the Sun Rises', canzona: underlying canon 9 parts in 1

(a) As a single melodic line with entry points labelled **i–ix**

(b) As a repeating nine-part complex

nine-voice collection,[38] and if we add in the possibility that up to five parts might be resting in a given bar this number rises to just over 200,000, or approaching six days of constantly sounding music![39] The situation is complicated, however, by the fact that some of the parts shown in Ex. 8.11b are not intrinsically compatible. Purcell uses 'free' parts and even small changes to the material itself to compensate for many of these problems; for typical examples see bars 25 (Va), 27 (Vn2) and 27 (Vn1) in Ex. 8.12a. Even so, there remain two pairs of voices, b/c and f/g (see the shading in Ex. 8.11b), which must be treated as alternatives – for the same reason, indeed, which is that the basic canon after one bar at the unison runs into trouble in the third bar. While taking this into account reduces the number of potential permutations considerably, many thousands remain that Purcell could have made use of – ample material for two fugal sections of a combined length of just 23 bars.

The sheer number of permutations available here begins to resemble the mathematics of change-ringing (hence the brief campanological reference

---

[38] $\frac{9!}{(9-6)!} = 60{,}480$ permutations of six voices selected from nine.

[39] The number of distinct selections available given one resting part is obtained by multiplying the number of combinations of five playing parts from an ensemble of six ($\frac{6!}{(6-5)! \times 5!} = 6$) by the number of permutations of five bars of music when selecting from the nine available parts ($\frac{9!}{(9-5)!} = 15{,}120$). This calculation (giving 90,720) must then be repeated for ensembles with between four and one (out of

at the start of this section). Whether Purcell was making a conscious reference to this practice is impossible to know, but there is a clear allusion to bells in the second of the two ground-bass songs that follow the Sonata, a countertenor duet that concludes '[Let] the arch of high Heav'n the clangour resound'. The tradition of ringing in the dawn in celebration of feasts and festivals was well established in many places by the late seventeenth century,[40] and is clearly used here to mark the importance of Oberon's birthday; thus it is tempting indeed to imagine Purcell's canzona as a fugal equivalent to the pealing of bells 'while the sun rises' on stage.

That not every canonic entry shown in Ex. 8.11a remains viable throughout is itself an indication that the canon formed part of Purcell's experimentation with the materials rather than having been the original impetus for their design; in other words, it belonged to the *elaboratio* rather than the *inventio* itself. It should be clear by now that Purcell would have been quite capable of devising a strict six- or even nine-part canon had he planned the movement in such a way; thus the fact that the music remains faithful to the polyphonic skeleton it shared with the Stradella and Corelli sonatas, despite the allure of greater artifice offered by the large canon, could even be taken as further indication of Purcell's conscious appropriation of those materials. It is also important to recognize that although Purcell's conception of the nine-voice canon effectively devised all imitative entries at one fell swoop, it left many other compositional decisions still to be taken. These can best be understood by arranging the canonic entries into a form that more closely resembles Purcell's eventual score for the canzona (Ex. 8.12a–b).

As Ex. 8.12a shows, in bars 16–29 Purcell incorporated complete canonic entries **iv**, **v**, **vii**, **viii** and **ix** in relation to the leading **i**, which is stated three times in succession; in both bars 20 and 24 Purcell took advantage of the identity of **ix** and **i** to begin the process again, making the texture in effect a perpetual canon. In addition to this, he also made use of numerous shorter sections of canonic entries, the unused sections of which are shown with crossed noteheads (which do not in this case indicate rejected entries as such, but rather are included to show how the materials that were used relate to the underlying canonic framework). The three entries not present in full in this first fugal section are all problematic in one way or another, but Purcell still incorporates their usable elements where possible: most of **vi** turns up in the first violin from bar 20, while the sequence of entries in bars 21–3 incorporates all three of **ii**, **iii** and **vi** if one places a notional **i** in bar 23 (this is **iii** relative to the Tpt1 entry in bar 20, but of course the perpetual canon means that any tonic entry can be

---

six) playing parts, and all five numbers added to the figure calculated in n. 38 for an ensemble with all six parts playing. The sum of these six possibilities amounts to 207,774 distinct selections, or 5.77 days of music at 100 crotchet beats per minute. I thank Katie Howard for assisting with this calculation.

[40] Ronald Hutton, *The Rise and Fall of Merry England: The Ritual Year, 1400–1700* (Oxford University Press, 1994), 248 and note 106.

Ex. 8.12 'Sonata while the Sun Rises', canzona: derivation of final texture from canonic voices

(a) bb. 16–29

Ex. 8.12(b)   bb. 38–48

understood as **i**). The opening of **iii** is saved, however, for the end of the second fugal section in bars 38–48, where it plays a vital role in the achievement of harmonic closure discussed below.

Attention to the selection and disposition of canonic voices also reveals much about the way Purcell structured the two fugal sections of the canzona, both in thematic and harmonic terms. The three statements of **i** that control the imitative contents of bars 16–29 do not exercise a corresponding influence over the sense of phrasing. In the first place, Purcell distinguished between the two fugue subjects **A** and **B** in his orchestration: the first two statements of **i** are each split between different instruments (Vn1 and Tpt2 in bb. 16–19, Tpt1 and Vn2 in 20–23), and throughout this section instruments may enter with either **A** or **B**. Through careful attention to the relative disposition of the two subjects, Purcell uses the structure of this passage to showcase the fact that **A** and **B** function both as subjects in a double fugue and as consecutive members of a single canonic leading voice. Thus the canzona begins in bar 16 with statements of **A**, which is then heard in combination with **B**; not until bar 22 do we hear **A** and **B** in succession in the same part, in the second trumpet and then again in the first violin at bar 24. The section ends with a series of close entries of **B** exploiting its cadential qualities (Tpt1, Vn2, Tpt2, bb. 27–8; the trumpet parts are derived from complete canonic entries analogous to the **iii** and **v** shown in bb. 21–2).

Harmonically, meanwhile, Purcell selects specific canonic entries in order to harness the inherent tension of the modulating tonic statement, with its cadence on the pitch A, together with the additional potential of overlapping entries to evade cadences and avoid regular phrase lengths. Thus although the first statement of **i** is congruent with a simple move to the dominant and back to a cadence in the tonic, the use of **B** in the bass at bar 19_3 – founded on a putative **iii** in bar 17 – prevents a strong sense of cadence at bar 20. In the second and third statements of **i** Purcell pushes this technique further, using the entry of **iii** in the second trumpet (b. 22) to preclude any sense of tonic cadence in bar 24. The result is a ten-bar phrase (bb. 21–30) which repeats the trajectory of bars 16–21 at greater length, the return to the tonic arriving only after a sustained emphasis on dominant harmony produced by the suspensions in bars 22, 24 and 26. Just as he would in the later pieces analysed above, Purcell uses such techniques to build and sustain harmonic tension across longer passages than those implied by the obvious phrasing of the fugal materials. The result in the *Fairy Queen* canzona is far more expansive than the workings either in Corelli's *Sonata a Quattro* WoO4, with its uncharacteristically restricted tonal range (its only harmonic contrast deriving from repetition of the main dominant-modulating subject) or in Stradella's *Il barcheggio* canzona, in which tension derives instead from the inventive transposition of the subject (to G, E minor and even C) but the basic imitative framework is left intact.

The unusual return in this canzona to a second fugal section at least as intricately worked out as the first (Ex. 8.12b) can perhaps be attributed to a desire on Purcell's part to exploit more fully some of the possibilities afforded by the canonic design. Certainly the second passage, in bars 38–48, is more densely worked than the first, with eight substantially complete canonic entries in its eleven bars as against nine in the fourteen bars of 16–29 (in both cases counting subjects **A** and **B** as one canonic entry even if distributed among two parts). As we have seen, the second section also makes effective use of entry **iii** for the first time.

The impression gained is that of a compressed reworking of the first fugal section, with entries closer together and redistributed among the available parts. As in bars 16–29, there are three complete statements of **i**, and this time each reinforces the integrity of the canonic structure by remaining in the same part (Vn2, b. 38; BC, b. 40; Tpt2, b. 43). The most obvious change is that Purcell now overlaps these entries of **i**, making use of the perpetual canon to draw the canonic voices closer together (another means of achieving the by now familiar increase in tension through heightened contrapuntal artifice). The first new entry of **i** in bar 38 is actually analogous to that in the first fugal section at bar 20, through the matching of this entry with **iv, v** and **viii** in both passages. Recognition of this parallelism helps to explain the considerable alterations to **i** in the second violin in bars 40 and 41: the appearance of **v** as a bass part (rather than **iv** as in bar 21) demands the removal of the melodic dominant cadence in bar 40. Purcell responded with the minimum necessary revisions while retaining the overall contour of the entry. The resulting removal of the dominant emphasis in this phrase further means that this section never builds the same harmonic tension as bars 16–29, instead performing a reprise-like affirmation of the tonic – though there is compensation in the density of the fugal texture.

The second complete statement of **i** in this section also draws its canonic parts from the first, this time the sequence **i, iv, vii** of bars 16–19. It is the return to the start of the canon at bar 43, though, in which Purcell again builds the level of artifice by exploiting thus far unused material: the sequence **i, iv, v** is joined for the first time by **vii**, creating a pair of entries a bar apart – analogous to the pairing of **i** and **iii** – in the first trumpet and first violin in bars 45–6. Just as we have already seen in the later *Come ye Sons* canzona, in this passage Purcell uses imitative processes to force the resolution of tension inherent in the subject and thereby provide a sense of closure: entries **i** and **iii** are incompatible at the third bar of **i**, which produces the voices labelled 'b' and 'c' in Ex. 8.11b. The solution is to remove the suspension, with its resolution to $g\sharp''$, and instead incorporate material that cadences in the tonic, while also making similar adjustments at the end of the dominant entry in the second violin in bars 44_3–48_1 . This is achieved particularly deftly in the first trumpet part, in which Purcell simply skipped straight to subject **B** on arrival on a'' at bar 46_3, effectively jumping to a voice derived from another canonic entry a bar earlier. In order to avoid unnecessary clutter this putative entry is not shown in Ex. 8.12b, but it is worth noting that the reason it so successfully masks the omission of the dominant-emphasizing suspension is that it builds on a process that began much earlier in the canzona, with a modified combination of these same two entries in the viola in bars 18–21, and a further combination split between the trumpet parts in bars 22–5. Purcell thus uses the demands of this particular combination to strip the tonic entry of its modulation, exploiting the potential of alternative interlocks to provide a new form of the subject that seems to arise naturally from what has gone before. By adopting this strategy at this point in the movement he is able once again to achieve a sense of closure which arises directly from the fugal process, and which has only to be strengthened in the closing bars with the return to material derived from the episodic middle section.[41]

* * *

When Michael Tilmouth described the works discussed in this chapter as 'Italian sonatas in orchestral garb' he went on to comment that 'it [was] in the earlier trio sonatas that Purcell made his most interesting formal experiments, compensating for the absence of the more obvious effects of the orchestral medium with a greater subtlety of design'.[42] On the contrary, however, the late canzonas analysed above if anything display far greater subtlety than Purcell was able to muster in most sonata fugues. If there is one overriding conclusion to be drawn from this analysis it is that the core techniques at work in the canzonas of the early 1680s and those of the 1690s were fundamentally the same; indeed, it would be no exaggeration to say that the latter would not have been possible without the earlier experimentation represented in the former. To the end of his life Purcell continued to employ permutational approaches to fugal exposition, both in a form recognizable from his sonatas (in *Come ye Sons*) and more experimentally through the application of the principle to shorter segments of the overall melodic subject. The latter gives rise to the remarkable texture of the *Fairy Queen* canzona – to appropriate a phrase from Michael Talbot, the *'ne plus ultra* of a "permutational" fugue'[43] – but also helps to explain the facility with which Purcell was able to research

[41] On the episode in bars 29–37 and its relationship to the closing bars of the canzona see Adams, *Henry Purcell*, 149–50.
[42] Tilmouth, 'The Technique and Forms', 109.
[43] Michael Talbot, *Albinoni*, 92. The phrase in question is there applied to the second movement of an anonymous 'Sonatta *a* 5' preserved at Durham Cathedral (MS M.175, pp. 59–68), which Talbot tentatively associates with Albinoni and considers may predate 1694, though when it arrived in England is not known. Further discussion of continental parallels with Purcell's interest in permutational counterpoint is to be found in Chapter 3 above.

imitative combinations throughout his career. After all, the difference between the construction of a large multi-voice canon and research of available imitative interlocks is in fact very small – the former involving the composition of melodic lines capable of mutual combination, and the latter, their recognition. If Purcell was indeed capable of marshalling in his head the permutational possibilities inherent in the materials he employed in the *Fairy Queen* canzona, he would surely have found that the less stringent application of similar strategies to derive the climactic passage in bars 24–9 of the *Indian Queen* trumpet overture cost him little mental exertion.

There is no doubt that the stylistic watershed Martin Adams associates with *The Fairy Queen* is conspicuous in the immediate impression projected by these late sinfonias and overtures, and indeed Adams's suggestion (which in fact he makes only to reject) that these changes to Purcell's style are 'so comprehensive that they might be taken to suggest some foreign intervention'[44] may seem to gain new weight in the light of the specific Italian precedents for Purcell's *Fairy Queen* canzona. Yet what is particularly impressive about this 'significantly new level of stylistic conflation' is not Purcell's greater maturity in reining in his youthful enthusiasm for audacious contrapuntal feats – in fact, the contrary is true, as we have seen – or even his submission to the melodic restraint and tonal circumspection of the Italian sonata repertoire, but his ability, just as with the deployment of *fugeing per augmentation* explored in Chapter 7, to yoke together his earlier technical strategies and later stylistic resources in order to produce a true synthesis. Thus his increasing design of thematic materials to delineate a limited range of tonally directed middleground models actually carried the potential to increase the available imitative combinations, those models relying as they often did on exactly the kinds of simple scales and sequential patterns that were ripe with imitative possibilities. The converse was also true: high contrapuntal artifice when deployed as an inventive principle will often result in a restriction of melodic individuality and harmonic complexity, so that the Italianate directness of these works seems to arise directly out of their underlying contrapuntal ingenuity. It was, surely, exactly this synthesis of which Purcell wrote in 1694 when he described the 'great deal of Art mixed with good Air' that he admired in the Italian canzona: not a judicious balance or careful negotiation, but a symbiotic relationship whereby each necessitates the other. No doubt readers in the know recognized then, as now, that few composers of Purcell's generation – Italian or otherwise – had achieved this 'Perfection of a master' to the degree that Purcell himself exhibited during the 1690s.

---

[44] Adams, *Henry Purcell*, 77.

Bibliography

MUSIC

Corelli, Arcangelo, *Werke ohne Opuszahl*, ed. Hans Joachim Marx, Arcangelo Corelli: Historische-kritische Gesamtausgabe der musikalischen Werke, v (Cologne: Arno Volk Verlag Hans Gerig KG, 1976).

Complete Violin Sonatas and Trio Sonatas, ed. Joseph Joachim and Friedrich Chrysander (originally *Les Oeuvres de Arcangelo Corelli*, Vols 1–3, London: Augener, 1888–91; repr. New York: Dover, 1992).

Cunningham, John and Peter Holman, eds, *Restoration Trio Sonatas*, Purcell Society Edition Companion Series, IV (London: Stainer & Bell, 2012).

Dowland, John, *A Pilgrims Solace (1612), Three Songs from* A Musical Banquet *(1610)*, ed. Edmund H. Fellowes, rev. Thurston Dart (London: Stainer & Bell, 1969).

Dowland, Robert, *A Musicall Banquet* (London: Thomas Adam, 1610).

Draghi, Giovanni Battista, *From Harmony, from Heav'nly Harmony*, ed. Bryan White, Purcell Society Edition Companion Series, III (London: Stainer & Bell, 2010).

Eccles, John, *Rinaldo and Armida*, ed. Steven Planck, Recent Researches in the Music of the Baroque Era, 176 (Middleton, WI: A-R Editions, 2011).

Gibbons, Orlando, *Hosanna to the Son of David*, ed. Edmund H. Fellowes, rev. edn Anthony Greening (London: Oxford University Press, *c.* 1976).

Holman, Peter and John Cunningham, eds, *Restoration Trio Sonatas*, Purcell Society Edition Companion Series, IV (London: Stainer & Bell, 2012).

Locke, Matthew, *Chamber Music II*, ed. Michael Tilmouth, Musica Britannica, 32 (London: Stainer & Bell, 1977).

Lonati, Carlo Ambrogio, *Sonata in D major*, ed. Michael Tilmouth (London: Stainer & Bell, *c.* 1960).

Simfonie a 3 [in g, g and A], ed. Peter Allsop, Italian Seventeenth-Century Instrumental Music, Series I: Rome, I (Crediton: New Orpheus Editions, 1990).

Purcell, Henry, *Sonnata's of III Parts* (London: the author, 1683).

The Prophetess, or the History of Dioclesian (London: the author, 1691).

Ten Sonata's in Four Parts (London: Frances Purcell, 1697).

Orpheus Britannicus (London: Henry Playford, 1698).

Orpheus Britannicus, books I and II, 3rd edn (London: W. Pearson, 1721).

271

Fantasias for Strings, ed. André Mangeot, transcrib. Peter Warlock (London: Boosey & Hawkes, 1927).

Fantasien, ed. Herbert Just, 2 vols (Berlin: Nagels Musik-Archiv,1930–35).

Ten Sonatas in Four Parts, 2 vols, ed. Christopher Hogwood (London: Ernst Eulenberg, 1978).

A Purcell Anthology: 12 Anthems, ed. Bruce Wood (Oxford University Press, 1995).

Come ye Sons of Arts, reconstruct. Rebecca Herissone (London: Stainer & Bell, 2010).

The Purcell Society Edition, 32 vols (London: Novello, 1878–1962; rev. edn London: Novello, 1964–2007; Stainer & Bell, 2007–):

Vol. 1, *Three Occasional Odes*, ed. Bruce Wood (Purcell Society Edition, Vol. 1).

Vol. 5, *Twelve Sonatas of Three Parts*, ed. John A. Fuller-Maitland (1893).

Vol. 5, *Twelve Sonatas of Three Parts*, rev. edn, ed. Michael Tilmouth (1976).

Vol. 7, *Ten Sonatas of Four Parts*, ed. Charles Villiers Stanford (1896).

Vol. 7, *Ten Sonatas of Four Parts*, rev. edn, ed. Michael Tilmouth (1981).

Vol. 8, *Ode on St Cecilia's Day 1692*, rev. edn, ed. Peter Dennison (1978).

Vol. 11, *Birthday Odes for Queen Mary, Part One*, rev. edn, ed. Bruce Wood (1993).

Vol. 12, *The Fairy Queen*, rev. edn, ed. Bruce Wood and Andrew Pinnock (2010).

Vol. 17, *Sacred Music, Part Three – Seven Anthems with Strings*, rev. edn, ed. Lionel Pike (1996).

Vol. 19, *The Indian Queen*, rev. edn, ed. Margaret Laurie and Andrew Pinnock (1994)

Vol. 22, *Catches*, rev. edn, ed. Ian Spink (2000).

Vol. 23, *Services*, ed. Bruce Wood and Margaret Laurie (2013).

Vol. 31, *Fantazias and Miscellaneous Instrumental Works*, ed. Thurston Dart (1959).

Vol. 31, *Fantazias and Miscellaneous Instrumental Music*, rev. edn, ed. Michael Tilmouth (1990).

Taverner, John, *'Gloria tibi Trinitas': Mass for Six-Part Unaccompanied Choir*, ed. Hugh Benham (London: Stainer & Bell, *c.* 1971)

Tomkins, Thomas, *Musica Deo Sacra* (London: William Godbid, 1668).

Services, ed. Percy Buck, Edmund H. Fellowes *et al.*, Tudor Church Music, VIII (Oxford University Press, 1928).

LITERATURE

Ackroyd, Peter, *Albion: The Origins of the English Imagination* (London: Vintage, 2004).

Adams, Martin, *Henry Purcell: The Origins and Development of his Musical Style* (Cambridge University Press, 1995).

Addison, Joseph and Richard Steele, *The Spectator* (London: [n. pub.], 1711–14), ed. Donald F. Bond, 5 vols (Oxford University Press, 1965).

Allsop, Peter, 'Problems of Ascription in the Roman *Simfonia* of the Late Seventeenth Century: Colista and Lonati', *The Music Review*, 50/1 (1989), 34–44.

The Italian 'Trio' Sonata from its Origins until Corelli (Oxford University Press, 1992).

Arcangelo Corelli: 'New Orpheus of our Times' (Oxford University Press, 1999).

Arnold, Franck Thomas, *The Art of Accompaniment from a Thorough-Bass as Practised in the XVIIth and XVIIIth Centuries*, 2 vols (Oxford University Press, 1931; repr. New York: Dover, 1965).

Arundell, Dennis, *Henry Purcell* (Oxford University Press, 1927).

Ashbee, Andrew, *The Harmonious Music of John Jenkins. I: The Fantasia for Viols* (London: Toccata, 1992).

Ashbee, Andrew and Peter Holman, eds, *John Jenkins and his Time: Studies in English Consort Music* (Oxford University Press, 1996).

Austern, Linda Phyllis, 'Music and Manly Wit in Seventeenth-Century England: The Case of the Catch', in *Concepts of Creativity in Seventeenth-Century England*, ed. Rebecca Herissone and Alan Howard (Woodbridge: Boydell, 2013), 281–308.

Avison, Charles, *An Essay on Musical Expression*, 3rd edn (London: L. Davis, 1775).

Barclay Squire, William, 'Purcell and Italian Music', *MT*, 58 (1917), 157.

Barnett, Gregory, 'Modal Theory, Church Keys, and the Sonata at the End of the Seventeenth Century', *JAMS*, 51/2 (1998), 245–81.

'Tonal Organization in Seventeenth-Century Music Theory', in *The Cambridge History of Western Music Theory*, ed. Thomas Christensen (Cambridge University Press, 2002), 407–55.

Bedford, Arthur, *The Great Abuse of Musick* (London: John Wyatt, 1711).

de Beer, Esmond S., ed., *The Diary of John Evelyn*, 6 vols (Oxford University Press, 1955).

Bent, Ian, 'The "Compositional Process" in Music Theory 1713–1850', *Music Analysis*, 3/1 (1984), 29–55.

Bent, Margaret, 'The Grammar of Early Music: Preconditions for Analysis', in *Tonal Structures in Early Music*, ed. Cristle Collins Judd (New York: Garland, 1996), 15–59.

Bevin, Elway, *A Briefe and Short Instruction of the Art of Musicke* (London: R. Young, 1631).

Blow, John, 'Rules for Playing of a Thorough Bass, upon Organ & Harpsicon.' [London, British Library Add. MS 34072, fols 1–5], ed. Franck Thomas Arnold, in *The Art of Accompaniment from a Thorough-Bass as Practised in the XVIIth and XVIIIth Centuries*, 2 vols (Oxford University Press, 1931; repr. New York: Dover, 1965), i, 163–72.

Boyd, Malcolm, *Bach* (London: Dent, 1983).

Bridge, J. Frederick, 'Purcell's Fantazias and Sonatas', *Proceedings of the Musical Association*, 42 (1915–16), 1–13.

Bukofzer, Manfred F., *Music in the Baroque Era* (New York: Norton, 1947).

Burden, Michael, 'The Purcell Phenomenon', in *The Purcell Companion*, ed. Michael Burden (London: Faber & Faber, 1995), 3–17.

ed., *Purcell Remembered* (London: Faber & Faber, 1995).

Burney, Charles, *A General History of Music, from the Earliest Ages until the Present Period* (London: the author, 1789), ed. Frank Mercer, 2 vols (New York: Dover, 1957).

Butler, Charles, *The Principles of Musick* (London: the author, 1636).

Caldwell, John, *The Oxford History of English Music, vol. 1: From the Beginnings to c. 1715* (Oxford: Clarendon, 1991).

Campion, François, *Traité d'Accompagnement et de Composition selon la Règle des Octaves de la Musique* (Paris: [n. pub.], 1716; repr. Geneva: Minkoff, 1976).

Chappell, Vere, ed., *The Cambridge Companion to Locke* (Cambridge University Press, 1994).

Christensen, Thomas, 'The "Règle de l'Octave" in Thorough-Bass Theory and Practice', *Acta Musicologica*, 64/2 (1992), 91–117.

Cicero, *De Inventione, de Optimo genere oratorum, Topica*, trans. Harry M. Hubbell, Loeb Classical Library (London: Heinemann, 1949).

Collier, Jeremy, *Essays upon Several Moral Subjects in Two Parts* (London: R. Sare and H. Hindmarsh, 1697).

Collins, Denis, '"So You Want To Write A Canon?" An Historically-Informed New Approach For The Modern Theory Class', *College Music Symposium*, 48 (2008), 108–23.

  'William Byrd's motets and canonic writing in England', *Context: Journal of Music Research*, 33 (2008), 45–65.

  'John Bull's "Art of Canon" and Plainsong-Based Counterpoint in the Late Renaissance', in *Music Theory and its Methods: Structures, Challenges, Directions*, ed. Denis Collins (Frankfurt am Main: Peter Lang, 2013), 99–127.

  'Palestrina's *Missa Sacerdotes Domini* and Analytical Approaches to Renaissance Counterpoint', in *Histories and Narratives of Music Analysis*, ed. Miloš Zatkalik, Milena Medić and Denis Collins (Newcastle upon Tyne: Cambridge Scholars Publishing, 2013), 120–34.

Cooper, Barry, 'Problems in the Transmission of Blow's Organ Music', *ML*, 75/4 (1994), 522–47.

Coprario, John, *Rules How to Compose* [Huntington Library, California, MS EL6863, *c.* 1610–14], ed. Manfred F. Bukofzer, facs. edn (Los Angeles, CA: Gottlieb, 1952).

Corp, Edward T., 'The Exiled Court of James II and James III: A Centre of Italian Music in France, 1689–1712', *JAMS*, 120/2 (1995), 216–31.

Cumming, Julie E., 'Composing Imitative Counterpoint around a *cantus firmus*: Two Motets by Heinrich Isaac', *Journal of Musicology*, 28/3 (2011), 231–88.

  'From Two-Part Framework to Movable Module', in *Medieval Music in Practice: Studies in Honor of Richard Crocker*, ed. Judith Peraino (Münster: American Institute of Musicology, 2013), 175–214.

Cumming, Julie E. and Peter Schubert, 'The Origins of Pervasive Imitation', in *The Cambridge History of Fifteenth-Century Music*, ed. Anna Maria Busse Berger and Jesse Rodin (Cambridge University Press, 2015), 200–28.

Cummings, William H., *Purcell* (London: Sampson Low, 1881).

Dahlhaus, Carl, 'Zur Geschichte der Permutationsfuge', *Bach-Jahrbuch*, 46 (1959), 95–116.

Dart, Thurston, 'Purcell's Chamber Music', *Proceedings of the Royal Musical Association*, 85/1 (1958–9), 81–93.

Demarquez, Suzanne, *Purcell* (Paris: Éditions du Vieux Colombier, 1951).

Descartes, René, *Renatus Des-Cartes Excellent Compendium of Musick: with Necessary and Judicious Animadversions thereupon. By a Person of Honour* [William, Viscount Brouncker; see Herissone, *Music Theory*, p. 3] (London: T. Harper, 1653).

Dill, Charles, 'Music, Beauty, and the Paradox of Rationalism', in *French Musical Thought, 1600–1800*, ed. Georgina Cowart (Ann Arbor, MI: UMI Research Press, 1989).

Dixon, Graham, 'Purcell's Italianate Circle', in *The Purcell Companion*, ed. Michael Burden (London: Faber & Faber, 1995), 38–51.

Donington, Robert and Thurston Dart, 'The Origin of the In Nomine', *ML*, 30/2 (1949), 101–6.

Dreyfus, Laurence, *Bach and the Patterns of Invention* (Cambridge, MA: Harvard University Press, 1996).

'Bachian Invention and its Mechanisms', in *The Cambridge Companion to Bach*, ed. John Butt (Cambridge University Press, 1997), 171–92.

Dryden, John, *Annus Mirabilis: The Year of Wonders, 1666* (London: Henry Herringman, 1667).

Of Dramatic Poesie, An Essay (London: Henry Herringman, 1668).

Albion and Albanius (London: J. Tonson, 1685).

'A Parallel of Poetry and Painting', in Charles Alphonse Du Fresnoy, *De Arte Graphica*, trans. John Dryden (London: W. Rogers, 1695).

Selected Criticism, ed. James Kinsley and George Parfitt (Oxford University Press, 1970).

Dubowy, Norbert, 'Lonati, Carlo Ambrogio', in *Grove Music Online*, www.oxfordmusiconline.com.

Duncan, Cheryll, 'Henry Purcell and the Construction of Identity: Iconography, Heraldry and the *Sonnata's of III Parts* (1683)', *EM*, 44/2 (2016), 271–88.

Favre-Lingorov, Stella, *Der Instrumentalstil von Purcell* (Bern: Eisler, 1947).

Field, Christopher D. S., 'Consort Music I: Up to 1660', in *The Seventeenth Century*, ed. Ian Spink, The Blackwell History of Music in Britain, III (Oxford: Blackwell, 1993), 197–244.

Field, Christopher D. S. and Michael Tilmouth, 'Consort Music II: From 1660', in *The Seventeenth Century*, ed. Ian Spink, The Blackwell History of Music in Britain, III (Oxford: Blackwell, 1993), 245–81.

'Fantasia: 1. To 1700', in *Grove Music Online*, www.oxfordmusiconline.com.

Field, Christopher. D. S. and Benjamin Wardhaugh, eds, *John Birchensha: Writings on Music*, Music Theory in Britain, 1500–1700: Critical Editions (Farnham: Ashgate, 2010).

Fisher, Stephen C., 'Italian Overture', in *Grove Music Online*, www.oxfordmusiconline.com.

Ford, Robert, 'Purcell as His Own Editor: The Funeral Sentences', *Journal of Musicological Research*, 7/1 (1986), 47–67.

Garber, Daniel and Roger Ariew, eds, *Descartes in Seventeenth-Century England*, 10 vols (Bristol: Thoemmes, 2002).

Gelber, Michael W., *The Just and the Lively: The Literary Criticism of John Dryden* (University of Manchester Press, 1999).

Gianturco, Carolyn, 'Music for a Genoese Wedding of 1681', *ML*, 63/1 (1982), 31–43.

'Stradella, Alessandro', in *Grove Music Online*, www.oxfordmusiconline.com.

Grimshaw, Julian, 'Morley's Rule for First-Species Canon', *EM*, 34/4 (2006), 661–6.

'Sixteenth-Century English *Fuga*: Sequential and Peak-Note Subjects', *MT*, 148 (2007), 61–78.

'*Fuga* in Early Byrd', *EM*, 37/2 (2009), 251–65.

'Compositional Phenomena in the *Missa Papae Marcelli*', *Recercare*, 24/1 (2012), 5–33.

Hammond, Paul, 'Classical Texts: Translations and Transformations', in *The Cambridge Companion to English Literature, 1650–1740*, ed. Stephen N. Zwicker (Cambridge University Press, 1998), 143–61.

Harley, John, *Music in Purcell's London* (London: Dobson, 1968).

Hawkins, John, *A General History of the Science and Practice of Music* (London: T. Payne, 1776), ed. Charles Cudworth, 2 vols (New York: Dover, 1963).

Herissone, Rebecca, 'The Compositional Techniques of Henry Purcell as Revealed Through Autograph Revisions made to his Works' (unpublished MMus thesis, King's College, London, 1993).

'Purcell's Revisions of his own Works', in *Purcell Studies*, ed. Curtis Price (Cambridge University Press, 1995), 51–86.

'The Theory and Practice of Composition in the English Restoration Period' (unpublished PhD thesis, University of Cambridge, 1996).

Music Theory in Seventeenth-Century England (Oxford University Press, 2000).

'"Fowle Originalls" and "Fayre Writing": Reconsidering Purcell's Compositional Process', *The Journal of Musicology*, 23/4 (2006), 569–619.

'Robert Pindar, Thomas Busby, and the Mysterious Scoring of Henry Purcell's "Come Ye Sons of Art"', *ML*, 88/1 (2007), 1–48.

'Performance History and Reception', in *The Ashgate Research Companion to Henry Purcell*, ed. Rebecca Herissone (Farnham: Ashgate, 2012), 303–51.

Musical Creativity in Restoration England (Cambridge University Press, 2013).

Higney, John, 'Henry Purcell: A Reception/Dissemination Study, 1695–1771' (unpublished PhD thesis, University of Western Ontario, 2008).

Hobbes, Thomas, *Humane Nature* (London: F. Bowman, 1650).

   Leviathan, or the Matter, Forme, & Power of a Commonwealth Ecclesiasticall and Civil (London: A. Crooke, 1651), ed. John C. A. Gaskin (Oxford University Press, 1998).

Hodge, Brian, 'A New Frescobaldi Attribution', *MT*, 122 (1981), 263–5.

Hogwood, Christopher, *The Trio Sonata* (London: BBC, 1979).

Holland, Arthur K., *Henry Purcell: The English Musical Tradition* (London: Bell, 1932).

Holman, Peter, *Four and Twenty Fiddlers: The Violin at the English Court, 1540–1690* (Oxford: Clarendon Press, 1993).

   Henry Purcell (Oxford University Press, 1994).

   'Consort Music', in *The Purcell Companion*, ed. Michael Burden (London: Faber & Faber, 1995), 254–98.

   '"Evenly, Softly, and Sweetly Acchording to All": The Organ Accompaniment of English Consort Music', in *John Jenkins and his Time: Studies in English Consort Music*, ed. Andrew Ashbee and Peter Holman (Oxford University Press, 1996), 353–82.

   Dowland, Lachrimae (1604), Cambridge Music Handbooks (Cambridge University Press, 1999).

   'Compositional Choices in Henry Purcell's *Three Parts upon a Ground*', *EM*, 29/2 (2001), 250–61.

Holman, Peter and Robert Thompson, 'Purcell: (3) Henry Purcell (ii)', in *Grove Music Online*, www.oxfordmusiconline.com.

Holst, Imogen, ed., *Henry Purcell, 1659–95: Essays on his Music* (London: Oxford University Press, 1959).

Howard, Alan, 'Purcell and the Poetics of Artifice: Compositional Strategies in the Fantasias and Sonatas' (unpublished PhD thesis, King's College, London, 2006).

   'Composition as an Act of Performance: Artifice and Expression in Purcell's Sacred Part Song *Since God so Tender a Regard*', *JRMA*, 132/1 (2007), 32–59; reprinted in *Purcell*, ed. Peter Holman, The Baroque Composers (Farnham: Ashgate, 2011), 353–80.

   'Understanding Creativity', in *The Ashgate Research Companion to Henry Purcell*, ed. Rebecca Herissone (Farnham: Ashgate, 2012), 65–113.

   'Compositional Strategies in Purcell's Second Three-Part Fantazia', *Music Theory Online*, 21 (2015), www.mtosmt.org/issues/mto.15.21.3/mto.15.21.3.howard.html.

   'A Midcentury Musical Friendship: Silas Taylor and Matthew Locke', in *Beyond Boundaries: Rethinking Music Circulation in Early Modern England*, ed. Linda Phyllis Austern, Candace Bailey and Amanda Eubanks Winkler (Bloomington, IN: Indiana University Press, 2017), 127–49.

'A New Purcell "Borrowing" from Orlando Gibbons', paper delivered at the 2014 Biennial Conference on Baroque Music (Queen's University, Belfast, 30 June–4 July 2010.

Howes, Frank, *The English Musical Renaissance* (London: Secker and Warburg, 1966).

Hughes-Hughes, Augustus., [n. tit.], *MT*, 37 (1896), 85.

Hurley, David Ross, *Handel's Muse: Patterns of Creation in his Oratorios and Musical Dramas, 1743–1751* (Oxford University Press, 2000).

Hutchings, Arthur, *Purcell* (London: BBC, 1982).

Hutton, Ronald, *The Rise and Fall of Merry England: The Ritual Year, 1400–1700* (Oxford University Press, 1994).

Johnson, Douglas, 'Beethoven Scholars and Beethoven's Sketches', *Nineteenth-Century Music*, 2/1 (1978), 3–17.

Kassler, Jamie C., *The Beginnings of the Modern Philosophy of Music in England: Francis North's A philosophical essay of musick (1677) with comments of Isaac Newton, Roger North and in the Philosophical Transactions* (Aldershot: Ashgate, 2004).

Keates, Jonathan, *Purcell: A Biography* (London: Pimlico, 1996).

Kerman, Joseph, 'Byrd, Tallis, and the Art of Imitation', in *Aspects of Medieval and Renaissance Music*, ed. Jan LaRue (New York: Pendragon, 1966), 519–37.

Kolneder, Walter, 'Der Generalbass in der Triosonaten von Purcell', in *Heinrich Schütz e il suo Tempo [Atti del 1°Convegno Internazionale di Studi, Urbino, 26–31 Iuglio 1978]*, ed. Giancarlo Rostirolla (Rome: Società Italiana del Flauto Dolce, 1981), 281–99.

Lamprecht, Sterling P., 'The Role of Descartes in Seventeenth-Century England', *Studies in the History of Ideas*, 3 (1935), 179–240.

Lester, Joel, 'The Recognition of Major and Minor Keys in German Theory: 1680–1730', *Journal of Music Theory*, 22/1 (1978), 65–103.

  Between Modes and Keys: German Theory, 1592–1802 (Stuyvesant, NY: Pendragon Press, 1989).

  Compositional Theory in the Eighteenth Century (Cambridge, MA: Harvard University Press, 1992).

Libby, Dennis, 'Interrelationships in Corelli', *JAMS*, 26/2 (1973), 263–87.

Lionnet, Jean, 'Fede, Innocenzo', in *Grove Music Online*, www.oxfordmusiconline.com.

Locke, John, *Essay Concerning Humane Understanding*, ed. John W. Yolton, 2 vols (London: Dent, 1961).

  Second Treatise of Government, ed. C. B. MacPherson (Indianapolis, IN: Hackett, 1980).

Locke, Matthew, *Melothesia; or, Certain General Rules for Playing upon a Continued-Bass* (London: J. Carr, 1673).

Love, Harold, 'Constructing Classicism: Dryden and Purcell', in *John Dryden: Tercentenary Essays*, ed. Paul Hammond and David Hopkins (Oxford University Press, 2000), 92–112.

Luckett, Richard, '"Or rather our musical Shakspeare": Charles Burney's Purcell', in *Music in Eighteenth-Century England: Essays in Memory of Charles*

Cudworth, ed. Christopher Hogwood and Richard Luckett (Cambridge University Press, 1983), 59–77.

Mabbett, Margaret, 'Italian Musicians in Restoration England (1660–90)', *ML*, 67/3 (1986), 237–47.

Mace, Thomas, *Musick's Monument* (London: the author, 1676).

Marshall, Robert Lewis, *The Compositional Process of J. S. Bach* (Princeton University Press, 1972).

Marvell, Andrew, *An Account of the Growth of Popery and Arbitrary Government in England* (1677), facs. edn (Farnborough: Gregg International, 1971).

McCrickard, Eleanor, 'The Roman Repertory for Violin before the time of Corelli', *EM*, 18/4 (1990), 563–73.

McGuinness, Rosamond, 'The Ground Bass in the English Court Ode', *ML*, 51/3 (1970), 118–40 and 265–78.

Mellers, Wilfrid, 'The Heroism of Henry Purcell: Music and Politics in Restoration England', in *Music and the Politics of Culture*, ed. Christopher Norris (London: Lawrence & Wishart, 1989), 20–40.

Meyer, Ernst Hermann, *Early English Chamber Music: From the Middle Ages to Purcell* (as *English Chamber Music*, London: Lawrence & Wishart, 1946; rev. edn 1982).

Milsom, John, 'Analysing Josquin', in *The Josquin Companion*, ed. Richard Sherr (Oxford University Press, 2000), 431–84.

'Absorbing Lassus', *EM*, 33/1 (2005), 99–114.

'Crecquillon, Clemens, and four-voice *fuga*', in *Beyond Contemporary Fame: Reassessing the Art of Clemens non Papa and Thomas Crequillon*, ed. Eric Jas (Turnhout: Brepols, 2005), 293–345.

'"*Imitatio*", "Intertextuality" and Early Music', in *Citation and Authority in Medieval and Renaissance Musical Culture: Learning from the Learned*, ed. Suzannah Clark and Elizabeth Eva Leach (Woodbridge: Boydell, 2006), 141–51.

'Josquin and the Combinative Impulse', in *The Motet around 1500: On the Relationship of Imitation and Text Treatment?*, ed. Thomas Schmidt-Beste (Turnhout: Brepols, 2012), 211–46.

'Cipriano's Flexed *Fuga*', in *Cipriano da Rore: New Perspectives on His Life and Music*, ed. Jessie Ann Owens and Katelijne Schiltz (Turnhout: Brepols, 2016), 293–329.

'Style and Idea in Josquin's *Cueur langoreulx*', *Journal of the Alarime Foundation*, 8/1 (2016), 77–91.

Monroe, Mary, 'From "English Vein" to "Italian Notes": The Stylistic Evolution of Purcell's Chamber Music for Strings' (unpublished PhD thesis, Columbia University, 1994).

Morley, Thomas, *A Plaine and Easie Introduction to Practicall Musick* (London: P. Short, 1597).

Morris, Stephen, 'William Young's Fantazias *a* 3, by Another Name, Still Sound as Sweet . . . ', *Journal of the Viola da Gamba Society of America*, 41 (2004), 5–35.

Neighbour, Oliver, *The Consort and Keyboard Music of William Byrd* (London: Faber & Faber, 1978).

Newman, William S., *The Sonata in the Baroque Era*, 4th edn (New York: Norton, 1983).

Oddie, Jonathan, 'Counterpoint, "Fuge", and "Air" in the Instrumental Music of Orlando Gibbons' (unpublished DPhil thesis, University of Oxford, 2016).

Owens, Jessie Ann, 'The Milan Partbooks: Evidence of Cipriano de Rore's Compositional Process', *JAMS*, 37/2 (1984), 270–98.

'Concepts of Pitch in English Music Theory, c. 1560–1640', in *Tonal Structures in Early Music*, ed. Cristle Collins Judd (New York: Garland, 1998), 183–246.

'"El foglio rigato" Revisited: Prepared Paper in Musical Composition', in *Uno gentile et subtile ingenio: Studies in Renaissance Music in Honour of Bonnie J. Blackburn*, ed. M. Jennifer Bloxam, Gioia Filocamo and Leofranc Holford-Strevens (Turnhout: Brepols, 2009), 53–61.

Penna, Lorenzo, *Li Primi Albori Musicale* (1672), facs. of 1684 edn (Bologna: Forni, 1969).

A Poem Occasioned on the Death of Mr. Henry Purcell, late Musician-in-Ordinary to his Majesty [. . .] By a Lover of Music (London: J. Whitlock, 1696).

Price, Curtis A., *Henry Purcell and the London Stage* (Cambridge University Press, 1984).

The Early Baroque Era, ed. Stanley Sadie, Man and Music (London: Macmillan, 1993).

'New Light on Purcell's Keyboard Music', in *Purcell Studies*, ed. Curtis Price (Cambridge University Press, 1995), 87–93.

Purcell, Henry, 'A Brief Introduction to the Art of Descant', in John Playford, *An Introduction to the Skill of Music*, 12th edn (London: Henry Playford, 1694), 85–143.

Reese, Gustave, 'The Origin of the English "In Nomine"', *JAMS*, 2/1 (1949), 7–22.

Rifkin, Joshua, 'Miracles, Motivicity, and Mannerism: Adrian Willaert's *Videns Dominus flentes sorores Lazari* and some Aspects of Motet Composition in the 1520s', in *Hearing the Motet: Essays on the Motet of the Middle Ages and Renaissance*, ed. Dolores Pesce (New York: Oxford University Press, 1997), 243–64.

Sanguinetti, Giorgio, *The Art of Partimento: History, Theory, and Practice* (Oxford University Press, 2012).

Schab, Alon, *The Sonatas of Henry Purcell: Rhetoric and Reversal* (University of Rochester Press, 2018).

Scheibe, Johann A., *Critischer Musikus* (Leipzig, 1745; facs. Hildesheim: Georg Olms, 1970).

Schubert, Peter, 'Counterpoint Pedagogy in the Renaissance', in *The Cambridge History of Western Music Theory*, ed. Thomas Christensen (Cambridge University Press, 2002), 503–33.

'Hidden Forms in Palestrina's *First Book of Four-Voice Motets*', *JAMS*, 60/3 (2007), 483–556.

'Thomas Campion's "Chordal Counterpoint" and Tallis's Famous Forty-Part Motet', *Music Theory Online*, 24/1 (2018), http://mtosmt.org/issues/mto .18.24.1/mto.18.24.1.schubert.html.

Schubert, Peter and Julie E. Cumming, 'The Origins of Pervasive Imitation', in *The Cambridge History of Fifteenth-Century Music*, ed. Anna Maria Busse Berger and Jesse Rodin (Cambridge University Press, 2015), 200–228.

Schubert, Peter and Marcelle Lessoil-Daelman, 'What Modular Analysis Can Tell Us About Musical Modeling in the Renaissance', *Music Theory Online*, 19/1 (2013), http://mtosmt.org/issues/mto.13.19.1/mto.13.19.1 .schubert_lessoil-daelman.html.

Scott, Jonathan, *England's Troubles: Seventeenth-Century English Political Instability in European Context* (Cambridge University Press, 2000).

Selfridge-Field, Eleanor, 'Vivaldi's Esoteric Instruments', *EM*, 6/3 (1978), 332–8.
'Instrumentation and Genre in Italian Music, 1600–1670', *EM*, 19/1 (1991), 61–7.

Shaw, Watkins and Robert Ford, 'Gostling, John', in *Grove Music Online*, www.oxfordmusiconline.com.

Shay, Robert S., 'Henry Purcell and "Ancient" Music in Restoration England' (unpublished PhD thesis, University of North Carolina, Chapel Hill, 1991).
'Purcell as Collector of "Ancient" Music: Fitzwilliam MS 88', in *Purcell Studies*, ed. Curtis Price (Cambridge University Press, 1995), 35–50.
'Purcell's Revisions to the Funeral Sentences Revisited', *EM*, 26/3 (1998), 457–67.

Shay, Robert S. and Robert Thompson, *Purcell Manuscripts: The Principal Musical Sources* (Cambridge University Press, 2000).

Sietz, Reinhold, *Henry Purcell: Zeit – Leben – Werk* (Leipzig: Breitkopf & Härtel, 1955).

Simpson, Christopher, *The Division-Violist* (London: W. Godbid, 1659).
The Division-Viol, 2nd edn (London: Henry Brome, 1665).
A Compendium of Practical Musick (London, H. Brome, 1667).

Smith, David J., 'Continuity, Change and the Emergence of Idiomatic Organ Repertoire in Seventeenth-Century England', in *Studies in English Organ Music*, ed. Ian Quinn (London: Routledge, 2018), 122–41.

Smithers, Don L., *The Music and History of the Baroque Trumpet before 1721* (London: Dent, 1973).

Soo, Lydia M., *Wren's 'Tracts' on Architecture and Other Writings* (Cambridge University Press, 1998).

Spink, Ian, 'Music and Society', in *The Seventeenth Century*, ed. Ian Spink, The Blackwell History of Music in Britain, III (Oxford: Blackwell, 1993), 1–65.
Restoration Cathedral Music, 1660–1714 (Oxford University Press, 1995).

Stevens, Denis, 'Purcell's Art of Fantasia', *ML*, 33/4 (1952), 341–45.

Talbot, Michael, *Tomaso Albinoni: The Venetian Composer and his World* (Oxford University Press, 1990).
Benedetto Vinaccesi: A Musician in Brescia and Venice in the Age of Corelli (Oxford: Clarendon, 1994).

'Vivaldi and the "Violino in tromba marina"', *The Consort*, 61 (2005), 5–17.

Vivaldi and Fugue (Florence: Olschki, 2009).

'Corelli, Arcangelo', in *Grove Music Online*, www.oxfordmusiconline.com.

Temperley, Nicholas, 'The Origins of the Fuging Tune', *Royal Musical Association Research Chronicle*, 17 (1981), 1–32.

Theile, Johann, *Musikalisches Kunstbuch*, ed. Carl Dahlhaus, Denkmäler norddeutscher Musik, I (Kassel: Bärenreiter, 1965).

Thompson, Robert, 'Purcell's Great Autographs', in *Purcell Studies*, ed. Curtis Price (Cambridge University Press, 1995), 6–34.

'Sources and Transmission', in *The Ashgate Research Companion to Henry Purcell*, ed. Rebecca Herissone (Farnham: Ashgate, 2012), 13–63.

Thompson, Robert and Robert S. Shay, *Purcell Manuscripts: The Principal Musical Sources* (Cambridge University Press, 2000).

Tilmouth, Michael, 'The Technique and Forms of Purcell's Sonatas', *ML*, 40/4 (1959), 109–21.

Tilmouth, Michael and Christopher D. S. Field, 'Consort Music II: From 1660', in *The Seventeenth Century*, ed. Ian Spink, The Blackwell History of Music in Britain, III (Oxford: Blackwell, 1993), 245–81.

Van Tour, Peter, *Counterpoint and Partimento: Methods of Teaching Composition in Late Eighteenth-Century Naples* (University of Uppsala, 2015).

Tyson, Alan, *Mozart: Studies of the Autograph Scores* (Cambridge, MA: Harvard University Press, 1987).

Walker, Paul Mark, 'The Origin of the Permutation Fugue', in *The Creative Process*, Studies in the History of Music, III (New York: Broude Brothers, 1992), 51–91.

Theories of Fugue from the Age of Josquin to the Age of Bach (University of Rochester Press, 2000).

Walls, Peter, 'The Influence of the Italian Violin School in 17th-Century England', *EM*, 18/4 (1990), 575–87.

Wardhaugh, Benjamin, ed., *Thomas Salmon: Writings on Music*, 2 vols (Farnham: Ashgate, 2013).

Wardhaugh, Benjamin and Christopher D. S. Field, eds, *John Birchensha: Writings on Music*, Music Theory in Britain, 1500–1700: Critical Editions (Farnham: Ashgate, 2010).

Weidner, Robert, 'The Early *In Nomine*: A Genesis of Chamber Music' (unpublished PhD dissertation, University of Rochester, 1960).

Wessely-Kropik, Helene, 'Henry Purcell als Instrumentalkomponist', *Studien zur Musikwissenschaft. Beihefte der 'Denkmäler der Tonkunst in Österreich'*, 22 (1955), 85–141.

Westrup, J. A., 'Foreign Musicians in Stuart England', *MQ*, 27/1 (1941), 70–89.

Purcell, 6th edn (New York: Oxford University Press, 1995).

White, Bryan, *Music for St Cecilia's Day from Purcell to Handel* (Woodbridge: Boydell & Brewer, 2019).

Wienpahl, Robert W., 'English Theorists and Evolving Tonality', *ML*, 36/4 (1955), 377–93.

Willetts, Pamela, 'Stephen Bing: A Forgotten Violist', *Chelys*, 18 (1989), 3–17.

Wilson, John, ed., *Roger North on Music* (London: Novello, 1959).

Winemiller, John T., 'Recontextualizing Handel's Borrowing', *Journal of Musicology*, 15/4 (1997), 444–70.

Wing, Donald G., *Short-title catalogue of books printed in England, Scotland, Ireland, Wales, and British America and of English books printed in other countries 1641–1700*, ed. Timothy J. Crist (vol. 2) and John J. Morrison (vol. 3), 2nd rev. and enlarged edn, 3 vols (New York: Modern Language Association of America, 1972–88).

Wintle, Christopher, 'Corelli's Tonal Models: The Trio Sonata Op. III, n. 1', in *Nuovissimi Studi Corelliani III*, ed. Sergio Durante and Pierluigi Petrobelli (Florence: Olschki, 1982), 29–69.

Wood, Bruce, 'Only Purcell e're shall Equal Blow', in *Purcell Studies*, ed. Curtis Price (Cambridge University Press, 1995), 106–44.

Purcell: An Extraordinary Life (London: Associated Board of the Royal Schools of Music, 2009).

Youngren, William H., 'Addison and the Birth of Eighteenth-Century Aesthetics', *Modern Philology*, 79/3 (1982), 267–83.

Zimmerman, Franklin B., *Henry Purcell, 1659–1695: An Analytical Catalogue of his Music* (London: Macmillan, 1963).

Henry Purcell, 1659–1695: His Life and Times (London: Macmillan, 1967).

Zwicker, Steven N., ed., *The Cambridge Companion to English Literature, 1650–1740* (Cambridge University Press, 1995).

Index of Compositions

General Index

Adams, Martin, 3, 16, 17–18, 146–7, 154,
    187–8, 202 n. 9, 203, 237, 244, 249,
    258, 270
Addison, Joseph, 123–4
    'Pleasures of the Imagination, The', 126–8,
    131
affections, doctrine of, 127
agency (of composer), 11, 19, 23
air, *see* ayre
Allsop, Peter, 76, 107
alterations, manuscript, 24, 25–6, 27–30, 216
Amphion, 8
analysis, musical, 4, 10, 23–4, 35
answer, fugal, *see* subject
antiphony, 183, 236–7, 238, 242, 247, 255–7
architecture
    classical, 19, 42–3
    Gothic, 123
artifice, compositional, 3–4, 19, 35–45, 53,
    56–63, 71–4, 76–7, 83, 105, 122–4,
    127, 130–32, 136–9, 240–41, 257
    as compensation for harmonic simplicity, 188,
    233–5
    no compensation for musical sensuality, 130
    and interaction with verbal texts, 219–26, 235
'Art of Descant, The' (Purcell), 1–2, 10, 31–2,
    39, 44–6, 51–6, 71, 75–6, 79–80, 82–3,
    105–6; *see also* Playford, John:
    Introduction to the Skill of Musick
audience, 77, 125, 242–3, 250
augmentation, *see fugeing per augmentation*
Austern, Linda, 77
authority, arbitrary, 128–9
Avison, Charles, 130
    Essay on Musical Expression, 124
ayre (air, aire), 1, 38–9, 51–2, 56, 114, 122–3,
    124–6, 128

Bach, Johann Sebastian, 4, 12, 24, 81–3, 87,
    106, 124
balladry, 37, 130
Barclay Squire, William, 10–11
Bassani, Giovanni Battista, 10, 83 n. 18
Bedford, Arthur
    The Great Abuse of Musick, 127–32, 188
Beethoven, Ludwig van, 24

bell-ringing, *see* campanology
Bevin, Elway, 16
    Briefe and Short Introduction, 54
Birchensha, John, 65–67 (Ex. 2.13)
Blow, John, 11 n. 29, 104, 220, 236
    'Rules for Playing of a Through Bass', 86–7,
    88, 90, 106
body politic, 129
Bologna, 107, 236–7, 242
Bononcini, Giovanni Battista, 10
borrowing, musical, 149–50, 156–8; *see also*
    quotation, musical
    self-borrowing, 153, 157, 187
Brady, Nicholas, 146
Braganza, Catherine of, Queen Consort,
    Catholic chapel of, 106–7
Bridge, J. Frederick, 10–12
Brouncker, William, Viscount, 87
Bukofzer, Manfred F., 32, 86
Bull, John, 16
Burney, Charles, 8–10
Busby, Richard, 42
Butler, Charles, 51
Byrd, William, 167

cadence, 14, 25, 45, 51, 76, 88, 228
    created by calculated or strategic use of
    materials, 46, 100, 112, 254–5, 268–9
    evasion/delay of, 106, 107, 115, 118, 221, 267
    interrupted, 170, 224, 253
    Phrygian, 247, 255
    plagal, 230
    preparation for, 178, 227, 243, 246, 253–4
    structural, 257, 260
Calvisius, Seth, 51
campanology, 258, 264
Campion, François, 88
Campion, Thomas
    *Art of Setting, or Composing of Musick in Parts,
    The*, 45
canon, 11, 45, 49, 58, 161, 183 n. 25, 195–7,
    220, 262–9
    and augmentation, 194–5, 201, 226
    over ground bass, 1, 2
    and invertible counterpoint, 76–7
    and melodic inversion, 197